Debating
Nationalism

DEBATES IN WORLD HISTORY

Series Editor: Peter N. Stearns, George Mason University, USA

Editorial Board: Marc Jason Gilbert (Hawaii Pacific University, USA), Heather Streets-Salter (Northeastern University, USA), Sadiah Qureshi (University of Birmingham, UK)

Bloomsbury's *Debates in World History* series presents students with accessible primers to the key debates in the field of world history, from classic debates, such as the great divergence, through to cutting-edge current developments. These are short, argumentative texts that will encourage undergraduate level history students to engage in the practice of doing history.

Published:

Debating the Industrial Revolution, Peter N. Stearns

Debating Modern Revolution, Jack R. Censer

Debating Genocide, Lisa Pine

Forthcoming:

Debating the Great Divergence, Michael Adas, Joseph Schmidt, and Joseph J. Gilch

Debating Gender, April Haynes

Debating Nationalism

The Global Spread of Nations

FLORIAN BIEBER

BLOOMSBURY ACADEMIC
LONDON • NEW YORK • OXFORD • NEW DELHI • SYDNEY

BLOOMSBURY ACADEMIC
Bloomsbury Publishing Plc
50 Bedford Square, London, WC1B 3DP, UK
1385 Broadway, New York, NY 10018, USA

BLOOMSBURY, BLOOMSBURY ACADEMIC and the Diana logo
are trademarks of Bloomsbury Publishing Plc

First published in Great Britain 2020

Cover image: 1914, Map of Europe by W. Trier
(© akg-images/Alamy Stock Photo)

A catalogue record for this book is available from the British Library.

A catalog record for this book is available from the Library of Congress.

ISBN: HB: 978-1-3500-9811-4
         PB: 978-1-3500-9810-7
         ePDF: 978-1-3500-9813-8
         eBook: 978-1-3500-9812-1

Series: Debates in World History

Typeset by Integra Software Services Pvt. Ltd.

To find out more about our authors and books visit www.bloomsbury.com
and sign up for our newsletters.

For Marijana and Oskar

Contents

Figures and Tables

Figures

Tables

Acknowledgments

Nationalism and the importance of nations have been with me since childhood. Growing up in the multilingual and multinational environment of Luxembourg, where living with different nations, hearing and speaking multiple languages was normal. There, I identified as European and have since continued to do so, while being aware that this identity is itself heterogenous and confronted with the persistence of nationalism. It is radical nationalism and the wars fought on the grounds of national claims that enabled me to understand and explore the post-Yugoslav space. Not some tribal and supposedly ancient hatred could explain nationalism and mass violence there, but rather the persistence of nationalism as a powerful force in today's world provided for an explanation that extends well beyond Southeastern Europe.

I am grateful to Bloomsbury and Peter N. Stearns for giving me the opportunity to reflect more broadly, both in terms of space and time on the rise of nations. Over the years, I have benefited greatly from the intellectual community of the Association for the Study of Nationalities. The conventions, the journal *Nationalities Papers*—which I had the pleasure to edit for four years—and the exchange with colleagues, have been an inspiration and a source of continuous learning.

Furthermore, I am particularly grateful to the students who contributed to the classes on nationalism I have had the pleasure to teach at the University of Graz, the Central European University, Cornell University, and the Universities of Sarajevo and Belgrade. Their questions and thoughts have been a great guide for clarifying my thinking on nationalism.

I am also grateful to *Ethnopolitics* for having published a symposium on my article "Is Nationalism on the Rise? Assessing Global Trends" (*Ethnopolitics* 17, no. 5 [2018]: 519–540), which I draw on in Chapters 1 and 8, and the insightful comments by Erin Jenne,

Zsuzsa Csergö, and Siniša Malešević. Furthermore, I would like to thank Paul Butcher for his proofreading of this manuscript. Finally, I would like to thank the University of Graz for its financial support.

It is tempting and easy to dismiss nationalism as a retrograde and negative force that has brought about considerable human suffering over the past two centuries. However, such a perspective would ignore the importance of nationalism for many and the complexity of its multifaceted history. In this introduction I thus seek to understand the ubiquity of nations and the power of nationalism rather than to judge it.

Florian Bieber
Graz, June 2019

1

Introduction

In 1983, concluding his seminar study on nationalism, British historian Eric Hobsbawm noted that "the owl of Minerva which brings wisdom, said Hegel, flies at dusk. It is a good sign that it is now circling round nations and nationalism."[1] To this hopeful assessment, Antony Smith, himself an important scholar of nationalism, replied, "it is still nationalist high noon, and the owl of Minerva has not stirred."[2] Two decades into the twenty-first century the sun is not setting on nationalism.

Indeed, nations are still all around us. We talk about inter*nation*al relations, the United *Nation*s, the *nation* to describe a state or one's *nation*ality. These terms, including the UN's predecessor, the League of *Nations*, betray a confusion between state and nation. The UN currently brings together 193 states but not all nations. There are plenty of nations, such as the Kurds, who lack a state. In addition, many nations might transcend borders, such as Hungarians or Russians, but the members of the UN only represent states and their citizens, not all members of a nation. There are also members of the UN whose citizens do not necessarily identify with a distinct nation but consider themselves part of a larger transnational community, such as many Arabs.

Thus, the UN and its predecessor are misnomers reflecting the confusion between state and nation. Similarly, many use the word "nation" to describe a state. This is also reflected in other languages. In German, for example, international law is known as *Völkerrecht*, literally the law of peoples. Similarly, the terms "nationality" and "citizenship" are often used interchangeably. This creates particular confusion in multinational states, where nationality is not identical to the citizenship held.

The many ways in which we are confronted with the word "nation" and its symbols in everyday life, from sports competitions to the news, from "ethnic" foods to tourism advertisements, highlight the omnipresence of nations around us. For their (apparent) innocence, these often stand in seeming contrast to the "outbreaks of nationalism," ethnic violence, and far-right and other groups threatening expressions of nationalism. To understand nations and nationalism, we need to capture both: the everyday variant, which might seem normal and nearly invisible to most, and the violent, threatening kind that can lead to ethnic conflict and electoral success for radical political parties and candidates.

Nationalism and patriotism

The first big challenge for anyone writing about nationalism is the strong emotions, mostly negative, that the word evokes. While nations and nationalism are ubiquitous, few would describe themselves as nationalists. For instance, if a survey seeks to identify the relevance of nationalism in a given society, it cannot simply ask respondents to identify themselves as nationalists. This negative association is not only a challenge in identifying nationalism, but also poses a dilemma for understanding. As German historian Peter Alter noted, nationalism is usually seen in moral terms as aggressive and negative, unlike other concepts such as "national interest" or "national pride."[3] Yet, this negative association is far from universal however. Where nationalism is a force against a colonial rule or where it seeks to unite multiple ethnic groups under a common roof, nationalism might evoke positive associations.

Frequently, nationalism is distinguished from patriotism as a way to distinguish between "good" and "bad." In this case, "nationalism" acquires negative and "patriotism" acquires positive connotations. For example, in 2018, on the occasion of the 100th anniversary of the armistice that ended the First World War, French president Emanuel Macron argued that "patriotism is the exact opposite of nationalism:

nationalism is treason. By saying 'our interests first and what do the others matter!' we erase what a nation holds most precious, what makes it alive, what makes it great, that which is most important of all: its moral values."[4] His statement was widely viewed as a thinly veiled criticism of American president Donald Trump and his motto of "America first." However, the dichotomy between a "positive patriotism" that evokes universalist values and a "selfish nationalism" reflects a common misunderstanding. Nationalism and patriotism are not opposites but are intrinsically linked. "Patriotism is a form of nationalism. They are ideological brothers, not distant cousins," noted the Swiss sociologist Andreas Wimmer (1962–).[5] Both emphasize the importance of self-rule and a shared political community, and the distinction between "good" patriotism and "bad" nationalism offers little help in understanding the dynamics of either. The British writer Samuel Johnson is said to have remarked in 1775 that "patriotism is the last refuge of the scoundrel."[6] With this quip, he meant that claims of patriotism—or, for that matter nationalism—are an easy justification for a wide range of policies, including those of ill intent. Yet to understand nations we need to move beyond such categories.

Furthermore, the negative connotations of nations and nationalism in Europe and North America are not universal. In many societies and countries, the term evokes distinctly less negative associations, not least because the two World Wars, which helped bring nationalism into disrepute, were still primarily European wars, save for East and Southeast Asia and sporadic episodes in Africa. By contrast, in the "Global South" nationalism was often an important anti-colonial force that reclaimed colonies from European colonial rule.

Some scholars of nationalism, such as the Israeli political scientist Yael Tamir, have argued that nationalism is an essential force, and potentially a positive one, in contemporary society. Tamir thus argued that:

> Nationalism helps fortify well-functioning states; it can also serve as a tool to foster solidarity in government efforts to address localized social challenges, fight social and economic inequalities, and take care of social groups that have been left behind. As such it is better not to abandon nationalism, but rather to channel its beneficent features to recreate the social state.[7]

For Tamir and others, nationalism is not only about exclusion but also transcending other differences within a community, such as class.

Universalism and nationalism

Nationalism emphasizes membership in a particular group: a nation. Its opposite is not patriotism but rather universalism. Whereas universalism stresses commonalities among all of humanity and explores cooperation among all humans, nationalism emphasizes proximity and cooperation among the members of one nation, no matter how it is defined. This dichotomy can be useful in understanding nationalism and its links to other ideas, especially as nationalism is able to coexist with other political ideas ranging from communism to liberalism and conservatism.

First, all modern political ideologies can be considered to have both nationalist and universalist expressions.[8] Liberalism, socialism, and conservatism can all be directed to the confines of a nation or to a broader community. Most prominent have been the discussions among socialists and communists about whether to pursue a universal approach to workers' rights and empowerment or whether to focus on particular countries, and therefore nations, first.

Second, this distinction is also visible in how nationalist groups and movements oppose universalists, or others accused of not belonging to the nation. This pattern can be recognized in the recent rise of nationalist populism, which often demonizes "globalist elites." The discrepancy between the supposedly authentic population of the nation and an elite—a population that is universalist or not rooted in that nation—is a recurring feature in nationalist discourses. In the past, the accusation has been directed against monarchs, liberal critics of nationalism, and minorities, particularly Jews, who have often been the useful "other" for radical nationalist visions that juxtapose the "authentic national" and the "hybrid global." In the German Reich at the turn of the nineteenth to the twentieth century, the term "Vaterlandslose Geselle,"—literally "fellow without a fatherland,"—was a pejorative term to describe Marxists and social-democrats. More sinister was the anti-Semitism of the first half of the twentieth century, which viewed Jews not just as a different nation rather, instead but as a different race and an enemy within the nation.

Third, the national-universal antagonism does not mean that the nationalist worldview excludes cooperation among nationalists. The liberal nationalists of the nineteenth century in particular, assumed, as we shall discuss in Chapter 3, that the new nations arising from the empires and small principalities could coexist peacefully. The idea of harmonious coexistence of nations proved to be illusory, however, and cooperation among nationalists often came to an end as neighboring nationalists launched competing claims over particular land or people, rendering any alliance difficult. Thus, nationalists might envisage—or rather assume—that the world is divided into nations and therefore view nations as the normal building blocks of modern societies. But the practicality of cooperating might be a challenge despite the shared worldview.

Nationalism is not inherently directed against the global, as long as inter*nationalism* is based on the logic of the nation. In fact, many of the architects of the global system after the First and Second World Wars, in the shape of the League of Nations and the United Nations respectively, were not so much globalists hoping to overcome the nation through international cooperation, but rather statesmen convinced of nations and nationalism as the central pillars of international order.[9]

Defining nations and nationalism

So how does a nation constitute itself? The world today is shaped by the seeming paradox of global nationalism: the understanding that the world is built on nations. If societies around the world are shaped by nations, the question is how these nations distinguish themselves from one another. In fact, one of the important debates on nations and nationalism is how membership is defined. Historically, objective definitions have prevailed. When Joseph Stalin was tasked by Lenin to write a programmatic text on the national question in 1913, he argued that the "nation is a historically constituted, stable community of people, formed on the basis of a common language, territory, economic life, and psychological make-up manifested in a common culture." [10] The underlying assumption of the definition was the possiblity of defining fixed criteria that determine membership in a nation, including language and culture. Such objective criteria are challenged, however, as there are many nations that lack some or several of them. There are multilingual nations, such as the Swiss nation, and one language can be spoken by multiple nations, such as Germans, Swiss, and Austrians; there are nations spread over a large noncontiguous territory, such as Greeks or Germans prior to the First and Second World Wars respectively. Furthermore some criteria such as shared culture, are hard to define, such as a "shared culture," and may even be shared with neighboring nations. National movements claim a shared community with a shared culture, yet these claims often neglect both internal heterogeneity and possible cultural similarities with neighbors who might share the cultural "core", from music to cuisine. At best, the objective criteria of nations can identify features which are partially shared by most members of most nations and thus give an indication of the grounds on which nations emerge. The difficulty in identifying a conclusive list of criteria for what constitutes a nation also highlights the limitations of defining nations objectively, as the modes of exclusion and inclusion are often arbitrary and historically contingent. Of course, nations – or rather national movements – often imagine themselves in such objective terms, including a common reference to shared descent. Common descent is then traced to premodern times, sometimes even antiquity, such as the ancient Greeks, Macedonians, Aryans, and other real and mythological groups from which the contemporary nation is said to have descended. Such references are, in reality, mostly myths with little foundation in historical fact.

Instead of attempting to determine fixed objective criteria, the prevailing understanding in scholarship has focused on subjective self-definitions. The German sociologist Max Weber (1864–1920) noted that the "concept [of the nation] undoubtedly means, above all, that one may exact from certain groups of men a specific sentiment of solidarity in the face of other groups." [11] Weber thus underlines common solidarity as the foundation for nations and a marker of distinction from other nations. Rather than solidarity, Karl Deutsch (1912–1992), an American political scientist originally from Prague, emphasized communication, suggesting that "nationality means an alignment of large numbers of individuals from the middle and lower classes linked to regional centers and leading social groups by channels of social communication and economic intercourse."[12]

For Weber and Deutsch as well as other proponents of subjective definitions, objective markers are only indirectly relevant. A shared language might facilitate communication, just like a shared religion or sense of common history enables a sense of solidarity. But neither are prerequisites, and communication is possible in multilingual nations, as many citizens might be fluent in multiple languages (or at least those elites that forged the nation were). Likewise, solidarity can rest on particular historical events and narratives surrounding them, irrespective of shared or divergent objective criteria. Shared solidarity and the ability to perceive others as members of the same community is crucial. Those who rule need be seen as representatives of the larger political community. While democracy might be an obvious tool to secure this, autocratic rules have been effective in claiming to represent the nation. At the same time, democracies have been at times unable to convince some of their citizens that democracy constitutes self-rule. In the end, defining the nation is a deeply political process for determining membership in a shared political community. In essence, nationalism is about self-rule, or to cite one of the leading scholars of nationalism, British-Czech sociologist Ernest Gellner (1924–1995), "nationalism holds that they [nations and states] were destined for each other; that either without the other is incomplete, and constitutes a tragedy."[13]

The crucial question of when a nation is a nation is not a matter of fact, but rather, of mutually agreed fiction. This fiction is constituted by the mutual agreement of members of a community to belong to the same nation. Such a process could be called nation-building. Its success is facilitated by commonalities among its members, but not guaranteed. As Andreas Wimmer has noted, nation-building can succeed when there are earlier structures of cooperation, such as civic networks, and the state provides shared goods. This has allowed multilingual Switzerland to emerge as a single nation, whereas in Belgium the different linguistic communities—Flemish, Francophone, and to a lesser degree a small German-speaking group—identify as separate nations.[14]

Without individuals' choice to belong to a nation, and the ability to form a community with others, a nation cannot exist. Objective markers such as language and seemingly objective criteria such as a shared history or descent are, rather, features that facilitate the subjective sense of belonging to a nation, but they are not necessary. National belonging, however, is not just a feature of self-identification but also is often ascribed by others, both claiming or excluding certain persons.

National movements claim communities and individuals based on their definition of the nation. For instance, Turkish nationalism has traditionally claimed Kurds as Turks, sometimes using derogatory terms such as "Mountain Turks." Conversely, national groups might also exclude some of those who seek to be part of the nation. For example, in the first half of the twentieth century, anti-Semites across Europe considered Jews to be alien and thus excluded them from the nation and, in the case of the policies of National Socialist Germany and its allies, from citizenship.

Accordingly, belonging to a nation stands at the intersection between individual choice and collective acceptance. Individuals have to identify with a nation, but this identification requires the consent of the larger community to be effective.

Belonging to a nation is one of the more rigid markers of identity. While it might be easier to change than gender, it is harder to switch than social position or political conviction. Here, we can distinguish between inclusive and exclusive nations in the sense of the ability to join or leave the nation. Inclusive nations are frequently based on citizenship rather than descent. Examples include many nations founded on large-scale immigration, such as the United States, Canada, or Australia, or from republican origins, such as France. The more rigidly a nation emphasizes descent as a criteria, the harder it is to join for those who lack such ancestry. This is the case in Germany, at least historically, and Japan. The rigidity of the boundaries of inclusion and exclusion can also be institutionalized. Thus, countries as diverse as the Soviet Union, Afghanistan, Cuba, Singapore, and Rwanda had or still have citizens' ethnicity or race marked on ID cards. In some cases, citizens could choose their identity and in others, they were assigned one. In Rwanda, the first line of the ID card determined whether the holder was a Hutu, Tutsi, Twa, or naturalized. The data guided the *Génocidaires* in whom to kill during the 1994 genocide. It is no surprise that after the genocide, any public identification with an ethnic group is suppressed.

In sum, belonging to a nation might be the result of an individual choice or one imposed from the outside, by society or the state. This process of inclusion and exclusion is never complete and is subject to change. States are often at the center of defining who is a member of the nation as they determine citizenship, which, in the case of self-identified nation-states, is a proxy for membership of the nation. It is telling that citizenship is commonly called "nationality" both in legal documents and common language. A consequence of membership in the nation and citizenship might be what American sociologist Rogers Brubaker (1956–) has called "nationalizing nationalisms [that make claims] in the name of a 'core nation' or nationality, defined in ethnocultural terms, and sharply distinguished from the citizenry as a whole. The core nation is understood as the legitimate 'owner' of the state, which is conceived as the state of and for the core nation."[15] Such claims of ownership might entail a variety of inclusionary or exclusionary understandings of the nation and encounter citizens with varying degrees of willingness to "join" the dominant nation. Individuals who hold no strong national identity, who might be considered "indifferent" in terms of national identity (a term we will discuss later), can be convinced, coopted, or coerced into the nation. Those who already hold a clear and distinct national identity are less likely to be incorporated into the nation and might resist claims to belong to the dominant nation, or might not even be offered membership. In this respect, timing matters. Nations always make claims over individuals who might not feel strongly attached to that nation. A national movement might nevertheless succeed in incorporating them if they lack a strong attachment to another nation or can plausibly find a connection to the bidding nation. Such collective choices were made as nations emerged in the nineteenth century. But they were also made afresh by individuals as they migrated to new places. For instance, while the German nation did not include Turkish speakers and Muslims in the original understanding of the nation, many Turkish migrants and their children became German citizens who have identified themselves as Germans and been accepted as Germans—at least by most other Germans. While a person born in Turkey might not be a German, either by their own choice or through the acceptance of the majority of Germans, a German citizen of Turkish descent might make the transition to becoming a German. The combination of individual ability to join the nation and acceptance by the larger body of the nation is crucial in constituting the community. The criteria of who is "in" and who is "out" are not fixed but are inherently changing.

Accordingly, nationalism needs to be understood as changeable and focused on its members' identification with it. As outlined above in discussing definitions of the nation, political self-rule is an essential ingredient of the nation. One can define nationalism as a *malleable and narrow ideology that values membership in a nation more highly than belonging to other groups (i.e., based on gender, political ideology, socio-economic group, region), seeks distinction from other nations, strives to preserve the nation, and gives preference to political representation by the nation for the nation.*

Typology of nationalism

Contrary to the above definition, some scholars have remarked that nationalism broader and less well defined than other ideologies, describing it, instead, as a worldview or broad system. The underlying assumption of the importance of group membership and belonging, and its political and social implications, however, make it an ideology: a set of normative beliefs and values. Nationalism' significance and centrality in the lives of a community and its individual members are not fixed and will alter. Such a circumstantial variation of nationalism is best described through a distinction between "latent" and "virulent" nationalism. Latent nationalism is ubiquitous and sometimes hard to notice: it can serve both to include migrants or exclude minorities, but is constant and steady, described by Michael Billig as "banal nationalism," an endemic condition that shapes society.[16] Through flags, stamps, and advertisements, the world surrounding most citizens normalizes the nation. These markers remind us that it is better to buy French, American, or German than the products of other nations; that the weather is constrained to the national maps of weather forecasts; that the heroes we commemorate are national; that we fly, pledge allegiance to, or stand for, a particular flag. The organization of the world into states that are commonly called nations—hence "United Nations" rather than the more appropriate "United States"—has created the endemic sense that the world is and should be divided first and foremost into nations that also happen to be states—both are largely fictions. It is this type of nationalism that is often described as patriotism.

By contrast, the nationalism that receives more headlines, often described as violent, aggressive or a "wave," alludes to its revolutionary side. Historically, nationalism has been linked to revolutions, such as the French or the American Revolution. However, virulent nationalism can be directed not just against the *ancien régime*, but also against neighbors through war and mass violence, or against governments that draw on alternative sources of legitimacy, such as communism or liberalism. Virulent nationalism rejects the status quo and seeks to reassert the will of an imagined community over a political or cultural space. It is distinct from, but draws on, its quieter twin: endemic nationalism.

Virulent exclusionary nationalism does not emerge out of the blue. Rather, it requires that a series of factors align. While nationalism might be a latent feature of a given society and the level of exclusion might vary, this in itself does not trigger a virulent exclusionary nationalism that dominates political discourse, elections, and policy. For nationalism to become virulent, first, a critical juncture is required: a particular moment of crisis. Thus, virulent nationalism can be best understood as a response to indigenous or exogenous shocks to an existing system. These shocks might be ideological, economic, institutional, or social. The collapse of communism in the late 1980s was a "perfect" critical juncture for the emergence of virulent nationalism, as the communist system faced economic and political upheaval, that triggered comprehensive institutional and social changes which enabled its rise of.

Nationalism of course, is not a force of nature, but is man-made. Until the 1990s, scholarship mostly focused on the larger processes that shaped nationalism: literacy, communication, the emergence of the modern state and standardized languages. Research in recent decades however, has shifted attention to the actors: the "ethnic entrepreneurs." Nationalism does not exist in a vacuum; it has to be promoted, and the members have to be convinced to belong to this group.[17] This requires media, political, social, and cultural elites.

These find more fertile ground when the structures are in place that favor virulent nationalism.

It is misleading to talk of nationalism as a singular phenomenon. Within a given community there are often competing nationalisms, which define the nation differently and also incorporate other ideologies, from the Left or the Right. Besides their ideological versatility, nationalisms might also exclude or include members on different grounds. The most important distinction made in this respect is that between civic and ethnic nationalism. The categorization was introduced by Hans Kohn (1891–1971), an American historian born in Prague, in his influential *The Idea of Nationalism*, written during the Second World War, where he distinguished between Eastern and Western nationalism. The Eastern variant, according to Kohn, is defined by illiberal and exclusionary dynamics, and the Western as being more inclusive and based on civic criteria. Born as a Jew in the multiethnic Habsburg Monarchy and working as a scholar in the United States, his dichotomy reflects his own life and experiences of the Second World War.

Associating civic nationalism with the West and ethnic nationalism with the East has since been criticized. Certainly, Kohn's typology is too static and presumes a clear normative hierarchy.[18] Nevertheless, it remains useful to identify the "ideal types" of nationalism. Civic nationalism is defined by citizenship, whereby all citizens are members of the nation. Ethnic nationalism is defined by descent, where only those who are born into the nation are members of the community, and citizenship is irrelevant. This distinction is exemplified by the prototypical cases of Germany and France.[19] In France, citizenship has long been a decisive factor for being French. For the German nation, where the unified state emerged only in 1871, as Germans lived in multiple states, from multinational empires such as the Habsburg Monarchy to small principalities and the Prussian Kingdom being a German was defined by descent. This distinction is commonly reflected in law as *ius soli* versus *ius sangui*: citizenship defined by the soil where one is born versus citizenship defined by blood—the citizenship of parents.

The civic conception of the nation is more inclusive, allowing migrants not just easier access to citizenship but also the possibility of becoming a member of and belonging to the larger community.

Civic (citizenship) vs. ethnic (descent)
inclusive   exclusive

Civic nationalism can include 'nations' that don't want to be included

By disregarding common descent, such a nation can be more heterogeneous and include more diverse backgrounds in terms of origins, religion, and other markers of identity. Still, the civic nation also co-opts the state, excluding those who do not identify with the nation. Take, for example, Bretons or Corsicans in France who might not consider themselves French. The French state assumes that all citizens are also members of the French nation regardless, rejecting any minority rights, which are seen to undermine the idea of a singular French nation based on citizenship. Questions of language and other markers of diversity are thus easily dismissed as irrelevant. An alternative path is the Swiss approach. The Swiss nation is sometimes described as one, constituted by the will of its inhabitants (in German, *Willensnation*), where the communal support for the nation, rather than a strong state or a sense of ethnic belonging, constituted the founding principle of the nation.

The ethnic nation does not lay claim on other nations and thus can acknowledge minorities with greater ease. At the same time, the myth of common descent excludes all those who do not fit this category, not to mention the problematic assumption that a nation is based on common descent—as if there were an original Adam and Eve of the nation—and some degree of continuity and purity. Thus, minorities might be accommodated, but an ethnically defined nation will commonly preclude equal access to the state resources for those who are not members of the dominant nation.

Historically, some nations have been based on ethnic rather than civic criteria. This has usually been contingent on the evolution of the nation. The French and the Spanish nations emerged out of existing states, whereas the Italian and German nations had no states of their own and rejected the states in which they had begun to be constituted—be they too small, too foreign, or too large for the nation.

It would be wrong to assume that nations are permanently locked into this trajectory of "ethnic" versus "civic" nationalism. Rather, all nations have the two ideal types and oscillate between them over time. Even France – the putative "role model" of the civic nation – has had episodes of exclusion based on descent, be it the latent anti-Semitism that became visible during the Dreyfuss affair at the turn of the nineteenth to the twentieth century or the more recent discrimination against French citizens of North African descent. Germany, on the other hand, being the prime case of ethnic nationalism, has made it possible for migrants—with some difficulty—to become German citizens and thus also members of the German nation, even if some on the far-right continue to contest this. Therefore, today, there are French citizens and members of the French nation of North African descent, just as there are German citizens and members of the nation of Turkish descent, who experience comparable levels of inclusion and discrimination.

In sum, rather than viewing ethnic and civic nationalism as being irrevocably linked with one or the other nation, they are best understood as competing understandings of the community. Today, the key marker of nationalism is its level of inclusion and exclusion, which might be based on the concept of descent but equally can be grounded in narratives of being "natives" of a particular land or holding a particular set of shared values. The mechanism of exclusion deriving from these could also be labeled nativism, defined by the Dutch political scientist Cas Mudde (1967–) as claiming that "states should be inhabited exclusively by members of the native group ('the nation') and that non-native elements (persons and ideas) are fundamentally threatening to the homogenous nation-state."[20]

In fact, there is never just one nation or nationalism, civic or ethnic. Rather, each nation is constituted by competing nationalisms; competing and often conflicting ideas of how to define the nation. In a landmark essay on ethnicity in 1969, the Norwegian anthropologist Frederik Barth (1928–2016) noted that it is "the ethnic boundary that defines the group, not the cultural stuff that it encloses."[21] Yet, boundaries do not set themselves but are determined by societies, individuals, and elites. Ethnic boundaries often separate people who actually share many similarities: just think of the language boundaries in many places where the dialects spoken along the border are closer to one another than they are to the standard languages. In essence, defining the nation is essentially an exercise in inclusion and exclusion. No nation is static in its understanding of who can be a member. For example, fifty years ago it would have been hard to conceive that somebody called Cem Özdemir, born to Turkish parents, could be German, not only in terms of citizenship but also in being considered part of the nation and succeeding as a leading politician. Similarly, in many other European

Waves moving between inclusive and exclusive

Good example

countries immigrants are now considered members of the nation, even
if they still face exclusion and discrimination. The pattern can also be
reversed. In Germany until 1933, Jews were not just citizens but widely
considered Germans. Of course, there had been anti-Semitic groups
since the nineteenth century who denied Jews equality or inclusion in
the nation, but they were a minority until Adolf Hitler took office and
excluded Jews from jobs, the nation, and citizenship, denying Jews
basic rights, including the right to life.

In most nations, these boundaries not only shift over time but are
also interpreted differently at any given point in time. As nationalism
is a narrow ideology that can merge with other ideologies and ideas
such as racism, conservatism, or communism, the perception of who
belongs to the nation and who does not will vary.

We can thus categorize nationalism along two axes: one, its
level of inclusion and exclusion, and two, whether it is endemic or
virulent (see Table 1.1). This allows us a more precise identification of
nationalism as a force that threatens the status quo, versus a more
established nationalism that might display exclusionary features,
but lacks the virulent and potentially violent dimension. Inclusionary
latent nationalism is thus often described as "patriotism," whereas
exclusionary virulent nationalism is the type that grabs the headlines
when far-right parties or ethnic conflicts are the topic. However, both
are just part of the larger question of nationalism.

One challenge when writing about nationalism is what Andreas
Wimmer and Nina Glick Schiller (1945–) have called "methodological
nationalism."[22] They warn of a common risk when writing national
histories, where authors either ignore the importance of nationalism
and the nation as a defining feature of the contemporary world,
or, alternatively, they naturalize the nation, assuming that the
organization of the social world along national lines is "normal."

Table 1.1. Conceptualizing nationalism.

	Level of Intensity	
Level of Exclusion	Inclusionary latent nationalism	Inclusionary virulent nationalism
	Exclusionary latent nationalism	Exclusionary virulent nationalism

Methodological nationalism can also manifest itself by imposing the nation or nation-state framework as a unit of analysis: textbooks often discuss the history of the nation-state as if this were the only historically viable unit of analysis. To give an absurd but instructive, example, in 2016 a Serb historian, Čedomir Antić, and a political scientist, Nenad Kecmanović, published a "History of Republika Srpska," the predominantly Serb entity of Bosnia. This region was established in 1991/2 and recognized at the end of the Bosnian war in 1995 as one of two regions of the country. However, the authors begin their history in the prehistoric period and then discuss the history of the Serbs in great detail, going back a millennium. In this way the framework of a recently established subnational unit is used to fabricate a the history and naturalize both this recently-defined unit and the nation it is supposed to represent, while deliberatly neglecting that before its creation and the ethnic cleansing its founders promoted, nearly half of the region's population did not identify as Serbs. While in this example the alleged nation-state (without a state) is a deliberate effort of nation-building, more subtle forms of methodological nationalism are common, particularly in the writing of national histories. Hence when writing about nations and nationalism it is essential to avoid assuming that these phenomena are natural or inevitable.

Outline of the book

This book is organized mostly chronologically, beginning with the prehistory and the origins of nationalism and proceeding to the present day. In addition, the chapters seek to introduce key theories of nationalism, so that readers of this book will be familiar both with the evolution of nationalism and with the key authors on the subject. As a brief introduction, this book does not claim to offer a comprehensive discussion of nationalism. Nor is it a study of the theories of nationalism. While it takes note of key theories, this book is primarily focused on the historical processes, that shaped nations and nationalism from the eighteenth century to the present.

Following this Introduction, Chapter 2—The Beginnings of Nationalism and Nations—will consider how old the ideas about nations and nationalism are, examining on the controversies over the age and origin of nations and how nationalisms make reference to premodern history and traditions. It will also discuss precursors to modern nations, in a global perspective. In doing so, it will map out the debate over the age of nations and nationalism (modernists vs. primordialists vs. perennialists). In particular, this chapter will explore the extent to which proto-nationalism can be found beyond Europe, both in long-established polities such as China and among communities with long-shared histories, and will outline the historical developments such as the modern state that led to the emergence of modern nationalisms.

Chapter 3—The Spread of Nationalism and Nation-states in Europe—will examine the emergence of nationalism across Europe during the eighteenth and nineteenth centuries. It will argue that nationalism spread unevenly but rapidly across the continent. Here, the focus will be on the ways that nationalism interacted with existing states – transforming some into nation-states or undermining empires or smaller polities) and how it spread from top to bottom and took root, sometimes with significant delay well after the creation of nation-states. The key debates that will be the focus of this chapter are on the spread of nationalism—i.e., whether nationalism was a movement that spread from the French Revolution outward to Europe's periphery or a more simultaneous development of nationalisms—as well as on the different characteristics of nationalism based on their evolution. This includes discussions over civic nationalism that emerged in certain states it versus ethnic nationalism in cases in others, where eiether large empires or smaller states were rejected where nationalisms rejected either large empires or smaller states. While nationalism was not unique to Europe, the centrality of Europe in the global system meant that the global rise and spread of nationalism had its origin in Europe.

Chapter 4—The Global Spread of Nationalism and Decolonization— will raise the question of whether nationalism is a European concept that spread through colonial empires or whether nations emerged globally, independent of one another. It will also consider how the rise of colonialism, and corresponding global trade and communication, brought different and competing ideas of nations and nationalism into dialogue and conflict, as well as how European forms of nationalism were transmitted through colonialism and appropriated and transformed through anti-colonial nationalist movements. The chapter will explore the different forms of nationalism that emerged globally, based on European models and earlier regional experiences, and how they shaped the postcolonial state system. Finally, it will consider the debate over the drawing of borders in the colonial context and how the European disregard for precolonial polities and groups shaped the postcolonial state system and nations.

Chapter 5—Nationalism after the Establishment of the Nation-state—will explore how nationalism did not diminish in its ability to shape society and politics with the establishment of the nation-state. The creation of nation-states merely transformed the salience of nationalism. This chapter will explore how everyday nationalism shapers modern nation-states, through symbols, traditions, and other practices. By exploring the mechanism of how nations are (re-)created, the chapter will show how nationalism intersects with other important identities, including gender, religion, socio-economic status, and race.

In Chapter 6—Ethnic Conflict—this book will move from the evolution and spread of nations and nationalism to exploring the challenge of diversity and the causes of ethnic conflict. It will offer a critical view on how nationalism and ethnic identity have been instrumentalized in conflict. It will relate the debates on nationalism to the scholarship on ethnic conflict, explore the conditions under which ethnic conflict emerges, and identify patterns of identity-based conflict. These focus on the role of ethnicity or nationalism over other factors, such as economic inequalities, resources, and other sociodemographic factors. Furthermore, it will reflect on the discussion over whether an ethnic conflict is triggered by grassroots mobilization or whether it is rather a top-down, elite-driven process.

The next two chapters examine the challenges posed by nationalism in contemporary societies. Chapter 7—Migration and the Politics of Diversity—will focus on how migration in established immigration societies, as well as self-defined nation-states, shaped debates over national identity, inclusion, and exclusion. In this chapter, the main discussion outlined will center on liberal versus multicultural approaches toward diversity and different approaches toward established minorities and immigrant communities.

Chapter 8—New Nationalism and Populism—will examine the interrelationship between nationalism and the rise of populism and authoritarianism in contemporary politics. It will discuss whether there has been a global resurgence of nationalism and populism, and to what extent such a rise is linked to globalization and other phenomena, such as the internet and social media. In doing so, it will highlight the debate over the economic versus cultural causes of new nationalism and explore whether new nationalism can be understood as a country-specific or a global phenomenon.

Finally, Chapter 9—Further Reading and a Guide to Key Debates— will outline the key debates explored in the previous chapters and identify the most important texts in the field for further reading as well as providing internet resources for primary sources and key repositories of secondary literature.

This book seeks to offer a concise discussion on how nations and nationalism became universal and omnipresent. As any short introduction, it cannot claim to be either comprehensive or groundbreaking. Instead, its goal is to trace the emergence and spread of nations and nationalism, to offer a global perspective, and to highlight some of the most important debates.

2

The Beginnings of Nationalism and Nations

Nationalisms commonly rely on narratives of their particular historical traditions, continuity, and age. Cultivating these narratives or myths is a central feature of nationalism. Often, these myths have quasi-religious features, which include stories of a golden era, a kind of national paradise, stories of decline and corruption, and offers of redemption. As the French theologian Ernest Renan (1823–1892) noted more than a century ago in his famous 1882 lecture "What is a Nation?" ("Qu'est-ce qu'une nation?") at the Sorbonne in Paris,

> The nation, like the individual, is the culmination of a long past of endeavors, sacrifice, and devotion. Of all cults, that of the ancestors is the most legitimate, for the ancestors have made us what we are. A heroic past, great men, glory (by which I understand genuine glory): this is the social capital upon which one bases a national idea.[1]

This chapter will examine the claims nationalisms make about their origins and why these are mostly myths. It will then explore the nations that arose at the onset of modernity, even if this emerging world of nationalisms and nations drew on earlier proto-nations and mechanisms of exclusion, especially along religious lines.

The role of historical myths

Myths and national narratives about the past serve multiple purposes. First, they anchor the nation in the distant past, making it appear more natural and older than it usually is in reality. The nation thus seems to be "normal" rather than an invention of more recent times. Take the Federal Charter of 1291, signed between the three cantons of Uri, Schwyz, and Unterwalden, which would become the founding myth of Switzerland. The Charter only became commemorated as the founding document that constituted the nation in the late nineteenth century, when nation-building began following the brief 1847 civil war. August 1—the supposed date on which the Charter was signed that is closely linked to the legend of the three cantons' representatives' historic oath on a meadow next to Lake Lucerne (the *Rütlischwur*) only started to be celebrated in the late nineteenth century. It became the official Swiss national holiday only in 1994.

Second, these myths allow nationalism to trump other, more modern forms of identity, such as social position, class, or gender. The reference to national ancestors places the nation into a larger narrative that is harder to escape or ignore.

Third, national myths often compete with each other and thus serve to strengthen the claim of one nation over others. These can be claims of greater antiquity—the older the nation, the more legitimate it is. Take the case of Macedonia. The Slavic population gradually started to identify as Macedonians in the first half of the twentieth century. However, neighboring Bulgarian, Serb, and Greek nationalists denied the existence of the Macedonian nation and described it as constructed and artificial. For example, the Greek Foreign Ministry argued on its official website—prior to the name compromise between the two countries—that the "Former Yugoslav Republic of Macedonia declared its independence in 1991, basing its existence as an independent state on the artificial and spurious notion of the 'Macedonian nation', which was cultivated systematically through the falsification of history and the exploitation of ancient Macedonia purely for reasons of political expediency."[2]

Historical myths may also serve to claim territory, asserting that a given nation has lived longer on a particular land than another. The

Armenian Foreign Ministry, for instance introduces its claim to the Nagorno-Karabakh region of Azerbaijan, occupied by Armenia since the 1988 war, by looking back three millennia: "Artsakh (Karabakh) is an integral part of historic Armenia. During the Urartian era (9-6th centuries B.C.) Artsakh was known as Urtekhe-Urtekhini. As a part of Armenia Artsakh is mentioned in the works of Strabo, Pliny the Elder, Claudius Ptolemy, Plutarch, Dio Cassius, and other ancient authors."[3] This claim is countered by the Azeri Foreign Ministry, which makes a similarly ancient claim to the region:

> Garabagh is one of the ancient regions of Azerbaijan. The name of this inseparable part of Azerbaijan consists of two different Azerbaijani words: "gara" (black) and "bag" (garden). The combination of these two words is as ancient as the nation of Azerbaijan. The association of these two combined words with the definite part of Azerbaijan in every part of the world is an oracle. The word Karabakh given by the Azerbaijan nation to a part of their native lands was used for the first time 1,300 years ago (in the 7th century).[4]

Even though both countries are modern states that emerged after the Russian Revolution of 1917, the irrespective claims go back millennia, well before nations and modern states existed.

Projecting the nation into the past also includes the invention of tradition. Traditions evoke the past by associating the present with historical and national narratives. Many national traditions are products of the nineteenth century or later.[5] In 1810, the Bavarian king Ludwig marked his wedding by a celebration that was later revived as the *Oktoberfest* to bind the crown and the people together.[6] The Greek Sirtaki dance, today widely considered the embodiment of Greece, was invented for the film *Zorba the Greek* in 1964. The Dirndl – the "traditional" dress in Switzerland, Austria, and Southern Germany – emerged only in the late nineteenth century, based on rural Sunday dresses, just as the Scottish kilt was a Victorian invention. In this respect, Renan noted that "forgetfulness, and I would even say historical error, are essential in the creation of a nation, which is why progress in historical studies often constitutes a danger for nationality."[7] There is indeed an inherent tension between the mythical

"ancient" national traditions are often recent deliberate inventions or selections

claims of nationalism and their historical reality. Nationalism's claims to antiquity and continuity make it more challenging to identify the modernity of the nation.

The origins of nations

Nations and their national myths are unreliable guides of their origin and age. While they might view others as constructed, recent, and thus implicitly or explicitly "fake," their own claims often reaches back into antiquity and appropriate real and imagined historical figures and states. Most scholars of nationalism would date the beginning of nations and nationalism to the late eighteenth and early nineteenth centuries, but some disagree, and there are different views as to when to date the beginning of nations.

The origin of the word "nation" derives from Latin and later old French *natio*, literally referring to "that which has been born," conceptually, this encompasses both. It replaced the earlier term of *gens*, which described extended families sharing common ancestry in ancient Rome. This word can be found still in contemporary words such as genes, genealogy, or the French *gens*, meaning "people." While *gens* or *natio* described a distinct group of people, usually with common descent or origin, these did not constitute nations. The idea that members of a common nation, however defined, should be governed by themselves and for themselves is largely associated with modernity. Empires claimed political sovereignty based on universality and appointment by God, while city-states based their claims on the virtue of being a close-knit urban community.

Some scholars, commonly referred to as primordialists and perennialists, argue that nationalism has premodern origins. While primordialists contend that nationalism has been a feature of human society since the beginning of humanity, perennialists maintain that nationalism has been a feature of societies since well before modernity and the French Revolution—the more commonly recognized point of departure for scholars of nationalism.

In fact, there are few scholars who claim that nations and nationalism are natural or have been part of human development from the early stages. Edward Shils (1910–1995), a sociologist, and Clifford Geertz (1926–2006) have both shaped the term primordialism with regard to identity. However, they did not claim that nations were ancient or inherent in human nature, but rather, that nations' and other communities' belief in their primordial origins contributes to their potency. This point reinforces the importance of nationalist claims about their own primordial nature rather than their actual origins in antiquity.

Adopting aspects of the primordialist approach, the British sociologist Anthony Smith (1939–2016), argued that while nations are modern, they had ethnic precursors based on shared myths of origin, descent, and the idea of a common homeland. This approach is also sometimes known as ethnosymbolism.[8] Others, such as the British historian Adrian Hastings (1929–2001), have argued that particular nationalisms emerged well before the modern era:

> The English nation-state survived 1066, grew fairly steadily in the strength of its national consciousness through the later twelfth and thirteenth centuries, but emerged still more vociferously with its vernacular literary renaissance and the pressures of the Hundred Years War by the end of the fourteenth. … English nationalism of a sort was present already in the fourteenth century in the long wars with France and still more in the sixteenth and seventeenth. Indeed, without the impact of English nationalism, the history of England's neighbors seems virtually unintelligible.[9]

Hastings, like other scholars, drew on particular cases to argue that nations emerged in England, Armenia, China, and elsewhere prior to modernity. However, such claims are a distinct minority among the academic community.

The dominant view recognizes that, indeed, there were precursors to the nation that matter in understanding the rise of the nation. Since early humanity, people have lived in groups and developed an attachment to these groups. Such collectivities might have organized in tribes along lines of descent, villages or towns in terms of geographic clustering or religion and language, or along other lines of similarity. All of these features would be incorporated into nations in the course of time. However, just as it would be simplistic to claim that nations are solely the product of modernity without any antecedents, it is also not plausible to describe these communities as proto-nations in waiting. While, such collective identities certainly existed before the rise of the nation, they lacked the global dominance that nationalism would achieve. Furthermore, ethnic or premodern proto-nationalism laid no claim to statehood or self-rule as modern nations would. Dominant scholarship maintains nations are intrinsically tied to the creation of the modern state. There is nothing inevitable about the dominance of the nation-state in the modern world. For most of humanity's history, including the time since the majority of humans adopted settled lifestyles, other forms of political organization prevailed. The nation-state is a recent form of organizing people. Half a millennium ago, the range of states varied from self-ruling city-states, small dynastic principalities, and lands ruled by a church or other religious institutions, to empires that (theoretically) claimed universal rule. The modern state is both more ambitious and more restrained in scope compared to most of its predecessors. More ambitious in that it exerts a great degree of control over its citizens; more self-limiting in that it only claims to govern a certain population, however it may be defined.

The modern state is often associated with the 1648 Peace of Westphalia that ended the Thirty Years' War. Yet, it was less the treaty itself as much as the larger transformation of Europe during the seventeenth century that led to the rise of the modern state. This state, unlike its predecessors, was characterized by clear boundaries and full sovereignty, i.e., the non-intervention of other states. On its territory, the government holds a monopoly over the legitimate use of force. Of course, these conditions of a modern state were often violated by bigger states interfering in the affairs of smaller ones, or by insurgencies challenging the monopoly of force, but overall it became the principle underlying international relations, law, and the modern state system.

The American sociologist Charles Tilly (1929–2008) has argued that the modern state arose through waging war, as described by the seemingly tautological statement that "war made the state and the state made war."[10] Modern states that were able to establish standing armies with an emerging capitalist system succeeded over other types of state that were either looser realms, such as the Holy

nation-state as distinct from kingdom, city-state, empire

modern state turns communities into nations

Roman Empire, or city-states and other smaller dominions. Standing armies and permanent taxation transformed the state's presence in its subjects' lives. While premodern states interacted with their inhabitants on an ad hoc basis, mostly through occasional taxation and sporadic security provision (with some notable exceptions such as China), modern states succeeded in linking their citizens to the state through armies and taxation, and in return they externalized conflict by putting an end to brigandage and establishing a monopoly of the legitimate use of force.

Thus, the key to understanding nationalism and its origins is the central link between nationalism and the state. Nationalism's claim to self-rule is most frequently expressed through the demand for statehood, either by transforming an existing state into a nation-state, unifying smaller units, or separating from larger multinational states. Nation-building projects often combine different dimensions. Take the creation of Italy, which unified the Grand Duchy of Tuscany, the Papal State, the Kingdom of the Two Sicilies, and the Kingdom of Sardinia, conquered Venetia and Lombardy which were part of the multinational Habsburg Monarchy and transformed them all into a single nation-state.

This dynamic was pertinent for Europe, where states were generally not exposed to the colonial intervention. Outside Europe, however, as we shall see in Chapter 4, colonial powers destroyed or subjugated most states in the Americas, Asia, and Africa, irrespective of whether they were weak or strong. Yet, precolonial state structures mattered. As Andreas Wimmer shows in his study on nation-building, the strong state structures in precolonial Botswana and the indirect colonial system provided the basis for the postcolonial state and nation-building.[11]

The emergence of nations

A premodern state that lacked universal education, a standing army, and a unified administration had only limited interaction with its citizens. Furthermore, premodern states often had only a vague understanding of where their borders were. In addition

building a connection between state, borders and citizens (not subjects)

their inhabitants were not citizens but rather subjects. The different polities, empires, royal dominions, and city-states did not base their claims to land and people on the idea of a shared past or future. Empires were universal in terms of laying claims—real or imagined—on the whole of the known world, such as China or Rome, or on royal domains, from small duchies to larger kingdoms, monarchs claimed to be ordained by God, not the people. (In fact, the monarchs often did not speak their peoples' language and had more in common with their fellow kings and queens in other states than with the lives and cultures of their subjects.) City-states emerged mostly as trading posts that enabled a greater degree of self-rule by their subjects than was the case with a dynastic rule.

In the premodern state, the official language was of little consequence to its inhabitants. In the Kingdom of Hungary within the Habsburg Monarchy, for example, Latin was the official language until 1844, yet few understood it. It is only when modern states started to use languages to teach, organize the army, communicate with citizens, or levy taxes that language became a highly visible feature of the state that included some and excluded others. A similar dynamic also occured when the state did not seek to assimilate its subjects but instead imposed a dominant language for pragmatic purposes. For example, when the Habsburg Monarchy began using German in most of its realm, it galvanized those who did not speak it even though it did not seek to impose a German national identity.

This example shows that the mere existence of a state did not translate to the emergence of a nation to match the state. The transformation of France from a state ruled by an absolutist monarch under the motto attributed to King Louis XIV, "L'état, c'est moi" ("I am the state") to a nation-state occured after the French Revolution. The Habsburg Monarchy, on the other hand, an absolutist monarchy like France, that marginalized the aristocracy which stood between the direct rule of the monarch and his (or her) subjects but did not attempt to build a nation. The Habsburg Monarchy, as we shall discuss in the next chapter, was first and foremost the collection of territories the Habsburg dynasty acquired through marriage and war, ranging from Spain to the Netherlands and Hungary, with the German and Czech language territories in today's Austria, southern Germany, and the Czech Republic at its core. Although it had a modern state structure by the early nineteenth century, with an army and an educational system. Considering the linguistic, religious, and socio-economic diversity of the empire, it would have been a challenging endeavor to create an Austrian nation, it made no attempt to create either a nation based on the dominant German language, like the Russian Empire did, nor a multilingual nation as neighboring Switzerland did. This shows that the state helped to provide the infrastructure for the emergence of nations but was in itself not sufficient for nations to arise. The state was a sometime facilitator in the emergence of nations in unexpected ways: for instance, nations emerged against the state. In fact, numerous nations emerged out of nationalisms that were directed against existing states. As already noted, this happened when states centralized, imposed an administrative

Document: Emmanuel-Joseph Sieyès, What is the Third Estate? (1789) [12]

Emmanuel-Joseph Sieyès (1748–1836) was a French revolutionary and member of the third estate in the national assembly in 1789.

What is a nation? A body of associates living under common laws and represented by the same legislative assembly, etc. Is it not obvious that the nobility possesses privileges and exemptions which it brazenly calls its rights and which stand distinct from the rights of the great body of citizens? Because of these special rights, the nobility does not belong to the common order, nor is it subjected to the common laws. Thus its private rights make it a people apart in the great nation. It is truly imperium in imperio. As for its political rights, it also exercises these separately from the nation. It has its own representatives who are charged with no mandate from the People. Its deputies sit separately, and even if they sat in the same chamber as the deputies of ordinary citizens they would still constitute a different and separate representation. They are foreign to the nation first because of their origin, since they do not owe their powers to the People; and secondly because of their aim, since this consists in defending, not the general interest, but the private one.

linguistic uniformity had to be created

language and a universal educational system, where parts of the population felt excluded, making the creation of the modern state an important impetus for the formation of proto-nationalist identities and movements. This occurred for instance in Belgium with the imposition of French as the dominant national language after independence in 1830, despite a slight majority of the Flemish population.

Beyond the use of language by a modern state administration the creation of secular, standardized languages is closely intertwined with the emergence of nations in other ways, too. Not only did languages help to influence national self-perceptions through inclusion/exclusion, the converse is also true. As Benedict Anderson (1936–2015) has compellingly argued, the emergence of nations advanced the standardization of secular languages.[13] Earlier, a small elite would have been able to read mostly religious texts in Latin or Greek. With the standardization of language, however, new publications had to be written in English, Dutch, German, or French to be accessible to ordinary people. Literacy, print, and language standardization thus became interlocking processes that advanced the rise of nationalism.

A shared language spread by education, books, and newspapers also advanced a common space for communication and could advance a shared identity. At the end of the Middle Ages, less than 10 percent of European men were able to read and write. In the centuries that followed, the number of literate men and women increased, at first mostly among those economically better off. The Low Countries (todays Netherlands, Belgium and Luxembourg), England, France, and Germany saw literacy rise earlier than the South and the East of the continent. Key for this increase was, first and foremost, the invention of the movable-type printing press that drastically reduced the cost of printing, not just books but also pamphlets and newspapers. During the Thirty Years' War, printed propaganda became an important part of warfare, with the different parties spreading their versions of events.

Language provides the tool for imagining a common nation. This imagined community, to use the term coined by Benedict Anderson, is a nation that is bounded by members who share more in common with each other than with others, including a shared past and a future ✳ destiny. Such a concept of shared historical continuity both projected the present into the past and reinterpreted history through the lens of the nation.

The rise of the modern state, literacy and, with it, communication, were important preconditions for the spread of national ideas. As later examples highlight, weak states and fragile societies with high levels of illiteracy would also experience the rise of nationalism. However, for the early rise of nationalism, these factors were indispensable. An underlying feature is also the secularization of public life. State and language were previously dominated by religious justifications: the dynastic rule was legitimized by a God-given right to rule, whereas languages were reduced to communicate religious—not secular—messages, and priests, rabbis, and imams often monopolized this communication, rendering it unnecessary for ordinary believers to read and write. The rise of nations also correlated to the decline of religion and its institutions as political and social actors. In Western Europe, this decline was largely a product of the split of Christianity between Catholicism and Protestantism, which fragmented the Church and also politicized religious antagonism. Furthermore, the resulting competition not only undermined the different strands of Christianity but also introduced innovative practices, such as the Protestant emphasis on making the Bible accessible to believers without the intermediary of the church, resulting in translations of the Bible into vernacular languages and the promotion of literacy.

The premodern period was not devoid of ideas of national identity, however national awareness was not the structuring principle of the era. As some scholars have noted, collective identities had long been an intrinsic part of human society, and the transfer of identity from extended families and tribes or villages to larger groups precedes nations. However, these premodern identities often emphasized features other than the nation, such as religion or locality. Rulers and communities practiced exclusion, expulsion, and even mass murder of those who were different. From ghettos to the expulsion of Protestants, Catholics, Jews, or Muslims, the religious exclusion was a defining feature of state policy from antiquity to the early modern state. In these cases, the justification for inclusion or exclusion was religion, which shares some aspects with nations but is nevertheless distinct.

Early modern European states engaged in acts of excluding Others through forced conversion, expulsion, and murder. From the expulsion of the Jews from Spain in 1492 to the 1572 St. Bartholomew's Day massacre in France when Catholic mobs killed Protestants, religious minorities were frequently the target of discrimination, exclusion, and violence. The Thirty Years' War between 1618 and 1648 had a strong exclusionary element, as Protestants and Catholics struggled for supremacy in the Holy Roman Empire. Most European states imposed religion of their subjects and excluded those who did not fit in, as reflected in the principle *cuius regio, eius religio* ("whose realm, his religion") enshrined in the 1555 Peace of Augsburg, which sought to end religious wars and empowered rulers to choose and impose their preferred religion in their realm. Religious exclusion and nationalism do share certain traits. In some cases, nations are defined in religious terms: in conflicts in Northern Ireland and Bosnia, for instance, religion became a proxy for membership in a nation. Indeed, the expulsion and exclusion of Jews, Muslims, Protestants, and Catholics were ways to tie the majorities to the state and homogenize the population. These features are similar to nationalism. At the same time, religious homogeneity did not automatically translate into earlier or more successful nation-building. Spain underwent the most far-reaching process of exclusion through the Inquisition, the forced conversion of Jews and Muslims followed by their expulsion. Yet Spain remained a considerably weaker nation-state than others that transformed into nation-states in the early modern period: France and England. Furthermore, Spain's colonial empire ended more than a century earlier than the British one, yet this did not facilitate the creation of a strong Spanish national identity. This indicates that, the early modern state developed tools of exclusion based on religious grounds that would later be used against national, minorities this dynamic did not necessarily translate into the emergence of early modern nations.

In parallel to modes of exclusion and discrimination, stereotypes have their premodern origins. Before the rise of modern nations, stereotypes about the Other also existed. For example, the *Völkertafel*, or panel of nations, drawn up in the first half of the eighteenth century in the Habsburg Monarchy, lists European nations from Spaniards to Russians, Greeks, and Turks and attributes to each a particular appearance, character, and dress as well as preferences, religiosity, flaws, and strengths. In short, it is a list of early modern national stereotypes, according to which, the English are effeminate, the Spaniards masculine, and the French childish, the Italians like to chat, Germans drink, and Russians sleep. While some of these stereotypes might be recognizable today, others appear odd not least the confusion between Greeks and Turks. Such descriptions suggest that, even before the nineteenth century, categories such as Italians, Poles, Hungarians, and Swedes existed and were widespread, even if there were no such nations or nation-states yet. These categories that emerged during the early modern period to distinguish between different populations and attribute different identities to them. Of course, the stereotypes combined the obvious, such as Russians dressing in furs, with the bias of the observer, such cultivating particularly negative stereotypes towards the "Easterners". The further toward the east and south-east they hailed from, the more treacherous they became. Thus, national categories are not solely a function of self-identification but also of ascribing character traits to outsiders. This early process of boundary-making would resonate when these imaginary distinctions between the different groups mapped onto emerging political projects.

States with strong administrative capacities that strove to homogenize the population, such as China or Spain, could be seen as proto-nation-states. Even more than Spain, China displayed early features of a proto-nation-state. While in Europe and the Middle East there was a distinct rupture of statehood between antiquity and the medieval period, no such clear break existed in China, where the state persisted uninterrupted. There were, of course, changes of dynasty and invasions that ruptured the state structure—particularly the Mongol invasions in the thirteenth century—yet the Chinese Empire could boast historical continuity since the Qin and Han dynasties, beginning in 221 BCE. A number of scholars have argued that as early as the ninth to eleventh century, a distinct premodern Chinese nation had emerged grounded on a shared understanding of Han ethnicity, a Chinese territory, and a common kingdom during the rule of the Song dynasty between 960 and 1279. These features are closely tied to elites, however, whereas their broader resonance among the population is both hard to ascertain and unlikely. The Song dynasty incorporated fewer "outsiders" such as Tibetans, Japanese, Koreans, or Turkic tribesmen in the army or the service of the dynasty than did its precursor, the Tang dynasty (618–907), which is usually associated with the peak of medieval Chinese civilization. During the Song dynasty, especially the later Southern Song period, the term "Han" to designate the predominant ethnic group came into use.[14] At the same time the dynasty set boundaries to its realm, creating the borders that states needed and that are essential in the boundary-making process of modern states and nations.

If interpreted as an early nation-state, the rise of a Chinese nation would precede the emergence of European nations by half a millennium. The distinction between a premodern empire that lacked a national identity and a modern state with a nation is a distinctly European concept that does not apply to China.

However, China was based on centralized dynastic rule, not the ideas of the inclusion of the members of the nation, as became a central claim of national movements from the French and American Revolutions onward. More importantly, earlier proto-nations, including China, were not part of a global system of nations, neither in terms of the political units nor with regard to the ideas underpinning them. China as an empire with features of a proto-nation-state was an outlier in a world organized into unbounded empires, micro-states based on dynastic power, self-ruling cities, and religious states. In fact, the rulers of premodern China. Like other empires of antiquity, perceived themselves to be at the center of the world, not unlike other empires of antiquity, rather than a world divided into competing nations. Modern nationalism, which emerged as the central political force in the late eighteenth century, not only sought to transform states into nation-states or national empires but also saw the world as being organized into nations. When China emerged as a centralized state, which bound its population together with a script shared across different languages, it was still a universalist empire, ruled by a dynasty that saw itself at the center of the known world. Many centuries later, as the idea of the nation took hold, dividing the world into a multitude of nations, China met the conditions for becoming a nation-state. However, the weakness of the state and the rise of European colonialism would delay the formation of a Chinese nation-state in the global system.

To understand the rise of nations, it is thus not enough to identify singular cases of early nationalism, be they England or China. One must take into consideration the rise of nationalism as a global force that began shaped states and societies in the late eighteenth century. Reflecting on previous centuries, shows that nations did not emerge with a revolutionary bang in July 1789, but rather, that the shift toward a world based on nations and nation-states began well before that date and would continue for more than a century. Nations rose steadily and gradually over an extended period of time, and not in one or several revolutionary moments.

Most modern aspects of the nation: unity of identity across class and b/w people and state
2. idea that the world consists of nations

3

The Spread of Nationalism and Nation-states in Europe

Nationalism emerged with a bang. and with a whimper. The American and the French Revolutions fired the starting gun for the rise of nations around the world. At the same time, others appeared more silently, gradually. Some nations, such as that of the English, developed incrementally and without much revolutionary fervor. Even those countries that experienced revolutions against monarchs and foreign rule, such as France, the United States, and the Latin American countries, did not become nation-states overnight. The transformation of monarchies, empires, and former colonies into nation-states would take a century or more, and arguably remains incomplete even today. This chapter will outline the emergence of modern nationalism in Europe at the time of the French Revolution, in terms of dynamics of proliferation and causes. It will explore how different states across the continent responded to nationalism and how it both threatened empires and was coopted by them. The success of nation-states, especially after the First World War, was challenged by large minorities who were not willingly incorporated into the new states. More exclusionary notions of the nation, and the hardening of dividing lines between nations, eventually gave rise to virulent exclusionary nationalism, culminating in the biological anti-Semitism of Nazi Germany and other movements that shared its hierarchical, totalitarian, and exclusionary view of nations and races.

The spread of nationalism was not a linear process emanating from France following the French Revolution, or spreading from Europe to the rest of the world. As discussed in the previous chapter, Ideas of the nation had existed earlier in other parts of the world. But the French Revolution was significant because it combined the notion of the nation with that of the right of the people to rule themselves. This combination was all the more potent because it built on the modern state that had emerged over the centuries preceding the Revolution. In effect, the nation is a response to the question raised by the French revolution of who should rule. If they wanted to ensure loyalty, taxation and military service, as noted in the previous chapter, rulers could no longer claim to govern by the grace of God, or by conquest, or marriage. The idea of self-rule—that the rulers should reflect the will of the people—implied the notion that rulers should be chosen *by* those over whom they ruled. It also determined *who* the people were. In France, the Revolution was directed against the king because he did not address the concerns of the citizens. In the Americas, the revolutionary fervor was not aimed so much against a specific ruler, but rather against distant rulers in faraway capitals that the inhabitants in the New World did not view as their own—we will discuss this in more detail in the next chapter. The revolutions were not only about being misruled, but about "foreign" rule.

In Europe, the French Revolution and the subsequent Napoleonic Wars were both an inspiration to national movements more generally, and a catalyst for particular national movements that mobilized against French domination of much of the continent. As Napoleon's army relegated to history many medieval and early modern states such as the Venetian Republic, the Holy Roman Empire, and numerous city states, it brought in the modern state that would constitute the foundation for the rise of nations.

On the Italian peninsula and in the states of the Holy Roman Empire, Italian and German nationalism emerged not so much by emulating the French nation, but instead, by rejecting what intellectuals and politicians saw as French hegemony. The battle that led to Napoleon's decisive defeat in 1813 near Leipzig became known as the "Battle of the Nations." The name of the battle epitomized how the idea of the nation had spread over the two decades of the Napoleonic Wars. Yet only two decades earlier, in 1792 at the Battle of Valmy when the

Document: Johann Gottlieb Fichte, Addresses to the German Nation[1]

*L*ectures given by the German philosopher Johann Gottlieb Fichte in Berlin during the French Napoleonic rule in Berlin in 1812.

To begin with and before all things: the first, original, and truly natural boundaries of states are beyond doubt their internal boundaries. Those who speak the same language are joined to each other by a multitude of invisible bonds by nature herself, long before any human art begins; they understand each other and have the power of continuing to make themselves understood more and more clearly; they belong together and are by nature one and an inseparable whole. Such a whole, if it wishes to absorb and mingle with itself any other people of different descent and language, cannot do so without itself becoming confused, in the beginning at any rate, and violently disturbing the even progress of its culture. From this internal boundary, which is drawn by the spiritual nature of man himself, the marking of the external boundary by dwelling-place results as a consequence; and in the natural view of things it is not because men dwell between certain mountains and rivers that they are a people, but, on the contrary, men dwell together—and, if their luck has so arranged it, are protected by rivers and mountains—because they were a people already by a law of nature which is much higher.

Thus was the German nation placed—sufficiently united within itself by a common language and a common way of thinking, and sharply enough severed from the other peoples—in the middle of Europe, as a wall to divide races not akin.

French soliders exclaimed "Vive la nation!," the Prussian forces were confused, because they were not yet acquainted with the idea of fighting for a nation rather than a king. In Leipzig, French troops faced defeat by Russian, Prussian, Habsburg, and Swedish troops that now began incorporating the logic of nation as well as increasing national resistance in the German Confederation of the Rhine. Many former German soldiers created *Burschenschaften*—nationalist fraternities that became strong promoters of German unity and nationalism in the following decades.[2] In 1817, they met at the central German castle of Wartburg to commemorate the Lutheran Reformation, which had begun there 300 years earlier, and the fourth anniversary of the Battle of the Nations. The participants called for German unity and an end to the post-Napoleonic restoration imposed after the defeat of Napoleon at the Congress of Vienna. Their successors in the 20th century would become proponents of radical exclusionary nationalism and anti-Semitism in Germany and Austria.

Rebellions against misrule were not new—peasant uprisings had been common across the continent, particularly during the sixteenth century—but they only gradually transformed into movements that based their claims not on improving the material or social positions, but on achieving national self-rule. When Ali Pasha of Ioannina took control of the Ottoman town of Ioannina (present-day northern Greece) in the late eighteenth century, he created a self-ruling region that lasted for decades, forging international alliances and promoting local autonomy, including a rich cultural life but this never became a national project. By contrast, the uprising in 1804 in the Ottoman region of Smederevo to Ali Pasha's north, initially also focused on local misrule but gradually took on national claims, making demands for the Serb population, just as the Greek uprising in 1821 would. Thus, while uprisings and rebellions were nothing new, what changed was the underlying justification and its resonance with those affected. While empires and monarchies could remedy or repress previous uprisings, they now had to contend with more structural claims for self-rule that could not be easily addressed. These uprisings and revolutions of the early nineteenth century were still far from popular national revolutions that would come later, but they were commonly driven by elites, and to the degree that the wider population participated, they were driven by particular concerns.

The revolutionary claims against multinational empires were but one strand of the emerging national movements of the early nineteenth century. While nation-states like France came about through revolution, other nations gradually emerged, such as England and Spain, they were not congruent with the state. In both of these cases, some regions resisted absorption into new nations—Catalonia in Spain, and Scotland and Ireland in Great Britain. As such, 'the emerging nation-states' were not just imperial powers overseas but also nationalizing empires. Either way, the shift from absolutist monarchies, in whole or in part, to nation-states was a gradual and drawn-out process enabled by a number of factors, including literacy and the emergence of secular languages. Ernest Gellner, the British scholar of nationalism of Czech origin, argued that nationalism became a necessity in modern states and thus "it is nationalism which engenders nations, and not the other way around."[3] Nationalism not only transforms and changes the cultural basis it draws on, but also, according to Gellner, arises in the context of modern societies when industrialization and cultural homogenization create the preconditions for a shared nation in a given polity.

The emergence of new states

Empires and nation-states dominated the nineteenth century. While the pair might appear to be diametrically opposed, but in fact, by the nineteenth century nations and empires began to converge. It is true that empires existed for centuries and had been historically either hostile or at least ambivalent about the nations within their borders, whereas for nation-states the nation is a central marker. In empires, the ruler justified his or her rule through God and the dynastic acquisition of lands, while nation states required a shared identity of the ruler and his or her subjects. Nevertheless, empires ceased being universalist projects that could govern the whole "known world" and became bounded.[4] They also created unified administrative structures not unlike those of nation-states. With the creation of a standing army, administration, and school system, a development common to both empires and nation-states the relationship between rulers and citizens became more immediate. Even in the 17th and 18th centuries, the rise of absolutism meant that the ruler gradually broke the power of the nobility and ruled directly. Such direct rule required new forms of legitimacy, and at the same time, it increased the contact between the state and citizen, as discussed earlier. Now, the politics of identity mattered. As empires discovered the importance of national identity, and they could opt to either convert, transform into mono-national empires or cultivate diversity. In this respect, empires were not mono- or multinational from the outset; they became mono- or multinational as national identities emerged and became their structuring feature.

Most other forms of statehood besides nation-states and empires disappeared as Napoleon reorganized the European state system. The last city-states and the oldest republics of Europe, the Venetian Republic and the Republic of Ragusa, were all abolished unceremoniously by the new republic, France. The Holy Roman Empire, the loose confederation of predominantly German states under Habsburg dominance, was similarly abolished. Left in their wake were small German and Italian states, including the papal states, that would join the new nation-states during the 1860s and 1870s voluntarily or by force.

New states emerged across Europe as nation-states, from Greece in the Southeast, to Belgium in Western Europe, to Norway in Scandinavia. The most significant transformation of the map of Europe occurred within the two decades between the unification of Italy, which began in earnest in 1859, and the Congress of Berlin in 1878. During these twenty years, Germany, Italy, Romania, Serbia, and Montenegro, as well as Bulgaria, emerged as new countries, all of which defined themselves as nation-states.

Scholars and statesmen in the nineteenth century shared a general assumption that nations had to be a certain size to exist. The logic of the era held that states had to be relatively big in order to defend themselves and build a viable economy. If states and nations were to be congruent, the nation had to follow the military and economic logic of the state. Small communities thus could not hope to survive as nations. Nationalist activists furthermore tended to consider themselves as modernizers, and dismissed small and regional identity as backward. Nowhere is this better expressed than in John Stuart Mill's (1806–1873) classic treatise on representative government, where he argued that,

Nobody can suppose that it is not more beneficial to a Breton, or a Basque of French Navarre, to be brought into the current of the ideas and feelings of a highly civilised and cultivated people—to be a member of the French nationality, admitted on equal terms to all the privileges of French citizenship, sharing the advantages of French protection, and the dignity and prestige of French power—than to sulk on his own rocks, the half-savage relic of past times, revolving in his own little mental orbit, without participation or interest in the general movement of the world.[5]

This view stood in contrast with the reality of many small nation-states emerging in Southeastern Europe, the smallest of which was Montenegro with around 200,000 inhabitants at the time of independence in 1878. That said, the irredentist aspirations held by many of them their irredentist aspirations implied much larger potential nation-states.

Nations and pan-national movements

Just as the new national movements were expected to absorb smaller regional identities, the boundaries between regional, national and pan-national movements were not always firm. National movements often thought of themselves to belong to larger groups. For example, a pan-Slavic movement was strong in the nineteenth century, as Slavs outside Russia lacked their own state and were ruled by Prussia, the Habsburgs, or the Ottomans. Despite sharing Slavic identity with Poles and others, the Russian Empire itself was oppressive in its rule of other Slavs. The spread of pan-Slavic ideas was not in competition with emerging national movements but was a supplement to them. It was also often ambiguous whether a movement was pan-Slavic or national. For example, the Illyrian movement in the South Slav lands incorporated Slovenes, Croats, and Serbs but oscillated between being a Yugoslav and a Croat national movement.

This phenomenon was particularly pronounced among Slavs who shared a linguistic similarity and lacked self-rule, but such ambiguities also existed elsewhere. For the German national movement, it was unclear what the scope of a German state would be. The Habsburg Monarchy had historically dominated German-speaking lands, however, its conservative orientation and its fierce opposition to nationalism presented practical obstacles for the creation of a German nation-state. During the debates democratic minded representatives at the Frankfurt Paulskirche during the revolutionary year 1848, two approaches to German statehood crystalized. A "greater German" solution would include the Habsburg Monarchy, in order to integrate all German language areas. The prevailing option – the "smaller German" solution – excluded the Habsburg Monarchy and focused on creating Germany out of Prussia, Bavaria, and the smaller principalities and towns. As already noted, the Habsburg Monarchys repressive practices, and in particular its opposition to German nationalism, made a greater German option less appealing. Furthermore, the Habsburg Monarchy could not easily become the core of a German nation-state, because German speakers represented only a minority of the population with Slav speakers, Hungarians, Italians, and numerous other groups living on the empire's territory.

The Austro-Prussian War of 1866 also highlighted that the two largest German-speaking states would not cooperate in the formation of a united Germany. Germany's particular configuration as it emerged in the aftermath of the Franco-Prussian War of 1871 was thus the result of many factors that prevented a larger German state. It furthermore aligned the idea of German unity with the militarist and conservative Prussian state, which was by no means a given only a few decades earlier.

The making of nations

The creation of nation-states across Europe ranged from transformation of existing states into nation-states, such as France and Great Britain, to unification of smaller units into large nation-states, such as Italy, to the gradual emergence of expanding nation-states, such as Greece or Serbia. In none of the cases did the creation of nation-states end the process of nation-building, however. In fact, in many instances it took the creation of the nation-state to initiate nation-building. The observation of Massimo d'Azeglio (1798–1866), a politician and novelist from Piedmont, best expressed the concern of these nation-builders in his memoir: "We have made Italy. Now we must make Italians." Indeed, at the time of his death Italy was barely unified, and many of its citizens would not have identified as Italians.[6]

Even those nations that emerged in preexisting states and evolved over a much more extended period, such as the French or British, stood far from consolidated in the nineteenth century. Even France, the prototype of the European nation and a model for other European national movements, took a century to emerge. At the time of the French Revolution, France was a country, as Graham Robb has noted, that took three weeks to cross in each direction. Most of its citizens lived within a small radius around their village.[7]

The main frame of reference was the region, or *pays*, instead of the state or the nation. Not only did the lack of mobility contribute to a more localized identity, but it also limited the reach of the French language. Even a century after the French Revolution, only a fifth of the population was comfortable speaking French—mostly those living in the region around Paris in the North. Others spoke different languages, including Breton, Corsican and Basque, which had little in common with French. Most of the south spoke Occitan, a romance language distinct from French. Elsewhere, regional and local dialects known as *patois* were widely spoken, most of which were incomprehensible to each other and to speakers of standardized French. In 1851 the French economist Adolphe Blanqui (1798–1854) noted that the inhabitants were "two separate peoples living on the same land, living a life so different they seem foreign to each other."[8] Thus it required a massive state effort to transform citizens into Frenchmen and Frenchwomen. Over more than a century, the nation was imposed as the main identity framework through tools of the modern state, such as education, communication, the military, and administration, the nation was imposed as the main identity framework. In his landmark study of the creation of the French nation-state, Eugen Weber (1925–2007) noted that "the famous hexagon can itself be seen as a colonial empire shaped over centuries."[9] This claim is not as far-fetched as it may appear at first, as the state and the Parisian elite often viewed the rural French as "savages," and the official understanding of its citizens did not differ much from its views of its colonial subjects. Indeed, there are stiking similarities between colonial rule in Africa and the creation of the nation-state within France. In the eyes of the state, in both cases, the French and colonial subjects needed to learn about values, manners, language, the country, and the nation.

The only distinction—and not a negligible one is that while the center viewed the French in the rural periphery as backward and primitive, they could become French through assimilation. The subjects of colonial rule, meanwhile, could not acquire French citizenship and thereby become French, or could do so only with great difficulty. An important step in French nation building was taken by Jules Ferry (1832–1893), minister of public education and fine arts, who introduced mandatory secular primary education in 1881/2. The goal was to reduce the influence of the church and regional languages, which were not just eliminated from the school curricula but actively prohibited from being spoken in school grounds: some schools used the motto "It is forbidden to spit on the ground and speak *patois*." It was also Ferry who promoted France's colonial expansion in Africa and Indochina with the goal of carrying out a "civilizing mission."

The French pattern was by no means unique, even if linguistic diversity in France was higher than elsewhere. The century-long effort to convert the nominally French nation-state into a unified nation highlights that it is nationalism that made the nation, not the other way around.

If the French model of nation-building rested on the imposition of the French language and culture over regional dialects and languages, the Swiss approach instead incorporated the different languages into a shared nation. The loose collection of urban and rural cantons that had forged a confederal structure to resist outside dominance was by no means predestined to become a nation-state. It was religiously diverse; its inhabitants spoke German, French, and Italian as well as the romance language of Romansh, and the differences between rural and urban centers were stark. With three large national movements across the border in France and in the German and Italian states claiming the three Swiss linguistic communities, one would expect the Swiss state to have disappeared like other early modern state structures that failed to effectively contend with the rise of the nation-state. However, the emergence of a civil society that cut across linguistic and religious lines fostered a level of cohesion that survived Napoleonic attempts at centralization, as well as the brief civil war in 1848 that resulted in a federal state. The emerging Swiss nationalism included French, Italian, and Romansh speakers, despite them amounting to only around a third of the population in total. The Swiss example highlights that, while a common language can facilitate the emergence of a common nation, it is by no means a prerequisite.

Of course, as the Andreas Wimmer has shown, molding a unified nation out of a multilingual population was not always successful. Belgium followed the French model of imposing the French language on the population, even though a slight majority spoke Flemish. The prestige of the French language, combined with a Francophone Flemish elite, propelled its predominance. The exclusion of Flemish did not lead to its marginalization, however, but rather to resistance and the rise of a Flemish national movement. The consequence was the erosion of the Belgian national identity in the twentieth century, resulting in a state defined by two competing nationalisms.[10]

Yugoslavia and Czechoslovakia were other states that sought to forge a shared nation out of a multilingual and multireligious population. However, the idea of a Yugoslav or a Czechoslovak nation were state-driven, top-down initiatives, without much resonance in society. More importantly, distinct Czech (and to a lesser degree Slovak) as well as Croat, Serb, and Slovene national identities had emerged before the creation of the common state. Those who identified with these nations were loath to relinquish their national identity for a larger new identity. Antagonizing state policies consolidated substate national identities. The failure shows that once the population accepts a particular national identity change becomes difficult.

National identity is sticky: once adopted it is not easily disposed of or changed. While individual identity switches are common, large-scale shifts among established and moderately consolidated national categories are rare. Pre-national identities, be they linguistic or religious, can be subsumed and assimilated into a nation, yet if these identities have evolved to include the characteristics of a nation, they are likely to persist and render efforts to create overarching nations more difficult.

The concept of "national indifference" best captures the attitude of most Europeans during the nineteenth century, and not just in France. While nationalism became an important subject for scholars and political elites, the significance of belonging to a particular nation was by no means a given, and most citizens and subjects of European states felt indifferent to the concept of the nation. This does not mean they were indifferent to other categories of identity: they often identified as Catholics, as workers or peasants, as inhabitants of one particular village. While national indifference declined in the course of the nineteenth century, it did not disappear nor should it be understood as a premodern relic. Rather, national indifference was often a response to modern mass politics that imposed national identity on citizens of newly created nation states.[11] This hold true even in the twentieth and twenty-first centuries many citizens might be aware of what nation they do (or "should") belong to, but it holds little relevance in everyday life.

Nationalists assumed that they would convince or coerce those co-nationals who remained indifferent to the nation to identify with it.

The logic, whether based on descent or citizenship, dictated that everybody had to belong to a nation. Indifference is in many ways the greatest threat to the nation. In the words of Ernest Renan, nationalism is the "clearly expressed desire to continue a common life. A nation's existence is, if you will pardon the metaphor, a daily plebiscite."[12] Thus, if the citizens do not express this desire, if they do not "vote for" the nation, it ceases to exist. Convincing the undecided was therefore essential. Furthermore, if they could not be convinced to be members of their own nation, they might be persuaded to join another. Take the competition among four Balkan nation-states over the inhabitants of one of the last Ottoman possessions in Europe in the late nineteenth century. The *vilayets*—the administrative regions of the Ottoman Empire—of Monastir (present-day Bitola, North Macedonia) and Salonica (present-day Thessaloniki, Greece) were populated by Slavs, Albanians, Jews, Greeks, and Vlachs (a small Romance-speaking Balkan community), as well as Ottoman Turks and others. Serbia, Bulgaria, and Greece, and to a lesser degree Romania, all laid claim to the region known as Macedonia and its population. To underline these claims, all four states opened hundreds of schools in the region to educate children in their languages. In addition, they sent their officials to count the population and create population statistics to provide a largely pseudo-scientific basis for their claims. Often the population data and the ethnographic maps were dubious, yet they provided crucial justifications for demands on the land and taking control of it in the first Balkan War.

The transformation of a population mostly indifferent to notions of nationalism into convinced nationalists took decades. This process took place in stages, which the Czech historian Miroslav Hroch described for small nations in Central Europe.[13] When states could not be the driving force of nation-building, other actors became essential. These might be existing institutions, such as churches or other premodern structures. For example, the Kingdom of Croatia was part of the Habsburg Monarchy that retained its own assembly, the *sabor*, mostly containing members of the nobility. This proto-parliament would evolve into an institution that make national claims in the nineteenth century, even though it had existed for centuries as an assembly of nobles without being such nation-builders.

Intellectuals, often writers and scholars, played a crucial role in promoting the idea of the nation. Many emerging national intellectuals in Central Europe were guided by the German experience with figures such as Johann Gottfried Herder (1744–1803), Johann Gottlieb Fichte (1762–1814), and the brothers Jacob Ludwig Karl (1785–1863) and Wilhelm Carl (1786–1859) Grimm. Steeped in mood of the romantic period, they often imagined themselves as rediscovering the nation, and actively sought to shape it through their work. The collection of fairy tales by the Brothers Grimm not only served to tell children's stories but also to give voice to the nation, as these tales were supposed to reflect the nation neglected and forgotten by elites. Similarly, Herder published a collection of folktales, later known as the "Voice of the Peoples in their Songs," featuring not just German but also Spanish, Lithuanian, Italian, French, and South Slav tales. His collections and the Brothers Grimm inspired many in Central and Eastern Europe, including the Serbian scholar Vuk Stefanović Karadžić, to also collect folktales. As German-language universities were centers of learning in continental Europe, this transfer of ideas was not surprising. The resonance beyond elites was limited, however, as most people were illiterate and largely indifferent to the ideas of the nation. It took active dissemination for them to gain popular resonance. Much of this diffusion took place through new institutions such as the cultural centers established in the mid-nineteenth century, which promoted the new national languages and cultures.

The final step for national movements to succeed occurred when these institutions and the intellectuals they represented became mass movements. This occurred only toward the end of the nineteenth century when literacy and education gave the ideas a broader reach. Once more, where states were absent as carriers of nationalist ideas, the void was filled by associations, such as the Sokol movement that emerged in Prague in 1862 and later spread to other Slavic lands as a gymnastics organization with a national purpose.

This trajectory of national movements without the backing of the state, however, was only possible when the state itself allowed for such groups to emerge. The Habsburg Monarchy endorsed the emergence of national elites, as long as they accepted the Monarchy. As a dynastic realm with multiple languages and identities, it recognized different languages, nations, and religions, whereas the Romanov

Empire and the Prussian (and later German) state only permitted the mobilization of the dominant Russian and German nations. The different policies and their impact became particularly visible in Poland. By the late eighteenth century, the early modern Polish–Lithuanian Commonwealth had been divided among these three empires. In Prussia, Polish identity was largely repressed, while in Russia only the short-lived "Congress Poland"—established at the Congress of Vienna and abolished in 1831—offered some autonomy. In the Habsburg realm, by contrast, Polish was a recognized language and Polish elites could participate in political life. Intellectuals were thus able to contribute to the emergence of national movements with greater ease in the Habsburg Monarchy than in either of its two northern neighbors. There, open rebellion and clandestine organizations became the only channels to promote Polish national identity.

Nationalisms in Europe's empires

Nationalism challenged existing states across Europe. Some were absolutist monarchies; others were small and fragmented duchies, principalities and city-states; and there were also empires. Monarchies that ruled over a compact territory, such as France or Great Britain, were better suited to transform into nation-states. The others coexisted less easily with nationalism. The German and Italian unification movements directed their territorial claims against the Habsburg Monarchy, which ruled over Italian and German-speaking populations claimed by both national movements.

There were two types of European empires. The trans-oceanic empires of Great Britain and France could separate colonial rule overseas from nation-state building at home. As we will discuss in the next chapter, this gap posed its own challenges in legitimizing its overseas rule. By contrast, the idea of nation-states challenged the continental European empires more directly. The Russian Empire, the Habsburg Monarchy, and the Ottoman Empire had all emerged over the previous centuries as realms of the ruling dynasties, and they responded in different ways to the rise of nationalism.

The Ottoman Empire perceived its rule primarily in religious terms. The Sultan was also Caliph and thus the supreme leader of Sunni Islam. The empire tolerated other Abrahamic religions—Christianity and Judaism—and provided for a high degree of self-government for these religious communities. These communities, known as "millets," gave Jews, Orthodox Christians, and other non-Muslim groups the right to conduct their own education and administer their own legal code. Following military defeats and economic decline during the nineteenth century, the Ottoman Empire undertook several attempts to transform into a modern European empire, yet both traditionalists within the empire and great power intervention from outside prevented this transformation, or at least curtailed it. Only after 1908 did the Ottoman Empire try to reconstruct itself into a national empire after the Committee of Unity and Progress, known as the "Young Turks," took over. This attempt had only modest success and at the time of the empire's collapse a decade later, it had become, in effect, a multireligious empire in which national movements emerged mostly among religious minorities.

The transformation of a multinational or multireligious state as in the case of the Russian Empire, into a nation-state was difficult. The Ottoman Empire lacked a clearly circumscribed core nation. The Turkic-speaking Muslim population had become a majority with the loss of most European regions of the empire. Yet there was no Turkish national identity, and Ottoman elites looked down on the Turkic peasants of Anatolia. A radical transformation took place only in the context of the First World War, when the Turkish government led by the Young Turks increasingly radicalized, and considered non-Turks, particularly non-Muslims, as a threat. This culminated in a policy of genocide against the Armenian population, which the Young Turk leadership accused of supporting Russian expansionism against the Ottoman state. In 1915 the government ordered the mass deportation of Armenians, resulting in the deliberate death of around 1.5 million Armenians due to attacks by regular and irregular troops, and heat and deprivation they endured while forced to march to exile through the Syrian desert. The deportation was intended to kill most Armenians in the Ottoman Empire, and thus it constituted not only the displacement of a potentially hostile population in wartime, but also the deliberate mass murder of a group, based on its identity, in the shadow of war.

This was by no means the first genocide. The German colonial administration in German Southwest Africa (present-day Namibia) had committed genocide between 1904 and 1908 against the Herero and Nama populations that had rebelled against the oppressive colonial rule. History offers numerous examples of states engaging in mass murder against population groups, such as that against native populations in the Americas, against Muslims in post-Ottoman lands by the newly autonomous and independent nation-states in the nineteenth century, and similar campaigns. But the Armenian genocide is notable for being part of a wartime attempt to create a homogenous nation-state out of the remnants of a multinational empire. The homogenization of the state continued after the war with the mass expulsion of Greeks and, later, with the organized population transfer between Greece and Turkey. The Turkish nation-state that emerged under Mustafa Kemal Atatürk's leadership was thus largely homogenous in comparison to its Ottoman predecessor.

Not unlike the Ottoman Empire, the Habsburg Empire was multilingual and multi-religious, and had emerged over centuries as the realm of the Habsburg dynasty. The Habsburg Monarchy ruled over predominantly German-speaking lands; the corresponding dynasty may have presided over the Holy Roman Empire of the German Nation (a misnomer, as Voltaire famously quipped, that "was neither holy, nor Roman, nor an empire"[14]), but it certainly did not represent the German nation. Napoleon put an end to the empire as such in 1806, and the Habsburg Monarchy focused its energy thereafter on consolidating its rule over territories acquired by marriage and conquest. These territories were eclectic, extending from the Swiss to the Russian border, with a population speaking German, Italian, Czech, Slovak, Hungarian, Romanian, Croatian and Serbian, Slovene, Polish, Ruthenian, Ukrainian, and many other languages and dialects. Imposing a single national identity was unrealistic. Of course, as Switzerland shows, a single national identity could emerge in a multilingual environment. However, the territorial vastness of the empire, the variety of its population in terms of socio-economic development and the religious differences, made such an enterprise unlikely to succeed. United only by a monarchy, it was also hard to identify a common framework that could bind all the languages, religions, and, increasingly, nations. There was never a plan to transform the monarchy into a nation-state. Instead, plans focused on creating a more consistent federal state out of the eclectic collection of monarchical possessions, such as Aurel Popovici's 1906 plan for "the United States of Greater Austria."

This does not mean irrespective of the identity at the level of the empire, multinational or multilingual identities could emerge locally. In Dalmatia, the mayor of Split Antonio Bajamonti compared Dalmatians to the Swiss, with different languages spoken by different people who shared a place "living in the same land, rather than reuniting with their mother countries, they believed it more opportune for them to live in the same family, which the centuries and misfortunes ... gave the right to consider itself a nation."[15] These efforts eventually failed as Italian, Croatian, and Serbian nationalists convinced Dalmatians that they were Italians, Croats, and Serbs.

Within the Habsburg Monarchy German speakers were the largest group, but they still only amounted to a quarter of the population. Instead of imposing a single identity, however, the monarchy mostly sought to accommodate nationalist claims, especially after a more repressive approach—adopted at the Congress of Vienna—failed by the mid-nineteenth century. To accommodate Hungarian national demands, the monarchy split in two in 1867. The eastern half included the lands of the Hungarian crown, incorporating today's Slovakia, Hungary, Transylvania (Northwestern Romania), Vojvodina (Northern Serbia), and Croatia. The Hungarian elites engaged in transforming their realm into a nation-state within the empire, except for Croatia and Slavonia, which maintained its self-rule. In Cisleithania, as the Austrian half was informally known, the central policy sought to accommodated the competing national demands. National movements competed over local control and language rights in contested areas, such as in Cili/Celje, in present-day Slovenia, or in Bohemia and Moravia, which had both German- and Czech-speaking populations. Overall, the policy of the state was recognition and settling these disputes through group and language rights, most famously the Moravian compromise of 1905, which divided the regional diet (parliament) and protected the rights of the Czech and German speakers.

It is from this legacy that the influential Austro-Marxists drew their ideas for dealing with the national question. Otto Bauer and Karl Renner, leading figures of the Austrian social democrats, sought to find a solution to avoid conflict among workers from different nations within the empire. Bauer realized that the national question would not disappear without accommodation, and he also rejected the strong link between nations and territory that the Russian Marxists had proposed. In the diverse cities and lands of the monarchy, territorial solutions were dangerous, or at least impractical. Bauer proposed instead to decouple territorial and national claims by promoting non-territorial cultural autonomy. Thus, rather than nation-states, Bauer supported the continued existence of the state as a multinational Danubian Empire, with "a legal sphere of power, through national autonomy, for every nation" to "bring an end to the power struggle between the nations; if the cry for help by the Austrian nations is no longer heard abroad, foreign imperialism will lose its most effective means of winning the support of the masses of its respective nations for its policy of conquest." [16]

In the end, the empire dissolved after the four years of the First World War, during which the military and political weaknesses of the state became visible while its repressive policies made it less attractive for many citizens. Non-German and non-Hungarian national elites began advocating a future outside the monarchy.

In contrast to the Habsburg and Ottoman empires the Russian Empire took a different strategy, transforming into a national empire, dominated by the emerging Russian nation. Its population was similarly diverse, including Poles, Finns, Baltic populations, Jews, Germans, Ukrainians, and Belarussians in the West; Armenians, Georgians, Azeris, Chechens, and others in the Caucasus; and Turkic populations in Central Asia. Until the early nineteenth century, the Romanov Empire was ruled like a conventional empire. If Poles or other groups rebelled, it subdued them; if the population and their elites were loyal, it interfered little. However, as the rebellions took an increasingly national tone, so too did the repression, and the Russian Empire progressively imposed a Russian centralized system of rule across its vast territory. The 1830 revolution in Poland resulted in Russian repression and the de facto elimination of the last vestiges of autonomy Poland had enjoyed since the Congress of Vienna. The repression was not only military but also religious, favoring the Orthodox Church over the Catholic Church – a classic example of the use of religion in imposing the dominant nation. In the course of the coming decades, the formal separate administrative structures were abolished and the use of the Polish language outlawed. Assimilation efforts were less swift in the Baltics and Finland, but here too the Russian Empire gradually chipped away at their autonomy. Russification was the prevailing policy toward Orthodox Christians in the empire, from Ukraine to the Caucasus. Muslims in Central Asia and the Caucasus, however, were subject to imperial control but not assimilation.[17] In sum, while the Habsburg Monarchy moved increasingly to accommodate its different national movements, the Russian Empire moved in the opposite direction toward increased repression.

Self-determination and the success of the nation-state

No conflict better represents the shift from a confrontation between nations and empires to one among nation-states than the Balkan Wars. The First Balkan War was fought in late 1912 and early 1913 between the Balkan League, composed of Serbia, Montenegro, Greece, Bulgaria, and Romania, against the Ottoman Empire. The league was successful, and the empire lost almost all of its European territory except for a small area around the capital city Istanbul. The Second Balkan War broke out just a few months later when Bulgaria, dissatisfied with the distribution of territories gained during the war, attacked Serbia and Greece. This brought together all the former belligerents, including the Ottoman Empire, to fight against Bulgaria and defeat it by the summer of 1913. Rather than bringing about the defeat of the empire and the amicable distribution of territory, the nation-states were deeply divided about who would hold on to each part of the former Ottoman lands. The Carnegie Commission, a group of international experts, visited the countries and documented the war crimes committed. Their report included a map showing the competing territorial claims of the different Balkan nation-states, highlighting how they overlapped and made compromise difficult. As empires retreated, the main line of confrontation shifted toward competition between nation-states. The nation-states laid claim to the same populations and/or land, each advancing a variety of arguments in favor of their claims, ranging from history, language, or descent to other objective and subjective markers of national identity.

Similarly, the First World War was made possible by nationalism and the modern state, but its belligerents included three empires, which would dissolve from within at the end of the war. The Russian, Ottoman, and Habsburg empires collapsed through revolution and internal turmoil. Whether the multinational empires could have found a way to transform themselves in the era of nationalism is anyone's guess, but the Great War was the catalyst that led to their collapse.

At the end of First World War, with empires collapsing, the question emerged of which principle should guide the drawing of the new map of Europe. While the war was a victory for national movements, different ideas competed regarding how the new borders should be drawn. As earlier conflicts within the empires, as well as between emerging nation-states had shown, borders between nations were contested and therefore difficult to determine. European powers had envisaged conventional rewards for the victors, disregarding the will of those who found themselves living in a different country. From French claims to Alsace and Lorraine, to German claims to the east, and Italian claims to the Eastern Adriatic, national demands were at best serving an opportunistic argument. The competing ideas that would undermine this concept came from the emerging global powers, the United States and the Soviet Union, who sought to challenge conventional great power politics that paid little attention to the wishes of those whose land was being negotiated. The American president Woodrow Wilson (1856–1924) articulated the idea of self-determination, meaning that people would choose their own government, and that this idea guide the (re-)construction of states in Central and Eastern Europe, govern the dismemberment of the big empires, and be considered in making border adjustments. Some of these concepts found their way into the famous fourteen points he outlined in his speech to Congress in January 1918 defining the American principles for the postwar peace.

The notion of self-determination was by no means uncontested. The winners of the First World War, particularly France and the UK, were reluctant to allow the idea of national self-determination affect their colonial possessions, which they hoped to expand. Beyond the colonial territories, both had claims to territories in Europe against the clear will of their inhabitants. France claimed Alsace and Lorraine, which Germany had gained in 1871, and also sought the Saar region, despite a clear German population majority. The British Foreign Office, for their part, objected that,

> It would clearly be inadvisable to go even the smallest distance in the direction of admitting the claim of the American Negros, or

the Southern Irish, or the Flemings, or Catalans, to appeal to an Inter-State Conference over the head of their own government. Yet if a right of appeal is granted to the Macedonians or the German Bohemians it will be difficult to refuse it in the case of other nationalist movements.[18]

This skepticism was ironic, as Britain had justified its entry into the war with the claim of protecting smaller nations that were bullied by the Central Powers, such as Belgium and Serbia. Nevertheless, beyond the self-serving concerns for the winners of the war, the concept of self-determination was vague and could justify conflicting revolutionary claims. Woodrow Wilson's secretary of state Robert Lansing was highly skeptical of the idea, asking "When the president talks of 'self-determination' what unit has he in mind? Does he mean a race, a territorial area, or a community? Without a definite unit which is practical, application of this principle is dangerous to peace and stability."[19]

Even the countries of Central and Eastern Europe, which stood to gain most from the postwar arrangement, were reluctant to see their claims restricted by assertions of national self-determination by others. Asking for the wishes of those affected was, in fact, the exception. There were plebiscites in Schleswig to determine the border between Germany and Denmark, in Upper Silesia and Eastern Prussia, between Germany and Poland, in Southern Carinthia, between Austria and Yugoslavia, and in parts of Burgenland, between Austria and Hungary. Elsewhere, expert commissions sought to establish the new borders, considering not only the national composition and the will of the population affected but also the defensibility of the borders. This was one reason why the large German minority living in the hilly border regions of Czechoslovakia ended up in that country. (Ironically this turned out to be a greater source of instability for Czechoslovakia than if the minority had not been included: the Sudeten Germans were instrumentalized by Nazi Germany in its territorial claims against the country nearly twenty years later).

The Peace Treaties following the First World War also included comprehensive minority rights for the first time. Although national minority rights had existed earlier, and some peace treaties, particularly the 1878 Berlin Treaty for the Balkans, included minority rights provisions, with little effect. The post-First World War Minority Treaties were an Allied condition for the newly established countries of Central Europe. Minority protection was driven by the Great Powers' distrust of their Central and East European partners, and thus imposed on reluctant governments, who viewed the obligation as unfair. Irrespective of their commitments, governments tried to disregard the provisions, and the newly created League of Nations became inundated with petitions by minority representatives. In the end, the protection system failed to uphold minority rights, and with the abuse of national minorities by irredentist states, the minorities became an imagined and sometimes real threat to the states of interwar Europe.

These international minority rights obligations appeared to conflict with most European states' self-understanding as nation-states. Poland reemerged after having been partitioned by three empires in the late eighteenth century. Czechoslovakia, Hungary, Austria, Yugoslavia, and Romania all incorporated territories of the Habsburg Monarchy, while the Baltics and Finland gained independence from the Russian Empire, which in the meantime become the Soviet Union. In addition, many more ephemeral nation-states had a brief existence in the shadows of the Russian Civil War (1918–21), including Georgia, Ukraine, Armenia, and Azerbaijan. The defeat of the Ottoman Empire also created a stillborn Armenia and a Kurdish state in Ottoman lands, as well as the restive Arab regions under League of Nation mandates, de facto under British and French colonial rule.

After the end of the Russian Civil War and widespread unrest in Central and Eastern Europe, and once the territorial disputes were mostly settled in 1920/1, the new states consolidated themselves, yet most were far from being nation-states in anything but name. In Poland in 1921 only 69.2 percent of the population was Polish; Ruthenians made up 15.2 percent of the population, followed by Jews, Belarussians, Germans, and others. This was a little different from most other countries in Central Europe. In Romania, Romanians made up 71.9 percent in 1930, and in Czechoslovakia, Czechs and Slovaks comprised 65.3 percent of the population. The tension between the aspirations of a nation-state and the reality of a multinational state, which often incorporated territories that had been under different legal systems for decades, proved destabilizing. Irredentist states, such as Bulgaria, Hungary, Italy, and later also Germany, encouraged minorities to undermine the nation-states, while the new states distrusted and often excluded minorities. Minorities without a kin state, such as the Jews, were the most vulnerable, lacking protection and being subject to institutionalized discrimination such as restrictions on entering universities, as well as considerable social exclusion and hostility.

The rise of biological anti-Semitism

The position of Jews as a European minority raised the question of integration and a nations' boundaries. Jews did not constitute a majority anywhere and instead lived as minorities throughout the continent. In some regions and towns the Jewish population was large, including in the city of Salonika (where nearly half of the population in the late nineteenth century was Jewish), and the Western borderlands of the Russian Empire—regions it had gained in the partition of the Polish–Lithuanian Commonwealth in the late eighteenth century. Most Russian Jews were forced by discriminatory laws to remain in this "Pale of Settlement" and could not move to other parts of the Russian Empire. The second half of the nineteenth century brought about formal emancipation of Jews as discriminatory laws and policies were lifted in several European states, but at the same time, pogroms increased and secular anti-Semitism was on the rise. While anti-Semitism was a Europe-wide phenomenon, it was encouraged by the Russian state and resulted in a series of pogroms, particularly in 1881–1884 and 1903–1906.

Traditionally, the main option for Jews in European countries had been to live in rural or urban isolation. After the religious emancipation, the choice was either to assimilate into the respective majority or to retain an inward-looking identity. The anti-Semitism many Jews confronted, however, raised the question of whether assimilation was possible. While those who did assimilate were able to make careers—at least in Western Europe—anti-Semitic undertones remained potent (as highlighted, for instance, by as the Dreyfus Affair in France). Earlier religious anti-Semitism became incorporated into the new nationalisms, expressing itself through discrimination and exclusion, from stereotypes of Jews as "Orientals" who are inherently alien among the British ruling classes, to the already-mentioned pogroms in the western regions of the Russian Empire. Jews also became targets of the pseudo-biological racial anti-Semitism that emerged in the late nineteenth century. Inspired by Darwinism, this view assumed that humanity was divided into races that were distinct and hierarchical. Proponents of this idea, such as the French aristocrat Joseph Arthur de Gobineau (1816–1882), defined Jews not as a religious group but through pseudo-biological and pseudo-racial characteristics. These ideas were taken up by Houston Stewart Chamberlain (1855–1927), a British-born philosopher who worked in Germany and shaped the worldview of Hitler.

The emergence of pseudo-biological racism and anti-Semitism was not unique to Europe, as similar ideas and policies arose in South Africa leading to apartheid, and informed colonial policies elsewhere. The emergence of racial anti-Semitism could be seen as the most radical understanding of nationalism as determined by descent. It excluded some groups—in this case, Jews—from the nation by definition, irrespective of their attempts to assimilate. This virulent anti-Semitism would become the inspiration for a number of radical nationalist groups in early twentieth-century Europe, the most prominent being the National Socialist German Workers Party (*Nationalsozialistische Deutsche Arbeiterpartei*, NSDAP), led by Adolf Hitler.

The rise of radical, nationalist, authoritarian, and totalitarian movements that could be described as fascist or National Socialist was not exclusively linked to anti-Semitism. Italian fascism, for instance, had few anti-Semitic features and included Jews in prominent positions—at least in the early phases. Its anti-Semitic turn reflects rather Italy's later dependence on Nazi Germany than ideological conviction. What these groups shared was a hierarchical cult of the leader, be it Hitler or Mussolini. The focus on leadership reflected their anti-democratic and authoritarian worldviews. These groups were often explicitly violent, and rejected parliamentarism and a state based on the rule of law. They claimed to represent the nation as a collective, rejecting individualism. As totalitarian ideologies and systems, the goal was complete control of society and the state, and their subordination to the fascist worldview.[20]

The nationalism these movements incorporated was largely "organic" in the sense that the nation was understood as an organism—

Document: The Doctrine of Fascism[21]

Written by Giovanni Gentile and Benito Mussolini in 1932 for the Enciclopedia Italiana

To Fascism the world is not this material world which appears on the surface, in which man is an individual separated from all other men, standing by himself and subject to a natural law which instinctively impels him to lead a life of momentary and egoistic pleasure. In Fascism man is an individual who is the nation and the country. He is this by a moral law which embraces and binds together individuals and generations in an established tradition and mission, a moral law which suppresses the instinct to lead a life confined to a brief cycle of pleasure …

Fascism wants man to be active and to be absorbed in action with all his energies; it wants him to have a manly consciousness … It conceives of life as a struggle, thinking that it is the duty of man to conquer that life which is really worthy of him: creating in the first place within himself the (physical, moral, intellectual) instrument with which to build it …

This higher personality is truly the nation, in as much as it is the State. The nation does not beget the State, according to the decrepit nationalistic concept which was used as a basis for the publicists of the national States in the Nineteenth Century. On the contrary, the nation is created by the State, which gives the people, conscious of their own moral unity, the will, and thereby an effective existence.

The right of a nation to its independence is derived not from a literary and ideal consciousness of its own existence, much less from a de facto situation more or less inert and unconscious, but from an active consciousness, from an active political will disposed to demonstrate in its right; that is to say, a kind of State already in its pride.

hence the subordination of the individual. Threats were subsequently also portrayed in pseudo-biological terms, such as diseases or parasites. In his January 1943 speech Joseph Goebbels, the Nazi minister of propaganda, exclaimed that "Jewry is a contagious infection."[22] This view was propagated through propaganda films and Nazi publications. It complemented a conspiratorial worldview that saw Jews (and other enemies) as part of a larger coordinated threat against the nation.[23] Due to their rejection of the established states in terms of borders, political systems, and the political community (i.e., who is part of the nation), these groups radically rejected the status quo. They were thus not traditionalists but rather revolutionary nationalists whose nationalist and racial worldview endorsed violence as a central feature of politics. Some, such as Mussolini, succeeded in taking power, but many remained at the margins of politics in their countries. Electoral success was limited and often short-lived. Hitler's electoral success in Germany was exceptional, and his rise rapid. Throughout the 1920s, the Nazi Party was a fringe group, gaining only 2.8 percent of the vote in 1928. This figure increased to 18.3 percent two years later, and peaked at 37.4 percent in July 1932, closely linked to the economic crisis and the gradual hollowing out of German democracy by other conservative, anti-democratic parties. Elsewhere, fascists ranged from Sir Oswald Mosley's British Union of Fascists to the Legion of the Archangel Michael in Romania, led by Corneliu Codreanu. None achieved enough electoral support to take power, nor were they able to take power in a coup, as Mussolini had done in his March on Rome in 1922. When they did attain power, it was as puppet regimes during the German occupation in the Second World War.

The rise of Zionism

The rise of racial anti-Semitism is also an important trigger for the emergence of Zionism. Among the national movements emerging in Europe during the late nineteenth and early twentieth centuries, Zionism takes a peculiar place, but it also highlights some key features of minority nationalism.

The Zionist movement responded to European anti-Semitism and the implicit rejection of the notion that Jews could emancipate themselves and become part of the emerging nations. The response was a national project of its own: the idea of creating a nation-state in Palestine, although other potential sites such as Uganda, were debated among various Zionist factions. As a minority without a discernable potential kin state in Europe, the movement sought self-government in the historical Jewish homeland, even though Jews were a small minority in Palestine at the time. Migration to Palestine gathered pace in the first decade of the twentieth century, increasing after the League of Nations established a British mandate in Palestine and committed itself to creating a "national home for the Jewish people." Still, it was the mass murder of six million Jews during the Holocaust that transformed the goal of the Zionist movement into a reality. The Zionist movement highlights how not all national movements are cut from the same cloth, and how they do not automatically include all members of the community they appeal to. At first, Zionism was a minority political project among European Jews. The majority pursued different strategies. Many sought either assimilation or integration, which could mean practicing Judaism but otherwise considering oneself to be a member of the dominant nation, or conversion. Benjamin Disraeli, whose parents and siblings converted to the Church of England in 1817, and who would become the first British Prime Minister of Jewish descent, is one prominent example of the latter. Others, particularly in Eastern Europe where assimilation or integration was hardly possible, lived in Shtetl or even in larger towns, but separate from the mostly − hostile majority. Equally, Zionism was not the only possible response to discrimination, as many Jews opted to emigrate to the United States instead. Some two million Central and East European Jews left for the United States during the big migration wave between 1880 and 1924. Zionism thus had to contend with different individual choices and political and social options. Like so many other national movements, it was also divided internally among different ideological options, from socialist Zionists who supported the creation of kibbutzim, to revisionist Zionists, such as the groups led by Ze'ev Jabotinsky, focusing on a strong Jewish nation-state in Israel and advocating the expulsion of Palestinian Arabs. Furthermore, Zionists diverged on strategy, disagreeing on whether to build a Jewish homeland from the ground up, focus on lobbying with great powers, or accept self-rule in a territory that was not Palestine, as the founder of the Zionist movement Theodor Herzl contemplated toward the end of his life. Jews lived in different countries, both empires and nation-states, spoke different languages and differed on whether they were a distinct nation (or race, to use the common terminology of the time) or just a religious group. It is hardly surprising that the national project was contested and fragmented. However, there is nothing unusual to this level of diversity. National movements generally faced the competition from alternative political projects and their internal pluralism.

Communism and nationalism

Besides nation-states and fascist regimes, another pattern of state and nation-building in the twentieth century Europe took shape in Communist Europe. After the Russian Revolution, the politics of nationalism in the emerging Soviet Union differed radically from other European models. As noted earlier Lenin and the Bolsheviks offered an alternative approach towards self-determination in the aftermath of the Great War. Officially, the Soviet Union was neither a multinational empire, as Great Britain or the Habsburg Monarchy had been, nor a nation-state. The Soviet Union was unique, as even the multinational states of Yugoslavia or Czechoslovakia during the interwar period conceived of themselves as nation-states with different subgroups, but not distinct nations. Thus, the official language of the Kingdom of Serbs, Croats, and Slovenes was called Serbo-Croat-Slovene, and the understanding prevailed that the different groups constituted a single nation with different names. Similarly, in Czechoslovakia, the constitution of 1920 described the Czechoslovak nation as the core, with national minorities.

The Soviet Union was the only state in interwar Europe which explicitly defined itself as a multinational state. At the core stood Lenin's concept of self-determination, which echoed Wilson but differed in critical aspects. In a key 1914 article for the Bolshevist literary monthly *Prosveshcheniye* (Enlightenment), Lenin argued that the "repudiation of the right to self-determination or to secession inevitably means, in practice, support for the privileges of the dominant nation."[24] In effect, he argued that dominant nations, in the case of Russia, the Russian nation, were used by the bourgeoisie to oppress others, and thus self-determination was a tool for the workers to emancipate themselves from oppression. As a result, Soviet rule would be built on the principle of self-determination, which included the (formal) possibility to secede.

The first Soviet constitution of 1924 and the Stalinist constitution of 1936 contained a provision allowing Soviet republics to withdraw from the Soviet Union. In turn, the republics were organized along national lines, creating the concept of titular nations that would predominate in the respective republics, even if large minorities lived there. Combining a right to self-determination with an ethnofederal structure that gives the nations the possibility to govern themselves was a crucial innovation of the Soviet model, implemented in two steps. The first step was the recognition of different nations. In the first Soviet census of 1926, 176 separate nationalities were recognized, of which the smallest, Black Tatars, counted only twelve members. Russians made up half of the 120 million inhabitants. However, neither the recognition of nations nor the attribution of territory was straightforward. In particular, in Central Asia, modern nations had not yet emerged, and Soviet policy was in effect less one of recognition and more one of creation. The Soviet system effectively created a complicated set of *Matryoshka* dolls of multiple layers of territorial autonomy at the Soviet and republican level, often with the formally constituent nation being a minority on its territory. In the Georgian region of Abkhazia, for example, the Abkhaz made up less than 30 percent of the population yet they constituted the titular nation. The most absurd example is the Jewish Autonomous *Oblast*, which survives as an autonomous region in Russia's far east until today. Created in 1928 as a Soviet homeland for Jews, the population of this remote and thinly populated region on the Chinese border was never more than 25% Jewish.[25]

These oddities already highlight that the reality of Soviet nationality policy was entirely different from the theory. The right to self-determination was not understood in the totalitarian state as a genuine possibility of a unit (e.g. Ukraine or Belarus leaving) to leave the Soviet Union, but rather as a safeguard against the bourgeois, capitalist oppression. As the Soviet Union had become a socialist state, such secession was no longer relevant from the Leninist perspective. Furthermore, the republics were only partly proto-nation states. Initially, the politics of *Korenizatsiya*, literally "putting down roots", sought to replace Russian elites with indigenous leaders. The Party, including Lenin and Stalin, warned against Greater Russian chauvinism, and in practice, the Soviet Union had created a quasi-imperial rule, especially in the Caucasus and Central Asia. The new policy promoted new elites, institutionalized the languages and alphabets (impractically in Central Asia which had little written tradition), and promoted language and culture in education. However, by the 1930s, this policy went into decline as Stalin's purges expelled and killed many of the new elites and promoted greater Russification and centralization. During the 1930s and 1940s in particular, the Soviet state also engaged in systematic discrimination against certain groups. The largest group affected were the Ukrainians, millions of whom were deliberately exposed to mass starvation in the massive famine in 1932–3, but Kazakhs and others were also disproportionately affected. During the Second World War, nations suspected of collaboration with Germany were also targeted; examples include the mass deportation of Crimean Tatars and Chechens.

The Soviet model, as well as its practice, would become a template for nationality politics in other socialist countries such as China, Yugoslavia, and across Central Europe after the Second World War.

After the end of the war, the Soviet Union and successful partisans in Yugoslavia and Albania established Communist regimes across Central and Eastern Europe, reaching from Tallinn in Soviet Estonia to Albania. The Baltic countries lost their independence during the war and were turned into Soviet republics, while the other countries retained their formal independence, albeit with limited sovereignty under Soviet tutelage. The logic of Communism dictated that nationalism was a bourgeois anachronism that would be overcome by the new regime. Already in coming to power, this distinction from nationalism was rather more ideological than real. In Czechoslovakia, the Communists participated in the first postwar government together with liberal and social democrats under the leadership of President Edvard Beneš. The government sought to organize the expulsion and nationalization of German minority property in Czechoslovakia. Many Germans had already fled the Red Army or had been expelled as they feared retribution due to large scale support for Hitler and their abuse to justify the annexation of these regions and, later, the occupation of Czechoslovakia. The Communist Party was a staunch supporter of these expulsions along national and collective lines, ignoring individual responsibility. Similarly, the Communist-dominated Lublin committee in Poland expelled Germans, and signed an agreement with the Soviet Union agreeing to the displacement Poles from lands that were part of prewar Poland before becoming part of the Soviet Republic of Belarus. Likewise, Ukrainians from Poland were expelled to Soviet Ukraine. The creation of homogenous nation-states de facto became the desirable template for postwar Central and Eastern Europe. Both the Communist and non-Communist parties and politicians saw not just Germans but also other minorities as a threat to state stability.

Once established, these new regimes were at first strongly Stalinist, with a formal commitment to Soviet-dominated internationalism and little national autonomy. The initial leaders included many who had spent years in Soviet exile, and many belonged to minority communities thus less likely to draw on strong residual nationalism. However, in the last years of Stalin's rule, anti-Semitic currents gained ground throughout the Soviet Union and in countries under its control. This translated into trials such as the Slánský trial in Czechoslovakia where Rudolf Slánský, the general secretary of the Communist Party, was accused of being part of a Trotskyite-Titoite-Zionist conspiracy and hanged in 1952. Such persecution eventually abated with the death of Stalin.

Nevertheless, after a generational change of Communist leaders, nationalism gradually became more prominent. The principle of unconditional loyalty to the Soviet Union undermined the legitimacy of Communist rule in the eyes of citizens, as became evident during the workers' protests in East Berlin in 1953, the Hungarian uprising in 1956, and the Prague Spring in 1968. Communist leaders, therefore, sought to strengthen their legitimacy through nationalist measures, either by displaying (mostly fictional) independence from the Soviet Union or by targeting minorities. In Romania, Nicolae Ceaușescu promoted nationalist myths of the ancient Dacians and engaged in repressive policies against the large Hungarian minority. A similar campaign was launched in neighboring Bulgaria against the Muslim Slav Pomak minority and the Turks. In fact, Turks and Muslims had long been a target of nationalists due to their association with the long Ottoman rule. They had to change their names and Turks were no longer allowed to speak Turkish. This campaign eventually led to the emigration of over 300,000 Turks from the country in 1989 and ushered in the regime's collapse. Even East Germany, which was the least independent and most dogmatic member of the Eastern Bloc, began emphasizing its German national identity by celebrating the

500th anniversary of Marin Luther's birth in 1983 and promoting a positive association with Prussia despite its identification with conservatism and militarism.

Yugoslavia took a different path by being the only explicitly multiethnic Communist state in Europe besides the Soviet Union. The first model for Communist Yugoslavia was the Stalinist Soviet Union. After the Second World War the country became a federal state organized along ethnic lines, dominated by the Communist Party. Different nations were recognized and given self-government through the republics and provinces as a way to manage competition among nationalisms while also empowering national identity (a policy choice that would later facilitate the country's collapse).

To summarize, the nineteenth century was the period when nationalism gradually spread across the continent, and national activists convinced the population to abandon their indifference to the various nations laying claim to them. Nation-states were multinational while empires gradually became national. The mass politics of nationalism enabled European elites to fight the First World War, which transformed Europe into a volatile continent of mutually hostile nation-states. The Second World War was started by a totalitarian regime promoting a pseudo-biological violent worldview that sought to radically transform Europe into a German-dominated continent, while reconfiguring the nation, and not only through the Holocaust and the mass murder of other population groups. It also imposed a hierarchical and totalitarian view of the nation that was emulated by the allies. The defeat of National Socialism in 1945 ushered in not just the divide of the continent in Capitalist and Communist spheres, but also a Europe whose states were more homogenous than they had ever been before. While as nationalism appeared to be discredited by its association with Nazi Germany, at the same time, nation-states had become the norm.

4

The Global Spread
of Nationalism and
Decolonization

Nationalism and the nation-state may have had their origins in Europe, but they quickly spread around the world. This diffusion occurred on the back of colonialism and the economic and political dominance that European powers held during the period of the rise of nationalism. While centralized states such as China, and collective identities existed previously, and elsewhere, this particular combination spread from Europe, built on powerful mass-based collective identity and the modern state, and the strength of European powers.

There was a deep-seated paradox in this spread of the nation. The European powers imagined the world as European, with colonial possessions as extensions of European influence, and non-European populations as inferior on the basis of cultural, religious, and racial grounds. The understanding that the world was divided into nations was based on the assumption that these nations were European and that they would rule the world. While this disempowered and marginalized the rest of the world, the idea of the nation nevertheless spread from Europe and the United States through the colonies of Spain and Portugal, and later France, Britain, even smaller colonial powers of the Netherlands, Belgium, Italy, and Germany, as well as the indirect influence exercised by European and North American powers in other parts of the world. This spread was unintentional, because these powers sought to maintain a Eurocentric global dominance.

Yet the idea of self-rule by a territorially-bound community was appropriated by colonized populations and became a central demand of anti-colonial nationalism. From early nationalism in the Americas in the late eighteenth and early nineteenth centuries to global anti-colonial struggles in the twentieth century, national movements did not end once independence was achieved. Instead they went on to confront the transformation of colonial units that had been imposed on preexisting populations and polities, often by force, into states. This chapter will examine this processes, from the emergence of national movements to the types of nations they advocated. In particular, it will explore how the colonial unit mostly prevailed over larger nation-states that would combine multiple colonies or smaller, more homogeneous states. That would break apart the colonial borders.

Benedict Anderson outlines how European colonization facilitated the spread of nationalism and how the colonial nationalism emulated many features of European nationalisms. The notion that nationalism outside of Europe largely copied European models, however, has been critiqued from a postcolonial perspective by scholars such as the Indian political scientist Partha Chatterjee (1947–). Chatterjee contests the notion that "we in the postcolonial world shall only be perpetual consumers of modernity."[1] His observation correctly challenges the perception that nationalism outside Europe is merely an undistinguished copy of European models. While colonialism and the dominance of Europe and later North America in the global world system facilitated the spread of power structures and ideas, nationalism outside Europe is not just a mere copy. As nationalism became a key resource in the anti-colonial movements, they based their demands for self-rule on the nation, distinct from that of the colonial centers. Yet, authors writing from the perspective of postcolonial theory, such as Chatterjee, risk reifying nationalism by endorsing its anti-colonial dimension and defining it as a spiritual and positive force that has primordial and essentialist features: "the nation is already sovereign, even when the state is in the hands of the colonial power."[2] Would that it were so simple and that a precolonial nation existed. The attempt to link the nation to a pre and anti-colonial notion of community is an understandable but flawed effort to counter the reductionist claim that the global rise of nationalism constitutes the mere emulation of European models. Instead, the rise of nations around the world is the result of the interaction between colonialism and the military, political, and economic dominance of European and North American powers. In this sense, global processes are not that different from those taking place within Europe. The spread of the nation from elites to wider populations, from the center to the periphery, occurred in parallel within Europe and from Europe outwards. This process was never unidirectional. While those who wielded economic, political, and military power could impose languages, norms, and rules, those who were the subject of such processes could accept, modify, and subvert them. The spread of nations and nationalism thus resulted in a variety of nationalisms around the world that evolved differently than the European models; they were based on their local contexts, including the rejection of colonial experience.

The spread of nationalism outside Europe is not marked by a sharp distinction to nationalism in Europe. As the previous chapter has noted, many features of the spread of the nation in Europe had de facto a colonial dimension that imposed national categories on unwilling subjects. In some cases, assimilation worked; in others, a long struggle of resistance emerged. Similar to national movements in the colonial context, nationalisms emerged in Europe, in particular in peripheral regions in the north, east, and south, that lacked the economic preconditions, education, or literacy that appeared to shape early nationalism in Western Europe. What became an additional feature of the global spread of nationalism was the question of race. As the American feminist scholar Anne McClintock (1954-) has argued, "imperialism and the invention of race were fundamental aspects of Western, industrial modernity."[3] Race is a social construct and only gradually became an important notion in global entanglements as European powers sought to justify the slave trade and political and economic dominance in Africa. As we will discuss in greater detail in the next chapter, history of race and nationalism are closely intertwined.

Two waves of colonization

There were two distinct waves of colonization, and these shaped the rise of nationalism differently. Early colonialism subjugated the Americas and created territories under the rule of European powers: predominantly Spain and Portugal in South America and Spain, England and France in North America. These colonies achieved independence, between the late eighteenth and the early nineteenth centuries with a few notable exceptions such as Canada. The nationalisms that sought separation from the homeland were driven less by difference from the metropole in terms of language or origin, but rather by distance. In North America, the movements for self-rule were firmly controlled by European elites; in Latin America, there was also a strong current of "Creole nationalism," as Benedict Anderson calls it.[4] This Creole nationalism was built by new elites who were constituted from different backgrounds, drawing on indigenous populations as well as descendants of slaves and European settlers. In practice, however, the new elites often excluded groups of mixed heritage while seeking to distance themselves from Spain and Portugal not based on how they differed from the colonial centers, but rather out of a feeling of being marginalized and neglected.

The liberation movements were also only partially national in nature; or—they also contained a social agenda. Coherent national movements would emerge gradually later, in the course of the nineteenth century. A similar process unfolded in the United States; the rebellion against British rule opposed the lack of representation. When in 1773 protestors dumped tea from the East India Company into Boston Harbor, they were not rebelling against high tea prices but against "taxation without representation," as well as more mundane grievances. The tea tax was seen as an infringement by the British Parliament on the autonomy of the colonies. The movement that would lead to the American Revolution in 1776 and the creation of the United States over the subsequent decade was not a national movement initially, nor did it envisage a particular American nation pitted against British rule. The original Articles of Confederation that governed the former British colonies highlighted the primacy of the thirteen states over the loose confederation. In fact, the creation of a strong national government through the constitutional convention was by no means inevitable—instead, the colonies might have kept a loose federation, or the states could have evolved into separate countries, as they did in Latin America. The critical difference was the relatively small size and economic weakness of the North American colonies, which drove them toward cooperation and integration by necessity rather than by default. The new American nation, like most of its counterparts in Latin America, emerged gradually after the new elites rejected rule by the colonial metropole that shared a language, customs, and descent.

The first country to seek independence whose elite was distinct from that of the homeland was Haiti. Haiti achieved independence in 1804 after a thirteen-year struggle. Ironically, but also typical of later anti-colonial nationalisms, the independence movement was inspired by the French Revolution, yet it was revolutionary France, particularly Napoleon, that violently sought to repress it. The Haitian national movement was first and foremost a revolt of African slaves led by Toussaint Louverture (1743–1803), a former slave himself. After achieving independence, Haiti would, for the most part, remain an exception to the rest of the Americas in, being governed by kings and presidents the majority of which were of African descent. This differed from the rest of elsewhere in the Americas, elites of European origin prevailed, whether they constituted a minority or majority.

In Latin America, the wars of independence from Spain and Portugal in the first decades of the nineteenth century followed the lines of the colonial administrations. The attempts by Simón Bolívar to unify Spanish America and establish a state called Gran Colombia, which included most of the northern regions of South America, such as Venezuela, Ecuador, Colombia, Panama, and parts of Peru and Brazil, ultimately failed. The country was more centralized and distinctly less democratic than the United States. It also had to fight a continuous war against Spain and rebels. Other attempts in Latin America to unify multiple colonial states after independence also failed, including the Federal Republic of Central America (1823–1841).

By the early nineteenth century, colonialism in the Americas had largely come to an end. The result was more fragmented states in Central and South America despite attempts at creating federal states, and the United States expanding in the North. With a few exceptions, such as Haiti, the elites of these states that opposed the colonial rule of the European metropoles of Spain, Portugal, and the UK, mirrored those of the European centers. The overall population was more diverse, with a significant non-European population, be they indigenous, former African slaves, or of mixed descent, but these groups stood largely at the margins of political, social, and economic influence.

The end of the early colonial phase spurred a new wave of colonization in the nineteenth century, mostly in the second half that extend beyond the Americas. This new phase transformed coastal trade outposts and indirect control into large territorial colonies, culminating in the Berlin Conference of 1884/5 that divided up Africa into colonial possessions. Beyond Africa, the UK consolidated its rule over India, France in Indochina, and the Netherlands in the Dutch East Indies. At the same time, European powers established ports under their control in China. Where the colonial expansion encountered preexisting states, these were mostly unable to resist European colonial domination. Only a few countries, such as Liberia, Ethiopia, Siam, Japan, and China in part, managed to resist European colonial rule. Overall, however, colonial subjugation did not trigger nationalism at first because—with the exception of Japan and China, in part—these states were too weak and their societies too fractured for a cohesive national identity to emerge before the twentieth century.

Drawing colonial borders

While colonial borders largely ignored earlier political units this does not mean that state tradition was without consequence. The intensity of precolonial rule differed significantly across Africa, ranging from centralized kingdoms such as the Kingdom of Dahomey, to weak political structures with populations organized primarily into small village communities. Where precolonial kingdoms existed and were reflected in the colonial borders such as the Jolof Empire in todays Senegal and Gambia, the integrative potential of the colonial unit was stronger than in regions without strong institutional legacies, such as Congo or Somalia. The type of colonial rule also mattered. In some cases, the colonial governments exercised power through local elites and left many institutions intact, whereas in others colonial rule uprooted earlier hierarchies and institutions. This continuity or disruption would have direct repercussions on state and nation-building in the postcolonial era.

By the nineteenth century, colonial control was no longer justified by pure power politics or competition with other great powers, even if the "scramble for Africa" left little doubt that competition and claims to national glory drove colonialization. The two largest colonial states in particular, France and Britain, justified their empires through the concept of civilizing missions. They employed this idea of modernizing backward people both in their own peripheries—from Corsica and Brittany in France, to Ireland and Scotland in Great Britain—as well as overseas. Scholars such as the American political scientist Michael Hechter (1945–) have argued that the gradual expansion of the centers to the peripheries in Britain and France were colonial projects.[5] Thus, the notion of spreading civilization was an extension of earlier and parallel processes in the homeland. However, in the latter cases, those who were subject to such pressure could become equal citizens. By contrast, within the colonies this was mostly not possible, nor were independence and self-rule expected for non-Europeans. Nor were they offered until pressure from anti-colonial national movements proved impossible to ignore.

The empires that were nation-states at home, such as France and Great Britain, clearly distinguished between those members of the nation at home, who could participate in political processes and were citizens, and those who lived in the colonies and possessed differentiated access to citizenship and political rights. While settlers of European origin usually had access to citizenship, indigenous populations were usually excluded. In the decentralized structure of the British Empire, none had access to a vote for the Westminster Parliament, but territories settled by Europeans could enjoy a higher level of self-governance than those where African or Asian populations prevailed. Britain thus created a hierarchy of colonies, distinguishing between dominions and colonies. Dominions enjoyed a higher level of democratic self-rule and autonomy. The first dominion was Canada, established in 1867, and others included Australia in 1901, New Zealand in 1907, and South Africa in 1910. India, Pakistan, and Ceylon were dominions only briefly in the years preceding independence.

France, with its more centralized colonial structure, eventually granted citizenship and the right to elect members to parliament to the four old colonies (three in the Americas—Guadeloupe, Martinique, Guyana—and Réunion in the Indian Ocean), as well as to the four original French colonial communes of Senegal. While non-Europeans were occasionally elected, the seats in parliament and the number of citizens corresponding from the colonies were minimal. In Algeria, besides European settlers, only Algerian Jews were able to gain the right to French citizenship.

In addition to lacking the citizenship of their colonizers, colonial subjects were separated from their neighbors by often arbitrary boundaries. The colonial borders paid little attention to local concerns, both separating long-established communities and throwing together very different groups in new polities. Countries such as Nigeria and Sudan straddled a religious dividing line, with a Muslim population in the North and a Christian or animist south. Few countries could be considered clear nation-states in waiting. At the time of independence, the only options were to either redraw the entire map of Africa prior to or during decolonization or to maintain the existing borders. Pan-African movements, such as the important "All African People's Conference" held in Accra, Ghana, in 1958, called for the "adjustment of existing artificial frontiers" and a subsequent creation of regional federations leading to the "United States of Africa."[6] And while the Pan-Africans correctly criticized the colonial borders, a massive change of existing boundaries was a challenge that the European colonial powers were unwilling to undertake. In addition, nor did most African elites supported keeping the colonial borders. Border changes were impractical partly because the European powers sought to withdraw quickly from Africa to avoid increasing costs and thus had no appetite for supporting such a risky endeavor. Pan-Africanists who explicitly rejected any colonial influence were unlikely partners of the erstwhile colonial powers. As a consequence, most African states that emerged in the decade after Ghana, which was the first sub-Saharan colony to become independent in 1957, inherited their borders from colonial times.

The central question for nationalism outside Europe was that of borders and states. The borders outside Europe, particularly in the Americas and Africa were not the product of shifting powers among local polities but, instead, of lines drawn in European chancelleries thousands of miles away, with little regard to the populations or the topography, and often mere decades before these units would become independent states. When the colonies of Spain and Portugal fought for independence in Latin America, the guiding principle for their territorial claims was *uti possidetis*, which means "as you possess" in Latin.

This principle of the international system holds that a state can claim a territory based on past control, unless that control is transferred through a treaty. (The principle avoided *terra nullis*, i.e., "no man's land").

In essence, the principle blocks rapid border changes, as it favors continuity and preexisting claims. The newly independent Latin American states agreed on the principle of *uti possidetis* to draw the borders among them based on previous colonial borders. By maintaining these earlier borders, the states reduced potential conflicting territorial claims—although there were still plenty of them—and also avoided any territory becoming a no man's land outside the control of any of the new states, which might then be reclaimed by the former colonial powers. A distinction was made between legal and de facto control, but territorial disputes were not laid to rest. The usefulness of this principle can be debated, but it nevertheless persisted as a standard, during the decolonization process in Africa and Asia more than a century later (as well as in the dissolution of Yugoslavia and the Soviet Union in the 1990s), but it produced quite divergent political dynamics in the different regional contexts. In Latin America, on one hand, the new borders divided mostly very similar populations, who spoke Spanish (except for Brazil) and included a mixture of settlers of European descent, former African slaves, and indigenous communities. In Africa by contrast, the number of settlers was mostly negligible, and colonial borders divided and combined African populations teeming with distinct languages, religions, and other markers of identity that could evolve into different nations or ethnic groups.

The elites in the colonial provinces also largely supported preserving colonial borders. Whereas a large Spanish speaking state in Latin America, a Francophone state in West Africa, or an English-speaking state in Southern Africa might have been conceivable, they did not emerge because the local elites were oriented inwardly toward the provinces where they built their power bases rather than outwardly. Kwame Nkrumah (1909–1972), the first president of independent Ghana, and a handful of other committed Pan-African politicians were the exception. Otherwise, most African leaders paid lip service to Pan-Africanism while pursuing politics in framework, based on colonial borders. Even in the run-up to independence, elites were oriented toward the colonial provinces, and no viable political project emerged to create larger states.

Document: Declaration on the Granting of Independence to Colonial Countries and Peoples[7]

Adopted by General Assembly resolution 1514 (XV) of 14 December 1960

1 The subjection of peoples to alien subjugation, domination and exploitation constitutes a denial of fundamental human rights, is contrary to the Charter of the United Nations and is an impediment to the promotion of world peace and co-operation.

2 All peoples have the right to self-determination; by virtue of that right they freely determine their political status and freely pursue their economic, social and cultural development.

3 Inadequacy of political, economic, social or educational preparedness should never serve as a pretext for delaying independence.

4 All armed action or repressive measures of all kinds directed against dependent peoples shall cease in order to enable them to exercise peacefully and freely their right to complete independence, and the integrity of their national territory shall be respected.

5 Immediate steps shall be taken, in Trust and Non-Self-Governing Territories or all other territories which have not yet attained independence, to transfer all powers to the peoples of those territories, without any conditions or reservations, in accordance with their freely expressed will and desire, without any distinction as to race, creed or colour, in order to enable them to enjoy complete independence and freedom.

6 Any attempt aimed at the partial or total disruption of the national unity and the territorial integrity of a country is incompatible with the purposes and principles of the Charter of the United Nations.

7 All States shall observe faithfully and strictly the provisions of the Charter of the United Nations, the Universal Declaration of Human Rights and the present Declaration on the basis of equality, non-interference in the internal affairs of all States, and respect for the sovereign rights of all peoples and their territorial integrity.

At the same time there have been numerous secessionist movements in postcolonial states, yet most have failed due to the consensus on the inviolability of borders. *Uti possidetis* also rejected unilateral border changes, and secessionist movements mostly failed to gain recognition. Secessionist movements, other than those seeking independence for colonial rule, could only succeed if the country from which they sought to separate agreed; obviously this occurred only in exceptional circumstances. They include Eritrea and South Sudan, which gained independence from Ethiopia and Sudan in 1991 and 2011 respectively after decades-long independence struggles. Otherwise, secessionist movements may achieve de facto statehood, i.e., achieving control of state functions on a given territory but lacking substantial international recognition. For example, Somaliland established de facto independence after 1991 when the Somali state collapsed. It has been able to maintain its autonomy since then, mostly due to the weak Somali authorities. The only case of a nonconsensual secession in the postcolonial world is Bangladesh, which seceded from Pakistan in 1971. While Pakistan sought to suppress the independence movement, including through mass murder, its geographic distance from the rest of Pakistan, and Indian intervention, enabled Bangladesh to become independent. The extraordinary circumstances—a distance of over 2,000 kilometers between what was formerly East Pakistan and the rest of Pakistan, with a large and hostile India in-between—made the secession hardly a model for elsewhere, however.

Two prominent secessionist movements during the 1960s—one in Katanga (1960–1963) and the other in Biafra (1967–1970)—demonstrated the limited chances of success, even with outside support. Katanga sought independence from Congo shortly after the latter had achieved independence from Belgium in 1960, while Biafra seceded from Nigeria in 1967. The secession of Katanga had little to do with ethnic tensions and more to do with economic motivations, as it was encouraged by the Belgian Mining Company *Union Minière du Haut Katanga*. Katanga was not unique, as Immanuel Wallerstein noted, but "every African nation, large or small, federal or unitary, has its Katanga."[8] Biafra was able to achieve some international recognition but was eventually defeated by the Nigerian Army. The secession was largely triggered by the polarization in Nigeria among the four largest groups, Hausa and Fulani in the North and Yoruba and Igbo in the South. These divisions were deepened by a religious divide between the predominantly Islamic North and the Christian South. Two coups in 1966 furthered ethnic polarization and led to mass killings of Igbo, which precipitated the secession.

The failure of Katanga and Biafra discouraged other secessionist movements in Africa. This failure has not prevented, however, ethnic conflicts albeit the conflicts have mostly been over the control of the government rather than secession—in Africa and beyond. We will explore these issues in Chapter 6.

Different paths of national movements

The anti-colonial experience crucially shaped national movements that emerged outside Europe. Their primary goal was emancipation from European colonial rule, for instance in India, or the threat of colonization, as was the case in China. In defining themselves in opposition to the colonial powers, the elites were often shaped and educated in the colonial centers and adopted ideas of nationhood that were grounded in European experiences. The nationalism of anti-colonial movements was thus based both on European nationalism and a rejection of it.

One of the earliest national movements in the colonial world emerged in India, where the Indian National Congress was founded in December 1885. The Congress was confronted with a widely diverse and fragmented population with a multitude of religious communities, including Hindus, Muslims, and Sikhs, as well as stark social divisions in terms of castes and economic differences. These were by no means a British invention. The largely indirect colonial rule nevertheless built on and reinforced the existing power structures and lines of fragmentation. For instance, the Indian Councils Act of 1909 created separate electoral rolls for Muslims, ensuring that only Muslims would be able to vote for seats reserved for Muslims. While protecting the Muslim minority, the measure also reinforced a political system that was fragmented along religious lines, rendering a pan-Indian opposition more difficult. The Congress had opposed the reforms, which were more in line with the demands of the All-India Muslim League, highlighting competing visions for India. The Congress was secular and rejected sectarianism as premodern. For the Muslim League, religion was the fundamental concern, and Muslims constituted a minority of around a quarter of the population. There were also Hindu nationalist groups, such as *All India Hindu Mahasabha*, founded in 1915. The Indian national movement was thus divided into an all-Indian civic movement and two separate religiously defined movements. (All three would persist, as the Congress Party and the Bharatiya Janata Party (BJP) vie for power in India today, and the Muslim League became decisive in establishing Pakistan.) Neither the Hindu nor the Muslim national movements defined themselves solely through religion, nor were they necessarily religious zealots. Instead, they envisaged a nation defined by religion but also marked by a distinct culture. In this vein, M.S. Golwarker, the general secretary of the Hindu nationalist *Rashtriya Swayamsevak Sangh* (RSS), conceived the nation as follows:

Living in this Country since pre-historic times, is the ancient Race—the Hindu Race, united together by common traditions, by memories of common glory and disaster, by similar historical political, social, religious and other experiences, living and evolving, under the same influences, a common culture, a common mother language, common customs, common aspirations. This great Hindu Race professes its illustrious Hindu Religion, the only Religion in the world worthy of being so denominated.[9]

The Hindu groups attacked the Congress for allegedly favoring Muslims. The Muslim League, on the other hand, mostly argued that the secularism of the Congress disguised majoritarianism. Muhammad Ali Jinnah, leader of the Muslim League, argued in a speech at the party congress in Lahore in 1940 that "Hindus and Muslims brought together under a democratic system forced upon the minorities can only mean Hindu Raj." Like M.S. Golwarker, he rejected the idea of a common Indian nation, believing rather that Islam and Hinduism "are not religions in the strict sense of the word, but are, in fact, different and distinct social orders; and it is a dream that the Hindus and Muslims can ever evolve a common nationality." [10] It was as at that party congress that the Muslim League adopted its call for the creation of a separate Muslim state, to be named Pakistan.

The conflict within India between different national movements was played out in many other anti-colonial national movements through the competition between those who sought to build a civic and inclusive national identity within the colonial territory as the new political unit, and those who focused on narrower criteria and drew on exclusive ethnic, religious, or historical identities. On a broader scale, these are the underlying tensions in all nation-building processes, which are rarely won conclusively by any one side. In India, the secular idea of India prevailed, at least initially, despite the partition of the country into India and Pakistan, as well as the massive expulsions and violence that would be called ethnic cleansing today. (When India and Pakistan were created in August 1947, more than fourteen million people fled to the presumed safety of their respective majority. In the run-up to independence and during the partition somewhere between 200,000 and two million people died. However, even after the partition, nearly 10 percent of the population of India were Muslims.) Congress Party dominated post-independence India, ruling until 1989 with only one brief three-year stint in opposition. The party maintained its secular outlook and thus built an India based on civic nationalism.

Unlike India, China never faced complete colonization. Yet the Opium wars (1839–1842, 1856–1860) threatend China, like Japan, with Western powers seeking to extend their influence in the weakened Asian states. The British forced China under the Qing dynasty to open to trade, establish treaty ports, and cede Hong Kong. The Boxer Rebellion (1899–1901) highlighted the emerging resistance to the pressure. The "Boxers" were, in fact, a secret society named "Society of the

Document: A Tryst with Destiny, Jawaharlal Nehru[11]

Speech delivered by Nehru at the Constituent Assembly of India on 14.8.1947

Long years ago we made a tryst with destiny, and now the time comes when we shall redeem our pledge, not wholly or in full measure, but very substantially.

At the stroke of the midnight hour, when the world sleeps, India will awake to life and freedom. A moment comes, which comes but rarely in history, when we step out from the old to the new, when an age ends, and when the soul of a nation, long suppressed, finds utterance.

It is fitting that at this solemn moment we take the pledge of dedication to the service of India and her people and to the still larger cause of humanity.

At the dawn of history India started on her unending quest, and trackless centuries are filled with her striving and the grandeur of her success and her failures. Through good and ill fortune alike she has never lost sight of that quest or forgotten the ideals which gave her strength. We end today a period of ill fortune and India discovers herself again.

The achievement we celebrate today is but a step, an opening of opportunity, to the greater triumphs and achievements that await us. Are we brave enough and wise enough to grasp this opportunity and accept the challenge of the future?

Freedom and power bring responsibility. The responsibility rests upon this assembly, a sovereign body representing the sovereign people of India. Before the birth of freedom we have endured all the pains of labour and our hearts are heavy with the memory of this sorrow. Some of those pains continue even now. Nevertheless, the past is over and it is the future that beckons to us now.

...

The appointed day has come – the day appointed by destiny – and India stands forth again, after long slumber and struggle, awake, vital, free and independent. The past clings on to us still in some measure and we have to do much before we redeem the pledges we have so often taken. Yet the turning point is past, and history begins anew for us, the history which we shall live and act and others will write about.

It is a fateful moment for us in India, for all Asia and for the world. A new star rises, the star of freedom in the east, a new hope comes into being, a vision long cherished materialises. May the star never set and that hope never be betrayed!

We rejoice in that freedom, even though clouds surround us, and many of our people are sorrow-stricken and difficult problems encompass us. But freedom brings responsibilities and burdens and we have to face them in the spirit of a free and disciplined people.

...

And to India, our much-loved motherland, the ancient, the eternal and the ever-new, we pay our reverent homage and we bind ourselves afresh to her service. Jai Hind [Victory to India].

Righteous and Harmonious Fists," which incorporated heterodox spiritual practices and proto-nationalism. While supporting the Qing dynasty, the Society rejected the increasing role of Christian missionaries, and the concessions China had to make to Western powers and Japan following defeat in the Sino-Japanese War (1894–1895). The movement began attacking missionaries, and following a power-struggle in the imperial court, the Boxers received backing from the Empress Dowager Cixi, who took de facto charge and declared war on the Western powers. As the foreign legations were besieged by rebels in Beijing, an Eight-Nation Alliance, consisting of Japan, Russia, France, Austria-Hungary, Germany, and Italy, intervened on the pretext of protecting the foreign citizens in the embassies. A peace agreement, known as the Boxer Protocol ended the war and further weakened the Chinese state. In this context, intellectual debates emerged on what constituted the Chinese nation. While China had features of a proto-nation-state centuries earlier, this confrontation with European and Japanese intervention triggered efforts to define the Chinese nation. Here, two streams emerged: some argued that the Chinese nation was defined by the ethnic group of Han, the dominant group in the empire. Others, such as the journalist and scholar Liang Qichao, argued that the nation was formed "through the intermingling of a great number of nations."[12]

When the last emperor was forced to abdicate in 1911, the republic and, its first president from 1912 to 1913 Sun Yet-sen, adopted a program stating that the Chinese state included five nations—the Han, Manchus, Mongolians, Hui, and Tibetans—making China not a mono-ethnic Han state but a republic composed of different regions and peoples. The core principles of this new republic defined by Sun Yat-sen included nationalism as well as democracy and the livelihood of the people. This principle of *Mínzú*, translated as "nationalism," emphasized an encompassing nation comprising the different groups, as reflected in the flag of the early republic that displayed five horizontal stripes to represent the Han, Manchus, Mongols, Hui, and Tibetans.

By taking control over Taiwan in 1895, and eying Korea, Manchuria, and Mongolia the rising power Japan threatend Chinas periphery and forced it to focus on its Han core. Due to the precarious condition of China amidst Japanese and other territorial claims, the focus on its Han identity would de facto relinquish the claim to the other groups and territories as part of a Chinese state.

Intellectual debates focused on whether the Chinese nation emerged through migration and outside influences or whether its origins lay in antiquity. The supposed direct line of continuity to antiquity echoed similar debates in Europe, such as those in Italy about its Roman heritage or Greece and the continuity of the Hellenic state or the city-states. Unlike India, which saw continuity of the national movement in the form of the Congress Party, in China, the republic movement led to the Kuomintang or Nationalist Party, which was defeated in the civil war in 1949 and retained power only in Taiwan. The Communist Party represented the other main alternative, yet it had cooperated with the nationalists earlier and also legitimized its rule through its national resistance to Japanese occupation— like other Communist partisan movements that combined national and socialist sources of legitimacy, such as in Yugoslavia. In fact, the Communist party was crucial in disseminating the ideas of nationalism during the Second World War "the peasant began to hear and use such terms as Han-chien (Chinese traitor), wei-chün (bogus army, i.e. puppet forces) .... the intrusion of these terms into the peasants' vocabulary signified the spread of a force that hitherto was prevalent only among the intelligentsia and city-bred people—namely, nationalism."[13] Thus, whereas in India the competition was between secular and different religiously-based national movements, in China,

Document: Constitution of the People's Republic of China[14]

Adopted in 1982 and amended in 1988, 1993, 1999, 2004 and 2018.

China is a country with one of the longest histories in the world. The people of all ethnic groups in China have jointly created a culture of grandeur and have a glorious revolutionary tradition.

After 1840, feudal China was gradually turned into a semi-colonial and semi-feudal country. The Chinese people waged many successive heroic struggles for national independence and liberation and for democracy and freedom.

Great and earthshaking historical changes took place in China in the 20th century.

The Revolution of 1911, led by Dr. Sun Yat-sen, abolished the feudal monarchy and gave birth to the Republic of China. But the historic mission of the Chinese people to overthrow imperialism and feudalism remained unaccomplished.

After waging protracted and arduous struggles, armed and otherwise, along a zigzag course, the Chinese people of all ethnic groups led by the Communist Party of China with Chairman Mao Zedong as its leader ultimately, in 1949, overthrew the rule of imperialism, feudalism and bureaucrat-capitalism, won the great victory of the New-Democratic Revolution and founded the People's Republic of China. Since then the Chinese people have taken control of state power and become masters of the country.

...

Both the victory in China's New-Democratic Revolution and the successes in its socialist cause have been achieved by the Chinese people of all ethnic groups, under the leadership of the Communist Party of China and the guidance of Marxism-Leninism and Mao Zedong Thought, by upholding truth, correcting errors and surmounting numerous difficulties and hardships. China will be in the primary stage of socialism for a long time to come. The basic task of the nation is to concentrate its effort on socialist modernization along the road of building socialism with Chinese characteristics.

...

Taiwan is part of the sacred territory of the People's Republic of China. It is the inviolable duty of all Chinese people, including our compatriots in Taiwan, to accomplish the great task of reunifying the motherland.

...

The People's Republic of China is a unitary multi-ethnic state created jointly by the people of all its ethnic groups. Socialist relations of equality, unity and mutual assistance have been established among the ethnic groups and will continue to be strengthened. In the struggle to safeguard the unity of the ethnic groups, it is necessary to combat big-ethnic chauvinism, mainly Han chauvinism, and also to combat local-ethnic chauvinism. The state will do its utmost to promote the common prosperity of all ethnic groups.

the main parties claiming control of the state used inclusive and anti-colonial elements. The two differed largely in terms of political ideology.

The rise of nationalism in Japan shared some similarities with China, in part as a result of confrontation with European and American imperialism. In Japan, the forced opening due to the American gunboat diplomacy of Commodore Matthew Perry in 1854 had a transformative effect on nation-building: the Meiji restoration fourteen years later was triggered by the elites' realization that Japan's fragmented feudal structure would weaken its position vis-à-vis the European powers. The Meiji restoration paved the way to a more centralized state. In the following decades, Japanese elites would study the European model of modernization and nation-states as a template for Japan. This does not mean that Japanese nationalism became a mere copy of European nationalism, but rather that Japanese elites adapted the European experience to their local context. The nationalism that emerged was just as top-down and state-driven as in Europe. The central role it granted the Emperor evoked historical continuity, but was in fact a product of late-nineteenth-century nation-building: "It is often characterized as intimately connected with the *Tennō* (the monarch, "the emperor") and with claims to the 'unbroken 2,600 year lineage of the emperor' as constituting the core of what supposedly makes the Japanese nation culturally unique."[15] Note that contrary to French nationalism, which was largely republican and saw in the king a vestige of premodern France, Japanese nationalism imagined a nation with a central role taken by the emperor. This understanding of the emperor more closely resembled that of Prussia/Germany, with which it also shared the central role of the bureaucracy and army in nation-building. However, the emperor was not just a promoter of the nation as in the German emporer or Italian king but also formed part of the claim to antiquity and historical continuity. During the late nineteenth and twentieth centuries, Japanese scholars and intellectuals widely debated how to define the nation, whether to focus on ethnic or civic criteria, and the role of the state, drawing on European literature and incorporating it into domestic debates and conceptualizations of the nation.[16] While Japan did not exist as a state or nation prior to the mid-nineteenth century, it nevertheless emerged as a coherent and homogenous nation that adopted an imperialist policy toward its neighbors by the early twentieth century. Being unsuccessful in including a clause on racial equality in the League of Nations in 1919, it adopted a critical view of European and Western Orientalism and racial hierarchies, while itself establishing an imperial state based on racial distinctiveness.

The experiences of India, China, and Japan highlight that national movements' different paths were based on the extent to which European colonial powers were able to establish their influence, and the divergent responses the Western intervention evoked. The varieties of nationalisms were thus both emulation and response to Western models.

Nation-building after independence

For most of Africa and Asia, the Indian experience of colonial rule was the model. Like India, most colonies in Africa were highly diverse, especially in sub-Saharan Africa. Not a single colony could be considered a nation-state in the sense of a large majority that identified with one nation. This diversity had multiple causes. For one, it is connected to geography, as more fragmented regions without easy transport links often maintain high levels of diversity.

Furthermore, as assimilation and nation-building in Africa did not occur under colonial rule, the countries were more diverse at independence than the European metropoles. At that point, Europe had seen a century or more of nation-states reducing the salience of local and regional identities and languages.

At independence, the new African elites could thus either further politicize ethnic divisions, employing the colonial divide-and-rule strategy or build a unified state based on a collective identity. In brief, there were two prevailing alternative nation-building models: one that would attempt to create a civic or multiethnic nation, and another that would emphasize sub-state nationalism and politicize ethnicity. The choices and the likelihood of success were not just based on the preference of elites, but also on other factors. These included the tradition of statehood that preceeded colonial rule, the extent to which colonizers politicized ethnicity, the origin of political elites, and the strength of institutions in the colonies at independence. The pattern of anti-colonial struggle also had an impact.

A differentiated treatment of groups was part of the divide-and-rule strategy of colonial rule, as well as the result of creating colonial elites, often composed of members from ethnic groups that the colonizers considered "racially superior" and more "advanced" than the other.[17] In this respect, not only was the often antagonistic relationship between ethnic groups a consequence of colonialism, but the very existence of ethnic groups was frequently a byproduct of colonialism. Colonialism created administrations and state institutions—often only in a rudimentary and exploitative manner—and these structures classified and categorized populations, establishing "groupness" where little had existed earlier. Nowhere is this more visible than in Burundi and Rwanda. Both were initially German colonies that came under Belgian administration after the First World War until 1962. While the distinction between Tutsis, Hutus, and the smaller group of Twa existed before colonial rule, the extent to which these amounted to distinct ethnic groups remains controversial. Many scholars argue that these were more akin to fluid socio-economic groups, where ownership of cattle determined who was a Tutsi and who a Hutu. Before colonial rule, the region was governed by two kingdoms with borders largely identical to the two countries today, which were dominated by a Tutsi hierarchy.

However, there was considerable variation in terms of the fluidity of the boundary between the Hutus and Tutsis.

In addition, there was no difference in language, religion, or culture among them. But colonial rule was indirect and favored the existing political and social hierarchy, further empowering the Tutsi minority. The stratification became more rigid, ethnified, and racialized. By the time of independence, both countries were deeply divided societies, marked by Hutus and Tutsis as distinct and antagonistic ethnic groups.[18]

Whether or not such antagonistic ethnic relations burdened the newly independent countries, they did shape the ability of the elites to promote either an overarching nation encompassing all citizens, or a narrower ethnic nation. The new states subsequently had to determine formal and informal institutions of inclusive or exclusive nation-building, best exemplified by language policies.

A critical question at independence was which language to adopt as the national language. While English and French remained associated with colonial rule, there were often no other nationwide languages available. Thus, the former colonial language often retained official status together with one or several local languages, as was the case in Senegal and Rwanda. Even when recognizing some new languages, others might remain unrecognized, such as Kurdish in countries such as Iraq and Syria, or Berber in Algeria. The language was a crucial aspect of nation-building, and different movements took divergent paths.

A different example comes from Indonesia, where a dialect of Malay became the national language, known as Bahasa Indonesia (Indonesian Language). The obvious choice for the national language would have been Javanese, spoken by around 45 percent of the population, while the dialect on which the new national language was based was initially used by traders—only 5 percent of the Indonesian population used it as their mother tongue. However, it was precisely the minority status of the language (and its simplicity) that made it attractive. As such, it could serve as a unifying language that transcended different groups in the vast state. It became the official language of the national movement in 1928 when the All-Indonesian Youth Congress adopted it as a crucial marker of unity. The efforts to promote the language as a pillar of nation-building thus began well before the country achieved independence from the Netherlands in

1945. On the other hand, India took a distinctly different path in terms of language, even though the starting point was similar. In India, a similar share of Indians spoke Hindi as Indonesions spoke Javanese. However, India adopted Hindi and English as the main national languages. Other significant languages, such as Tamil and Bengali, gained no countrywide status, although they were in official use in parts of the country. (In India, there are 122 languages, in total thirty of which are spoken by more than a million people each). With Hindi not being universally accepted as the lingua franca, English retained its status as an official language. Despite several deadlines to phase out English from official use, it has remained a language of government.[19]

In other aspects of nation-building, the different paths are best illustrated by the two neighboring East African states of Kenya and Tanzania. In Tanzania, the government of Julius Nyerere, one of the leaders of the pan-African movement, promoted Swahili to replace English as the national language, while more than 100 languages are spoken in the country. In addition, the schools vigorously promoted a shared Tanzanian identity. In local administrations, new structures replaced those that had been associated with the colonial systems and strong tribal connotations.

The situation was quite the opposite in Kenya. Here, Jomo Kenyatta and his successor Daniel Arap Moi favored their own ethnic groups and made fewer attempts to build a shared national identity. Swahili remains widely in use, but English and languages associated with different ethnic groups, such as Kikuyu, remained the main official languages, including in schools. Similarly, the curriculum has placed less emphasis on shared history and identity. Finally, Kenya retained colonial-era tribal institutions at the local level, giving greater weight to traditional ethnified structures.

While both countries had a similar ethnic and linguistic makeup at independence, within decades, the different nation-building policies bore fruit. Kenya has experienced several waves of ethnic violence and ethnicity remains a significant political cleavage. In Tanzania, ethnic identity and languages have not disappeared, but they have lost a lot of their salience, and attachment to the state identity is strong.[20]

Downplaying ethnicity can also be a strategy of a minority in power. For example, in Rwanda, the Tutsi-led Rwandan Patriotic Front that took power after the genocide in 1994 has banned reference to ethnicity, and officially, "divisionism" has become a criminal offense. Considering the mass violence committed in the name of ethnicity, such a ban is an obvious policy choice. At the same time, however, it has served to repress criticism of the authoritarian regime led by Paul Kagame and furthermore obscures the fact that the small Tutsi minority dominates the government. Similar attempts to engineer a common political identity elsewhere on the continent have most frequently taken the form of banning ethnically based parties or in some cases, such as Nigeria, presidential candidates were required to gain a certain percentage of the vote in a minimum number of regions to ensure that winners enjoy broad cross-ethnic support.[21] On one hand, such policies of political and social engineering can reduce ethnic polarization, but on the other, they can also often serve to either repress political pluralism or mask the rule of a minority.

The challenges of nation-building were particularly pronounced in settings where colonial rule had destroyed earlier polities and failed to preserve local structures. As European powers scrambled to unload their colonies as fast as possible, there were frequently neither institutions nor prepared elites to take over the state. The weakness of institutions was nowhere as visible as in the Congo, where Belgian colonial rule destroyed precolonial state structures and left few administrative structures behind. Combined with a repressive colonial episode, including the Free State of Congo under the direct and personal rule of King Leopold, there was not much of a state to govern. Independence was hasty and ill-prepared, as Belgium granted independence to Congo with merely a few months of preparation in 1960. What followed was a personalized authoritarian rule of Joseph-Désiré Mobutu (1930–1997). Mobutu came to power as a military leader shortly after Congo's independence from Belgium in 1960 with the support from Western governments, including the United States, France, and Belgium itself, whose extensive financial aid during the Cold War he used to retain power and enrich himself. Mobutu's corrupt dictatorial rule became the embodiment of all the autocrats that emerged in sub-Saharan Africa after independence. Yet despite nearly four decades of self-serving kleptocratic rule, his government also epitomized some efforts of postcolonial nation-building. Mobutu sought to discard the symbolic vestiges of colonialism, taking on the indigenous name Sese Seko Kuku Ngbendu Wa Za Banga; renaming the capital Léopoldville to Kinshasa; and encouraging a modern interpretation of traditional Africa dress as part of the *Authenticité* campaign. This effort collapsed in the 1990s with the end of Mobuto's rule. The failure of the state and identity construction should not just be reduced to the personality of Mobuto, who appeared to be a caricature of an African potentate (including hiring a Concorde to fly to Paris for shopping trips), however but also has to consider the colonial legacy.

The evolution of nationalism in Africa includes a distinct phenomenon of non-European nationalism: white settler nationalism. While Creole nationalism emerged in the Americas and also in Australia and New Zealand, European populations elsewhere were a small minority in the colonies. Even in Algeria, which had one of the largest shares of settlers from France and other European countries, the *pied noirs* only made up around one million people, or 10 percent of the population, in 1960. By contrast, in Southern Africa, a distinct white minority nationalism emerged, not connected to the colonial center or another European homeland. The core of white settler nationalism was the strong Afrikaner sense of identity, based on the language, which had evolved from its Dutch origins; Calvinism, represented by the Dutch Reformed Church; and a narrative of historical distinctiveness. The Afrikaner or Boer population originated from Dutch settlers and had established their own republics in the nineteenth century and were incorporated into the British Union of South Africa following the Boer Wars in 1902. After the victory of the National Party in 1948, the country established a system of racial segregation and white rule known as apartheid, and in 1961 it declared its independence from Great Britain. The Afrikaner-dominated ruling National Party built on existing racial segregation and sought to forge a white South African nationalism. Jan Smuts, the long-term South African politician and author of the preamble of the UN Charter, noted in 1917 "that the different elements in our white populations ought really to be used to build up a stronger and more powerful nation than would have been possible if we had consisted of purely one particular strain." This "desirable" mixing was, of course, restricted to European populations, and Smuts rejected the "mixing up of black and white in the old haphazard way." He further advocated that the regime should institute a "policy of keeping them apart as much as possible."[22] Besides South

Africa, white settler regimes also existed in Rhodesia (present-day Zimbabwe) between 1965 and 1980 and in Southwest Africa (present-day Namibia) under South African control. The logic of racial separation became more complex and institutionalized over time, with so-called Bantustans established in South Africa and Southwest Africa, which were nominally self-governing and in some cases independent (although only recognized by South Africa) and included mostly rural black populations who were stripped of their South African citizenship.

Eventually, the different variants of white settler nationalism in Africa failed. In Algeria, around 800,000 *pieds noirs* were evacuated from the country at independence in 1962 after many opposed the independence that French president De Gaulle had negotiated with the Algerian National Liberation Front after eight years of war. Minority rule in Rhodesia ended in 1980 when the country came under majority rule under the name Zimbabwe. Finally, the government of South Africa abandoned apartheid in a peaceful transition during the early 1990s. Many white settler communities disappeared after independence, partly through voluntary migration partly though pressure and expropriation by the new rulers who often targeted the white population for its association with colonial rule and the privileges it enjoyed. Only Afrikaner and English-speaking whites in South Africa were able to sustain a large community, in part due to their significant size as well as the peaceful transfer of power.

Pan-Arabism and the failure of transborder nationalism

Above we described the failure of, attempts to promote nations that transcended colonial borders. These efforts failed in the case of secessionist movements due to the rigid structure of postcolonial borders. But efforts to create transnational movements also failed. No case illustrates this better than the demise of Arab nationalism. Pan-Arabism—the idea of unifying all the Arab lands—emerged in the early twentieth century as a political idea directed against Ottoman rule. Like other national movements, it included the concept of creating and promoting a standard language. Arabic preserved its cohesion as a written language, largely due to its importance as the language of the Qu'ran. Yet the dialects spoken between Morocco in the West and Iraq in the East, Sudan and Yemen in the South, and Lebanon and Syria in the North varied to such an extent that speakers of the different varieties of Arabic could not easily communicate. The revival movement (Nahda), established by Lebanese writer and journalist Jurji Zaydan (1861–1914), sought to popularize a common Arab history and promote Arab unity.

The Arab revolt led by Sharif Hussein ibn Ali, the Sharif of Mecca, during the First World War was instigated by the British against Ottoman rule and associated with the (self-aggrandizing) account of Thomas Edward Lawrence (1888–1935). It was the first time Arab nationalism became a political project. It was limited to the Arabian Peninsula and the Mashreq—the regions that include today's Lebanon, Syria, Palestine/Israel, Jordan, and Iraq. The Arab areas in North Africa—the Maghreb—were no longer under Ottoman control at that time. They had come under European colonial rule between 1830 (Algeria) and 1911 (Libya) and were thus less affected by the revolt.

Despite some successes, the revolt could not prevent the division of the Ottoman Arab lands into mandate territories ruled by France and Great Britain, which thwarted the emergence of a unified Arab state in the Middle East. While the Western betrayal of promises of Arab self-rule encouraged Arab nationalism, it also fragmented Arab politics. The new states and their rulers, even if under colonial rule, gained the ability to build distinct polities, and often Arab and local identity clashed. Within this context, gender also began to matter, as women found a space for action in the national movements, in a break with earlier, more traditional patterns of acceptable behavior. For instance, women became important supporters of the nationalist Wafd party in Egypt after the First World War and in Palestine a decade later. [23]

Arab nationalism gathered momentum after the Second World War. The independence of Arab states, as well as the creation of Israel, facilitated its emergence. One of the political pioneers of Arab nationalism was Michel Aflaq (1910–1989), Syrian scholar and founder of the Ba'ath (Renaissance) party that advanced the ideas of the Arab nation and unity. Many other key figures in the Arab nationalist movements, originated from Lebanon and Syria. Many, including Aflaq, were also Christians rather than Sunni Muslim, the overwhelming majority of the Arab population.

Ba'athism and most other Arab nationalist movements drew on the widespread anti-colonial themes as well as on hostility toward Israel, which became closely associated with colonialism in pan-Arab discourse. However, the main objects of criticism were the rulers of the Arab states, whom Aflaq depicted as the main obstacles to Arab unity:

It is now the Arabs who quarrel among themselves over unity and federation, republic and democracy, freedom and sovereignty, or to put it more correctly and justly, the quarrel is between professional political cliques, which have sold themselves, and conscience to the foreigners ... We must be above such disputes, which have no connection with the real issue of nationalism, even though they are named after it and take on Arabic terms and nomenclatures derived from nationalist aims. But, they are in fact alien to it.[24]

Arab nationalism reached its zenith when Gamal Abdel Nasser (1918–1970) took power in Egypt after a coup against King Farouk. The Free Officers, led by Nasser, established a republic and drew on Arab nationalism and socialism, as well as non-alignment, as ideological pillars. One of the leaders of the anti-colonial movement, the charismatic Nasser became the most prominent figure of the Arab world. In 1958, Egypt established a political union with Syria called the United Arab Republic (UAR) and formed a looser union with North Yemen under the banner of the United Arab States, with the goal of uniting the Arab world. Both unions disintegrated in 1961, however. Egypt's dominance of the UAR led to a coup in Syria and the premature end of the joint state. With the defeat of Egypt and its allies in subsequent wars against Israel in 1967 and 1973, and the rising power of the oil-rich monarchies in the Gulf, the star of pan-Arabism and Arab nationalism began to decline. After Nasser's death in 1970, the movement lacked a charismatic speaker, and the two formally pan-Arab regimes in Syria after 1963 and Iraq between 1968 and 2003 became vehicles for the personal dictatorships of Hafez al-Assad and Saddam Hussein, respectively, who were not just hostile to each other, but also reduced Arab nationalism to lip service and tainted it by association.

Pan-Arabism and Arab nationalism thus became instrumentalized and discredited by the corrupt and brutal dictatorships of the Arab world. By the early 1980s, political Islam became a more popular alternative to Arab nationalism. In addition, the Arab populations proved to be too diverse and difficult to convince about political unity in the name of an Arab nation. While an Arab cultural space continues to exist, the notion of a common nation has faded. The efforts of intellectuals in promoting the idea of Arab unity did not translate into political reality, as the elites, a diverse group of kings, sultans, and presidents for life, remained divided.[25] Today, the Arab League is the only institutional reflection of the ambition of Arab unity: a weak international organization that is stymied by the fractious relationship among its members.

Well before political Islam became the dominant political movement and ideology in many Muslim countries, including the Arab world, religion mattered more than ideologues of Arab nationalism were able to admit. The former Ottoman lands that were divided between French and British mandates after the First World War were mostly Arab, but multireligious, with substantial Christian communities as well as other small denominations such as the Druze, and the crucial split between Shia and Sunni Muslims. Whereas pan-Arabism sought to overcome these divisions, they actually became more entrenched over time. Lebanon offers an instructive case study in this respect. Created by France as a predominantly Christian state on the Eastern Mediterranean, the 1943 Lebanese National Pact enabled the French mandate to become independent with an unwritten political agreement between the Christian and Muslim elites to govern the country jointly. The confessional power-sharing included Maronites, Orthodox, Sunnis, Shia, and Druze as well as other small communities. This created a fragile balance, which made the country one of the few electoral democracies in the Middle East, and at the same time, a volatile system that would lead to a fifteen-year civil war between 1975 and 1990. While the confessional identities did not coagulate into full national identities, they proved more politically relevant than the overarching Lebanese identity. In other states, Sunni elites initially dominated in combination with authoritarian rule. In Syria and Iraq, Shia communities were marginalized and, over time, the religious distinctions became increasingly relevant. In Iraq, Sunni dominance lasted until the fall of Saddam Hussein during the American invasion in 2003. In Syria on the other hand, Sunni dominance ended when Hafez al-Assad took power in the 1970s and consolidated his rule by including many fellow Alawis —a regious minority group—in the power structures. As a result, both Iraq and Syria were secular regimes in which religious minorities ruled over a majority that hailed from a different Islamic background. In all three cases, religion became a more important marker of identity than the state or Arab identity.

The quip attributed to the Egyptian diplomat Tahseen Bashier that "Egypt is the only nation-state in the Arab world; the rest are just tribes with flags"[26] might have been hyperbole, but it did reflect the weakness of states in the Middle East. All the same, despite the weak basis of statehood and national identity, pan-Arab efforts failed. Other transnational identities have not taken hold and therefore states based on colonial lines have persisted. Secessionist conflicts have been exceptional, and usually shaped by the colonial legacy, such as the conflict in Western Sahara over independence from Morocco or the splintering of Yemen and Libya, where the fault lines to a considerable degree follow the colonial divisions.

Conclusion

Nationalism outside Europe emerged first and foremost as a key feature of anti-colonial movements opposing the predominance of European powers but it was nevertheless based on European ideas. The discrepancy between idea of self-rule, accepted for Europe, but rejected for non-European countries thus undermined colonialism. The weakening of colonial powers during the two World Wars, and the experience of non-European soldiers fighting and dying for them undercut the logic of colonialism. Although the anti-colonial movement had strong pan-African and also pan-Arab themes, the independent states followed colonial borders, as did the nationalism, At independence, nationalism was often a weak force, restricted to small elites that were often educated in the European metropolis. Nation-building that followed independence took a variety of paths, drawing on earlier statehood traditions, the colonial tradition, and the pattern of the anti-colonial struggle, as well as reflecting the particular composition of the elite at independence.[27]

One of the defining features of the era of nationalism is the notion of the nation as the universal principle of organizing communities.

This concept spread as colonialism linked the world to Europe, but does not mean that the idea of nations was merely a copy of European models. Rather, nationalism around the world was based both on emulation and resistance. It became a force to confront colonial rule by anti-colonial movements from the nonviolent struggle of the Congress Party in India to the violent campaign of the National Liberation Front in Algeria. After independence, provided either an overarching identity to incorporate multiple ethnic groups, or the dominating logic to exclude minorities or marginalize majorities.

5

Nationalism after the Establishment of the Nation-state

As discussed in the previous two chapters, in the course of the nineteenth and twentieth centuries nation-states emerged around the world as the prevailing type of state. These states took varying strategies in converting or reaffirming their national natures. Thus, the establishment of the nation-state is not the end of nationalism. Even if a core goal of national movements is the creation of nation-states, to be achieved through transforming existing states, secession, unification, or decolonization, the result is not a ready-made nation-state. Instead, the institution of the nation-state usually preceded the widespread acceptance of the nation among its citizens. Transforming, or rather upholding, the nation as the central pillar of state and societal identity is a never-ending task. These processes might be directed toward migrants and minorities who do not fit into the prevailing conception of who is a member of the nation, or toward reaffirming the nation over other, competing identities. In addition, there is also competition between different nationalisms, namely divergent concepts about how to define the nation, be it inclusively or exclusively. The nation is never complete but is constantly changing and developing. Much of this nationalism fit into the category of latent nationalism, yet it could be either inclusive or exclusive. Nationalism is often reflected in state policy, top-down, or might also be part of a wide range of everyday practices performed by citizens, companies, and associations. These might be at times "banal" in the sense that they are little routines, not revolutionary acts of fighting for the nation. Using the term "banal nationalism," the British social scientist Michael Billig argued that everyday nationalism includes "routine practices and everyday discourses, especially those in the mass media, [through which] the idea of nationhood is regularly flagged ... Through such flagging, established nations are reproduced as nations, with their citizenry being unmindfully reminded of their national identity."[1] Banal in this instance does not mean meaningless or insignificant, rather it highlights that nationalism is not just reflected in high politics or deliberate mobilization by radical groups but also in much more everyday habits and signs. Everyday nationalism is thus far from extraordinary, unlike ethnic conflict, the topic of the next chapter. However, everyday nationalism is not inherently benign. It can be violent and exclusionary, such as discrimination against Roma or other minorities in many European countries.

In this chapter, we will explore some of the ways in which nationalism affects people in everyday life, from citizenship and other state policies, which give a particular meaning to the state and the nation, to the rise of regional nationalisms challenging the nation-state framework. Finally, the chapter will explore the intersection of nationalism with other markers of identity, such as class, gender, religion, and race.

Nation and citizenship

A central question for the state is how to organize citizenship, both in terms of formal rules for inclusion and exclusion and the many informal ways in which some groups are privileged over others. All states set boundaries in terms of their physical borders as well as membership in the political community, a category that largely coincides with citizenship. In terms of choices, Sammy Smooha, an Israeli sociologist, argues that we can distinguish between democracies that recognize nations and those that are formally blind to nations.[2] Of course, even being formally blind to the question of which nations exist does not mean that a state can easily be neutral or blind. Even the choice of state language may predetermine a preference given to a particular group. As modern states set official languages for use in public life, including education, this choice may give preference to one or several nations associated with that language. The only alternative is to use a "neutral" language, such as English or French, which are in use in former African colonies, or another lingua franca not associated with any specific group, as discussed in the previous chapter. Even if the question of language is settled, the history taught, the symbols used and other choices made by states often privilege one group over others.

Thus, while accepting the limitations of neutrality, one can distinguish between states that define themselves as states of their citizens, without the aim to build a national community, and those that seek to create a civic nation. The United States qualifies as a good example of the former type of individual liberal democracy that is less concerned with forging a coherent civic nation, whereas France exemplifies the latter, with the establishment of a civic nation that, at least in theory, offers membership to all. The United States might have been historically more agnostic about languages spoken outside the classroom than France, and less concerned about the formal affirmation of belonging to the nation, but there is a considerable social pressure to affirm membership in the civic nation, including its outward display through the flag and other symbols of "patriotism."

According to Smooha, there are three types of democratic regimes that recognize ethnicity or nationality: multicultural states, consociational states, and ethnic democracies. Canada is a good example of the former, with its state policy of multiculturalism, a topic discussed in more detail in Chapter 7. It explicitly recognizes the diversity of identities, but specific collective identities are not granted recognition per se and collective rights are not formally granted. Thus, multiculturalism is best understood as the state acknowledgment of diversity and its pragmatic and inclusive response. In consociational systems, nations or ethnic groups are formally granted recognition and incorporated into the political system through a set of institutional tools, such as executive representation, proportional representation in the public administration and legislature, veto rights, and autonomy. This approach, as we will explore in greater detail in the next chapter, is a frequent response to ethnic conflict and is used in deeply divided societies.

types of polyethnic states,
— useful models for final project?

Finally, ethnic democracies constitute a group of democracies in which one group, usually the largest nation, dominates the political system and excludes others. Exclusion can restrict access to citizenship or reduce access to social, economic, and political rights and power. In the most radical form, this can result in the disenfranchisement of a large population, even a majority. If one takes South Africa during the apartheid era or the United States before the civil rights movement, the nonwhite population was either legally excluded from citizenship and equal rights or marginalized through indirect tools of exclusion. These different regime types can be mirrored among authoritarian systems, merely without democratic representation among the dominant ethnic group.

How the state positions itself toward the question of national identity shapes a set of policies, from official languages to school curricula, and from national holidays to the group rights a state may offer or withhold. The first, and in many ways the most important, reflection of how the state views itself is its citizenship policies. As noncitizens are not able to vote (with exceptions), and they do not enjoy the same rights and protections as citizens, citizenship determines who belongs to the community and who does not.

The most fundamental distinction of citizenship is how access is granted. This may be based on residence in the country, often called *jus soli*, the right of the soil, i.e., a person born in a country is automatically its citizen. This approach reflects the logic of immigrant societies where migrants settle and seek to make their new country a permanent home, at least in theory. Today, most countries in the Americas still offer citizenship based on birth. A similar approach has been a feature of French citizenship rules. As the nation defined itself as being open to all inhabitants of France, citizenship was granted accordingly. The countermodel is termed *jus sanguinis*, the right of blood, in which citizenship is awarded based on descent. Traditionally, German has been the prototype of this approach to citizenship. Today, it is the prevailing model of citizenship around the world, yet even Germany has modified its laws and moved away from a rigid insistence on the descent. The two types of citizenship closely overlap with the respective conceptions of the nation, as we explored in earlier chapters, that is, a civic nation based on the population of a state or an ethnic nation in which descent prevails.

Today, most European countries follow neither of these concepts of citizenship rigidly, and especially since the late 1980s, many countries have moved toward a middle ground with few solely basing their citizenship on either descent or place of birth, allowing for naturalization to some, not based on descent, and in turn not offering citizenship to all those born in the country irrespective of the parents' citizenship.

The concept of descent can be defined both in ethnic and in civic terms, yet both easily result in exclusion. The Baltic states after independence in 1991 established citizenship laws that provided automatic access to their inhabitants who could demonstrate that they or their ancestors were citizens of the interwar Baltic republics. Latvia, Lithuania, and Estonia emerged after the collapse of the Russian Empire in 1917 and 1918 and retained their independence until it was ended in 1939 through Soviet and later German occupation, followed by renewed Soviet rule. Their citizenship was thus based on the descent but not officially described in ethnic terms, as descendants of Russian, German, Jewish, and other minorities in the Baltic states dating back to the interwar period could claim citizenship. Nevertheless, the laws excluded a large segment of the population. During the forty years of Soviet rule, millions of migrants moved to the Baltic republics from other republics of the USSR, particularly to Latvia and Estonia. At independence in 1991, several hundred thousand Russian speakers lived in the two countries, making up 30–40 percent of the population. Except for a small number of Russian speakers who could demonstrate that they or their ancestors lived in the interwar republics, most were not granted automatic access to citizenship. Acquiring it was not easy, as it required overcoming considerable obstacles, in particular learning the new state language. Despite these hurdles, many Russian speakers have acquired Estonian or Latvia citizenship since independence. Yet 15 percent of the inhabitants of Estonia in 2017, who were either Russian citizens or without a clarified status, were still de facto stateless.

If the Baltics based the principle of descent on earlier, interrupted citizenship regimes, Germany has historically based its citizenship on German descent. This became particularly visible in the immigration of ethnic Germans to Germany after the end of communism, the so-called *Spätaussiedler*, the late re-settlers. With the fall of the Iron Curtain, emigration became possible and attractive for many in Eastern Europe. Since the 1950s, West Germany had a law that enabled the immigration of Germans from Eastern Europe, but the Iron Curtain had limited immigration from communist countries. After 1989, the numbers increased drastically. From the 1950s to 1970s around one million Germans arrived in West Germany from Eastern Europe, followed by another million in the 1980s, mostly at the end of the decade, and two million in the 1990s. Most of these "Germans" who arrived in Germany had never lived in Germany but had lived as part of German-speaking minorities across Eastern Europe, from the Baltics to Romania, for centuries, well before the creation of the German nation-state. However, they were not just offered refuge in Germany but also granted citizenship based on their ability to prove either German descent or a discernible commitment to the German national culture, for example through a declaration, excellent knowledge of German, or demonstrating that they had learned German at home. For proof of descent, one grandparent was usually sufficient. Ironically, the notorious *Ariernachweise*, Aryan certificates, required of Germans during the Third Reich to prove their non-Jewish descent served as legitimate proof.

For many of these *Spätaussiedler* pragmatic considerations such as job prospects, were often more important than commitment to the German nation. Furthermore, many did not speak German nor had they been an active part of the German minority. However, the citizenship laws made it easier for individuals who could demonstrate a very tentative connection to the German nation in Kazakhstan, for example, to acquire German citizenship than it was for a Turkish citizen who was born to immigrant parents in Germany.

Citizenship policies also have a transnational dimension. Countries that offer citizenship based on descent have also offered citizenship to their ethnic kin elsewhere. Classic emigrant countries, such as Ireland and Italy, have thus enabled emigrants and their descendants to (re-)acquire passports with relative ease. Similarly, but more controversially, Hungary and Croatia give ethnic Hungarians and Croats in neighboring states passports and voting rights, raising concerns about the loyalty of minorities in those countries. Russia has similarly offered easy access to citizenship to ethnic kin and other groups in neighboring countries. This was used to justify Russian military intervention in South Ossetia and Abkhazia, two secessionist regions of Georgia, in 2008.

Questions of citizenship are particularly pertinent in countries where citizenship holds great value. Thus, discussions on who ought to be included or excluded are more intense in Europe and North America. However, the question of citizenship is also crucial elsewhere, especially when migration matters. For example, in Côte d'Ivoire citizenship became a salient issue in the mid-1990s. Aimé Henri Konan Bédié succeed the longtime dictator Félix Houphouët-Boigny in 1993, but faced strong challengers in 1995, including Alassane Ouattara, a highly regarded official from the International Monetary Fund (IMF). Considering that there had been significant migration from Burkina Faso, the parliament required candidates to have native Ivorian parents to run, resulting in Ouattara's disqualification. In total, there are around 700,000 stateless persons in Côte d'Ivoire, mostly migrants and their descents from Burkina Faso, many of whom were already living there when the country became independent. In addition to the use of citizenship to exclude political opponents, citizenship policies can be used for collective exclusion. In Myanmar, the Muslim Rohingya minority has been subject to an extensive experience of exclusion on the grounds of citizenship. Since independence, the Rohingya have been denied citizenship in the predominantly Buddhist state. State repression against the Rohingya increased in 2016 following clashes between the army and rebel forces. In addition to the dynamics of ethnic conflict, the topic of the next chapter, the military regime expelled more than one million Rohingya to neighboring Bangladesh, with the Myanmar authorities claiming that the Rohingya were in reality migrants from Bangladesh. This example illustrates how the politics of citizenship can underpin and justify deliberate policies of exclusion.

However, most of the time, citizenship creates a peacetime hierarchy between "owners" of the state and those who have a more tenuous status. The creation of European Union citizenship, which is complementary to state-based citizenship and offers freedom of movement and some political rights, has challenged the rigid distinction between citizens and noncitizens.

Citizenship might not guarantee equality, as other hierarchies privilege some citizens over others. Examples include the Jim Crow laws in the United States as well as anti-Roma laws and policies in Europe, which made them second-class citizens. This type of hierarchy can also be well illustrated in the case of Israel. Since its creation, Israel has been home to Arab Israelis who were not expelled and did not flee at independence. Unlike Palestinians in the West Bank and Gaza, these Palestinian Arabs hold Israeli citizenship, and they made up around 21 percent of the population of Israel in 2013. While Arab Israeli citizens can vote and participate in public life, they are structurally marginalized, as the state of Israel is defined as a Jewish state, from its symbols to many of its policies. This was legally enshrined in 2018 with a nation-state law that, in the words of Prime Minister Benjamin Netanyahu, ensured that,

> This is our state, the state of the Jews. In recent years there have been some who have attempted to cast doubt on this, and so to undercut the foundations of our existence and our rights. Today we etched in the stone of law: This is our state, this is our language, this is our anthem, and this is our flag.[3]

Such a distinction between majority and minority is also reflected in migration policies. Whereas Jews are able to migrate to Israel and automatically receive citizenship, Palestinians whose ancestors lived on the territory are not able to return. With such hierarchies of citizenship, states reaffirm their position as nation-states.

The relationship between states and identity is a complex one. As discussed above, states—both nation-states and multinational states—will enact their understanding of national identity through citizenship laws that provide for different criteria of inclusion or exclusion. However, citizenship is far from being the only context in which state policy and nations interact, even beyond the formative period of state, and particularly nation-state, construction.

As discussed above, the politics of language and education reflect the state's understanding of its population. The language choices made by the state can exclude or include some of its citizens. Besides, the educational system determines not just the language children learn *questions of what history gets taught...*

but also the history that is taught: does this history create a civic or an ethnic narrative of the nation, and how are earlier states and peoples portrayed? Some countries that recognize minorities might offer separate language training, history classes, and even separate schools for children from a minority background. Such separate educational systems can be both empowering and exclusionary. Thus in the Baltic states, which inherited a school system from Soviet times where different mother tongues were taught in different schools, not much was done to include Russian-speaking minorities, which further marginalized them. As the social prestige of the state languages grew, Russian-speaking parents often began to send their children to schools teaching in the state languages to give them a social advantage at the cost of not learning their mother tongue. Similarly, Roma children across Central and Southeastern Europe are often sent to special needs schools, which prevents them from advancing to high schools and university, resulting in segregation and discrimination.

Categorizing citizens

States also count and categorize their citizens. What might sound like a technical process, census taking, is a highly political method of creating identity categories and including and excluding population groups. The UN notes that "the traditional census is among the most complex and massive peacetime exercises a nation undertakes."[4] Much of census taking has little to do with identity and more to do with economic and social planning. However, censuses often ask citizens questions about their religion, mother tongue, or national identity. Such questions proved to be highly controversial in the multilingual Habsburg Monarchy of the nineteenth century, as well as in multiracial countries such as the United States. The census takers in modern states seek to create a complete and comprehensive picture not just to govern better but also to impose specific categories. As Benedict Anderson notes, colonial censuses introduced racial or ethnic categories that were not only part of "divide and rule" strategies but also borne out of a genuine, if misguided, desire to understand and to categorize.[5]

Censuses are thus not mere statistical exercises, in which real and fixed identities are counted. They create identities by recognizing some and ignoring others. Censuses set the boundaries by determining which categories are legitimate and implicitly exist: once a group is counted, it can be ignored by the state if it is small, or it might become the subject of state policy. However, this presupposes that the group is a coherent unit.[6] This assumption has been repeatedly challenged, particularly when it comes to Roma communities in Central and Eastern Europe, who are far from a single unified minority. Today there are around 10–12 million Roma living in Europe, making it the most significant transnational European minority. Yet official data is hard to come by as many Roma do not wish to identify as Roma in censuses. This is in part due to past discrimination and fear of negative consequences for identifying as Roma. It also reflects the desire of many to assimilate into the dominant nation to improve their social and economic position. Furthermore, there is often a weak sense of a unified Roma identity, based on the fact that the Roma speak multiple languages, often not Romani, which also varies significantly across the continent (and beyond), and practice different religions as well as having a strong sense of identity among smaller subcommunities. Unsurprisingly, censuses turn out to be too coarse to capture the complexity of this community, and others, highlighting the challenges that arise when a standardized bureaucratic process encounters the complexity of national identities.

Censuses also rank identities. This might occur when particular identities are promoted or demoted. In Socialist Yugoslavia, for example, the Slavic Muslim population was granted their own category as a nation in 1971, when they were listed as "Muslims," distinct from Croats and Serbs. The recognition in the census was a crucial step to the legal recognition and political promotion of the community.

Next to the functions of categorization, their purpose is also crucial. In the US censuses, there has been a shift from being a tool to uphold racial segregation toward one that enables affirmative action policies. Thus, censuses can serve to dominate, ignore, or empower particular groups. Counting populations can, therefore, reflect state policies toward diversity and national identity.

Responses to subnational identities

Nation-states and other states alike interact with the national identities of their inhabitants, be they citizens or not. States are of course not the only actors in shaping nations and nationalism. National movements emerged in multinational empires, absolutist monarchies, and small city-states, and when they were able to create nation-states, these often absorbed the movements that created them which became institutionalized, including in state institutions, from national academies of arts and sciences and universities to organized sports associations and theaters. Non-state actors, such as media, parties, and social movements remained important. The nations they built were often not without contestation, including from subnational regional, linguistic, and ethnic identities.

While nationalists assumed that regional identities could be assimilated into larger national movements, this process proved far more fragile and tentative than was supposed. After the Second World War, Europe's states had become more homogenous than at any time over the preceding centuries. Millions of minorities were killed or displaced during and after the war. Jews, who were a substantial minority across Central and Eastern Europe, were much diminished by the Holocaust, and survivors became subject to pogroms and discrimination in postwar Central and Eastern Europe, accelerating their emigration for Israel. Germans and others associated with Nazi occupation and terror were expelled, irrespective of personal responsibility. Thus, ironically, as European integration promoted the cooperation and integration of states across the Western half of the continent, it had become less diverse. In the 1950s, after the massive expulsion and murders of the Second World War and before the rise of large-scale migration, European states had been closer to being nation-states than ever before or since. Yet the monopoly of the nation-state was short-lived, as regional nationalisms emerged and made political claims. The regional nationalisms along the so-called Celtic fringe include the Scottish, Welsh, and Breton movements. Basques and Catalans sought more self-rule in Spain, whereas German-speakers in South Tyrol, Corsicans in France, and others rejected being subsumed into the larger nation.

Some had a long history of political demands, including the Catalans, who had a strong sense of regional identity that was suppressed by Franco's regime. Similarly, the Basque national movement emerged with the ETA (Euskadi Ta Askatasuna, or "Basque Homeland and Liberty") terrorist group fighting against Spain in 1959. In Northern Ireland, the Irish Republican Army (IRA) sought unification with the Republic of Ireland and rejected the unionist dominance in the province. This resulted in the twenty-five-year low-intensity conflict that began in the late 1960s.

What characterized many of these movements was the combination of leftist politics with regional nationalism. Groups such as ETA and the IRA saw themselves as national movements in the same vein as African and Asian anti-colonial movements. Thus, if nation-building within France or the UK had features of the *mission civilisatrice* of the peripheral regions that shared many similarities with colonial territories, the movements in those regions in the 1950s to 1970s rejected the quasi-colonial control of the center and what they saw as a fundamentally alien rule. While some aspired to join neighboring nation-states, such as the IRA, others aimed either for independence or merely more autonomy.

Not all such groups opted for violence. The Catalan national movement, like the German-speakers in Alto Adige/South Tyrol or supporters of Greenlandic autonomy sought to achieve their goals through negotiation and mostly aspired to greater self-rule rather than outright independence.

While these groups failed to achieve full independence, they were mostly successful in terms of attaining autonomy. For example, the 1998 Good Friday Agreement devolved government to Northern Ireland in the UK; the 1978 Spanish constitution granted the Basque region and Catalonia far-reaching self-rule; Greenland gained extensive autonomy and left the European Community in 1985, while Denmark remained in the EC; South Tyrol, with its German-speaking majority, achieved far-reaching autonomy and an advanced power-sharing arrangement within the region between the Italian and German speakers. Whereas some movements focused on regions where the nation and the state had not become congruent, such as in South Tyrol, other national movements were new and had not previously self-identified as distinct nations. Besides, not all nation-state-building projects convinced all their citizens to consider the nation as the main unit of identification. For example, in Italy, the gap between North and South extended beyond just regional rivalry and stereotypes. When the Lega Nord emerged under the leadership of Umberto Bossi in the late 1980s, it advocated the secession of the North and the creation of a state called *Padania*. Although the party eventually relegated Padania to party folklore and expanded to the South, it shows that the glue that holds nation-states together can stop working despite a century of nation-building.

Everyday nationalism

The ability of national movements and states to persuade populations to identify with the nation is thus by no means a given. Nations are therefore not made to become a stable category once and for all, but need to be remade and reinforced through continuous nation-building. This process functions not just through large acts but through little, common, and sometimes imperceptible everyday actions. These include the symbols on coins and stamps, and the TV weather forecast, which may be limited to the state borders or show the weather also where ethnic kin live.

One ritual that exemplifies this everyday nationalism is the pledge of allegiance that American schoolchildren recite each morning at the beginning of school. Following multiple revisions, the pledge in current use was adopted in 1942, and in 1954 "under God" was added: "I pledge allegiance to the flag of the United States of America, and to the republic for which it stands, one nation under God, indivisible, with liberty and justice for all." The pledge is recited in public schools, at different levels of government, and the opening of congressional sessions. Even if this is merely a ritual, it emphasizes the central importance of the nation *every* day. While the pledge is not mandatory, significant peer-group and at times teacher pressure make opting out very difficult.

Even more frequently, the nation is evoked not by using the term nation but by much simpler words, such as "we" or "us." A victory in sport is easily described as a collective success. Headlines in German

Documents: La Marseillaise. French National Anthem[7]

Written in 1792 by Claude Joseph Rouget de Lisle and became national anthem in 1795.

Arise, children of the Fatherland,
The day of glory has arrived!
Against us tyranny's
Bloody banner is raised,
Bloody banner is raised.
Do you hear, in the countryside,
The roar of those ferocious soldiers?
They're coming right into your arms
To cut the throats of your sons, your women!
To arms, citizens,
Form your battalions,
Let's march, let's march!
Let an impure blood
Soak our fields!

Document: Il Canto degli Italiani. Italian Anthem[8]

Written in 1847 by Goffredo Mameli and Michele Novaro, became national anthem in 1946.

Italian Brothers,
Italy has awakened,
She has wreathed her head
With the helmet of Scipio.
Where is Victory?
She bows her head to you,
You, whom God created

As the slave of Rome.
Let us band together,
We are ready to die,
We are ready to die,
Italy has called us.
We were for centuries
Downtrodden and derided,
because we are not one people,
because we are divided.
Let one flag, one hope
gather us all.
The hour has struck
for us to join together.

newspapers in July 2014, after the German national team won the soccer world cup, for example, proclaimed triumphantly: "Wir sind Weltmeister!" (We are world champions). Of course, not all ninety million Germans were world champions, only a team of top soccer players; but it was celebrated, as global sports events usually are, as a national victory.

The nation is also evoked when it comes to consumption. For example, the Buy American Act, passed in 1933, gives preference to American companies in government procurement, and the United States and other countries have seen campaigns to encourage citizens to buy products from their country, described as a national or patriotic duty. Similar laws and campaigns can be found across the world, encouraging buying products from their own country, based on a variety of arguments from environmental to patriotic, from food safety to economic. In all of these cases, the assumed frame of reference is the nation-state. Thus in 2017, 70 percent of Americans thought it to be very or somewhat important to buy products made in the United States.[9]

Such "nation-branding" is also central in tourism and global business, where states position themselves on the marketplace and sell their distinct identity to would-be visitors and investors. Nation-branding is thus not just an exercise in attracting tourists, thereby boosting the economy, but also about projecting a particular image of oneself as a state and, by extension, as a nation, thereby implicitly or explicitly shaping outside perceptions. The message is thus a reflection of the state and the government's view of the country—even if the campaigns are generally designed or at least assisted by professional advertisement agencies. Tourism and nation-branding are primarily directed toward the outside world. How a nation-state presents and sells itself is consequential for the outside world and, in turn, for the nation.[10] Tourism was an essential part of nation-building even in its early phases in the nineteenth century. The idea of visiting your own country to get to know it has similar functions in nation-building to military service or other ways in which citizens "discover" their country. Getting to know one's own country in this manner was an active part of consolidating Benedict Anderson's "imagined community."[11]

Starting in the nineteenth century, and increasingly with the rise of mass tourism in the twentieth century, visitors were encouraged by the state to discover their own country. In France, the state and its intellectuals highlighted the intrinsic value of the French discovering their own country through travel.[12] Only the rise of modern infrastructures, such as train and shipping routes or the expansion of road networks, and social welfare, including regular holidays for workers, led to the emergence of modern travel habits. If the traveler from within the nation could learn about their own nation and thus understand the nation-state as an organic unit, travelers from outside were no less critical. The outsider visitor provides for an audience back home to whom they may present and interpret the country and the nation. There are also symbiotic relationships emerging between, on the one hand, the invented traditions that nationalism often requires in order to project itself into the past and, on the other, newly invented "authentic" traditions that tourists desire to see. *Shopska* salad, today a common dish throughout the Balkans made of tomatoes, cucumbers, peppers, onions, and white brined cheese, has become part of the national cuisines in the region but was invented by the communist Bulgarian tourist agency *Balkantourist* in the mid-1950s to showcase a newly created national tradition that highlighted the abundance socialism could provide to the growing Western tourists on the Black Sea coast.[13] Elsewhere around the world, tourist agencies invented, blended, and created supposedly national traditions appropriate for tourists that would filter back into the national self-identification. Tourism, particularly in exotic places, often seeks out the "ethnic" and the "authentic," to contrast with globalized consumerism.[14] This often Orientalist view of the exotic produces and legitimizes ethnicity, not unlike how earlier colonialism did. The terms "ethnic foods" or "world music" thus reinforce the dichotomy between a globalized Western culture in music or food versus exotic and "ethnic" food and cultures elsewhere. Such a distinction and commercialization of "ethnic" or "national" foods suggests that food, clothing, or music are associated with a particular group defined in ethnic or national terms. While this might hold true in some contexts, it is often misleading. Cuisines, dress, and music cross cultures and are rarely the monopoly of one nation.

Gender, class, and nation

Beyond consumption and travel, nationalism interacts and intersects with other aspects of everyday life and social structures, such as class and gender. While nationalism might be a flexible ideology, it has critical defining features in terms of social relations. The role of class or socio-economic status matters in many contexts. In Northern Ireland, the "peace walls" built to divide Protestant and Catholic neighborhoods and the murals that mark who is in charge—Irish nationalists or British unionists—are not to be found everywhere. Instead, they are most common in working-class neighborhoods, whereas in middle-class districts there are far fewer markers of nationalism of either side, and these neighborhoods tend to be more diverse in terms of national background. Nationalism and class or socio-economic status can mutually reinforce each other and increase the significance of nationalism. The reasons are complex, and it is not just as simple as that poorer or less well-educated citizens are more nationalist than those with a middle or upper-class background. The difference depends on the opportunities for cross-national communication, which might vary depending on education and the workplace. Besides, nationalism might resonate more with groups that are suffering from economic or social deprivation. As we will explore in the next chapter, inequalities—real or perceived—between members of different groups can facilitate ethnic tension and become instrumental in conflict.

Socio-economic position also matters when it comes to immigration. Usually, wealthy migrants are not considered a threat by far-right groups, tabloid media, or nationalist discourse. The better-off who move to another country are also often not called or thought of as migrants but as "expats" or just mobile professionals. Migrants with lower socio-economic status, on the other hand, are seen more as a threat, both in terms of culture and economic position, to the native population, as we will explore in Chapter 8 on migration.

In addition to socio-economic relations, gender roles also intersect with nationalism. If nationalism is concerned with the creation of a political entity for the nation, usually a nation-state, it is also concerned with maintaining the polity and ensuring the survival of the nation. The concept of the nation, particularly when it is understood in terms of descent, is closely linked with the idea of its biological reproduction. The far-right "Alternative for Germany" party campaigned in 2017 with a poster showing a pregnant woman under the slogan "New Germans? We make them ourselves." The advertisement implied that instead of naturalizing foreigners, Germans should have more children to maintain the German population. While giving preference to descent rather than migration, it also points to the central role attributed to women in maintaining the nation. Natalist policies, i.e., measures to increase the birthrate among the population, are a common feature among nationalists. A variety of governments, from communist regimes, such as Romania under Ceaușescu, and Republican states, such as France, have actively encouraged families to have more children, but the link between nationalism and birth rates is particularly salient and such policies are usually framed in the context of preserving the nation. In 2019, the Hungarian prime minister Viktor Orbán unveiled a plan to reward families with four or more children by freeing mothers from paying income tax for life. In countries with declining birth rates, such natalist policies became more pronounced, in combination with national anxiety over extinction. A demographic decline is thus often framed as an existential threat to the nation. The strong anti-migrant sentiments in Central and Eastern Europe, as we will discuss in Chapter 7, are closely linked to the fear of national demographic decline.

In multiethnic states, other groups might also become demographic threats due to differentials in the birthrate. During the 1980s in Yugoslavia, for example, Serbian media and intellectuals worried about the higher birthrate among Albanians in Kosovo, suggesting that the difference explained the decline of Serbs in the region. Albanians were presented as sexually active and aggressive, and the difference in birthrate, which had primarily socio-economic causes, was reframed in national terms. Public debates suggested that the higher birthrate was a deliberate strategy by the Albanians. Ironically, the higher birthrates among migrants or particular minorities are a source of both perceived threat and of envy, as these groups appear in nationalist discourse as a challenge to the nation while also being a role model in terms of birthrates and national cohesion. In such a context, the primary role of women is thus focused on giving birth and raising children. As a consequence, politically and socially engaged women have often been attacked by nationalist parties for not living up to their expected role as mothers. Nationalism often reinforces patriarchal structures and traditional gender roles. One can understand the logic of nations in functioning like extended families, in which traditional patterns are extended and reproduced. Leaders are expected to be men, often circumscribed as "strong men" who offer to protect the nation, which is often defined as female, embodied most vividly by Marianne, portrayed in 1830 painting *Liberty Leading the People* by Eugène Delacroix as bearing her breast, thus reinforcing her female attributes.

The perception of women as key in preserving the nation is closely intertwined with narratives about purity and the threat posed by women having partners from other nations. This was particularly pertinent in the anti-Semitic rhetoric of the Third Reich, where women (and to a lesser degree, men) who had Jewish partners were denigrated as "race traitors". In the context of ethnic violence, sexual violence against women is often framed as undermining the enemy nation.

While nationalism has strong patriarchal features engrained, this does not mean that nationalist leaders do not claim to seek to advance the position of women as part of their program. In what has been called femonationalism, far-right parties have deliberately sought to position themselves as protectors of women from radical Islam.[15] Thus far-right politicians such as Geert Wilders, leader of the Dutch Party of Freedom, and Marine Le Pen of the French

National Rally argue that Islam constitutes a threat for women's rights, thus their anti-Islamic policies protect both women from the "indigenous" majority and Muslim women more effectively than conventional parties. The appropriation of women's rights by the far-right also counters nationalist and far-right groups' strong emphasis on masculinity and is often a deliberate strategy to soften the image of nationalist parties.

This relates to the relationship between nationalism and LGBTQ (lesbian, gay, bisexual, transgender, and questioning) communities. Homophobia and nationalism have often been closely intertwined. This is no surprise, considering nationalism's concern with reproducing the nation and traditional family roles, including patriarchal social structures. Nonheterosexual identities and communities have become more central in some nationalist discourses in recent decades, as LGBTQ rights have become a source of public debate. In 2013, for example, the Russian Duma passed a law "for the Purpose of Protecting Children from Information Advocating for a Denial of Traditional Family Values," with only one abstention, penalizing the promotion of "distorted ideas about the equal social value of traditional and non-traditional sexual relationships." The law, also known as the gay-propaganda law, was justified in terms of the defense of tradition against Western decadence. Similar laws and initiatives have emerged elsewhere, from sub-Saharan African countries such as Uganda to post-communist Europe often framed as protection of the nation. Elsewhere, LGBTQ rights have been appropriated by far-right and nationalist groups, similarly to women's rights. Thus, anti-Muslim parties and groups have claimed to defend Western liberalism, including LGBTQ rights, from conservative Muslim migrants. The appropriation of LGBTQ issues to improve the image of nationalist (and other) groups has been described as "pink-washing."

Thus, nationalism traditionally promotes a conventional understanding of gender roles and rejects LGBTQ communities and the complexity of identity they imply. At the same time, there have been efforts by nationalist groups to incorporate the liberalizing dynamics, particularly in Western societies, to claim the protection of LGBTQ communities and women's rights.

Not only are the roles of women defined by nationalist movements but those of men too. Nationalist masculinity defines men as strong and often militarized. This stands in contrast not just with the understanding of the role of women but also with the "effeminate" or weak men. For example, the Israeli and earlier Zionist vision of masculinity emphasized the physical ability to defend and tend to the land, contrasting it with the "Ghetto Jew" who is weak and victimized by discrimination.[16] As a result, nationalism does not just reinforce or instrumentalize particular gender hierarchies, it also engages with and appropriates changing gender roles. Nationalism as an ideology is flexible, but it is also restrained by the centrality of belonging to a particular nation. Other identities, including gender, are subordinated and commonly structured to emphasize hierarchy, which commonly includes the particular roles of men and women, including assumed respectable behavior.[17] What this respectability entailed, of course, shifted from nineteenth-century Europe to global nationalism in the twenty-first century.

Religion and nation

If the rise of the nation and the nation-state challenged universalist claims to rule, often based on religion, religion itself has not ceased to be a significant marker of identity. Nationalism has often borrowed many parts of its own master narrative from religion, from the notion of decline and redemption to the concept of martyrdom. Nations are products of the religions they are embedded in, even if the relationship between nation and religion is not always symbiotic. Confronted with religion as a defining marker of identity, nationalism had to define its relationship with religion. This relationship can be both antagonistic and mutually reinforcing. Some nations emerged following religious lines, such as Russian nationalism, which incorporated Orthodox Christianity as a core constituent marker, whereas other nations emerged across religious divides, such as the German nation, which includes Catholics, Protestants, Jews, and more recently other religions including Muslims. This relationship is subject to change. Early German nationalism was highly suspicious toward Catholics, whose loyalty was in doubt due to the alternative authority of the Vatican. Similarly, in India, Indian nationalism includes both a secular understanding, as promoted by the Congress Party, that includes non-Hindu Indians, and a more exclusive Hindu nationalism promoted by the Bharatiya Janata Party (BJP). Secular and religious, inclusionary and exclusionary religious nationalisms thus compete. The centrality of religion in the nationalist self-definition varies, even if a nation is relatively mono-religious. Polish or Greek nationalisms are cases of strong religious nationalism. In both nationalisms and states, Catholicism and Orthodoxy are privileged and form a constituent feature of national identity. French or Italian nationalism, on the other hand, define themselves in more secular terms, even though most French and Italians are Catholics. This variation is in part shaped by the historical development of the respective nationalism. French nationalism emerged as a revolutionary process against the monarchy and included the Church as a representative of the ancient régime. Similarly, in Italy, Italian unification in the 1860s challenged the Church's political power. Once Italian unification was completed with the conquest of Rome, the Pope would not leave the Vatican and endorse the new state until the Lateran Treaty signed between Mussolini and Pope Pius XI in 1929 normalized relations. Polish and Greek nationalism arose against larger empires, the Ottoman Empire in the case of the latter and the Russian, German, and Habsburg empires in the former. In both cases, the Church could serve as an institutional source of identity. In brief, the relationship between nation and religion is closely linked to the early phase of the nation-building process. If the religion and its institutions are aligned with the nation, the relationship was likely to be mutually reinforcing; if ecclesiastical hierarchies were associated with empires or other states hostile to the nation, the relationship was often more antagonistic.

Besides secular and religious nationalism, civil-religious nationalism takes a middle path. The United States constitutes a good example of such a relationship in which state, nationalism, and religion are not formally intertwined, yet Protestantism has long been the prevailing religion in the self-understanding of the state and nation. While not formally exclusionary, other religions have long been disadvantaged, and references to God in the symbols of the state, including the national motto "in God we trust," highlight the importance of religion. While the founders attributed importance to general religiosity, the symbolic references to God, similarly to the pledge of allegiance, are mostly products of the twentieth century. The motto was only introduced in 1956. From the initial prominence of Protestantism, the acknowledgment of other religions broadened toward including Catholicism and Judaism, represented by President Eisenhower's 1952 speech in which he argued that "our government has no sense unless it is founded in a deeply felt religious faith, and I don't care what it is."[18] Other nation-states often give one religion a privileged position, without religion being a formative feature of the nation. Schools in countries such as Italy and Austria feature crucifixes in classrooms, even though neither nationalism is particularly religious. The cooption of religious symbols and holidays is a reflection of the symbiotic relationship between nation and religion. Through migration, as we will explore in the next chapter, these symbols gain a new meaning. Migrants of different religious background are symbolically excluded from the nation, whereas exclusionary nationalists have reinterpreted the symbols to strengthen the Christian nature of the state and nation, often characterized as "Judeo-Christian" or "Western." By claiming religious symbols as part of a larger "European" or "Western" heritage, they are reinterpreted as markers in a confrontation with the non-European, non-Western other. This reframing of religious symbols as markers of nations or larger symbolic spaces, such as "civilizations," is deeply ambivalent, considering the secularization of many societies, particularly in Europe. With the rise of atheism and agnosticism, framing nationalism in religious terms risks undermining the nation.

Nationalism, particularly secular nationalism, often incorporates elements of a civic religion, drawing from a repertoire of religious symbolism and narratives and appropriating them for the nation. National myths of decline and redemption have strong religious motifs, as do the creation of secular holidays and ceremonies, from the aforementioned pledge of allegiance in American schools, which mention God, to the commemoration of war dead and other heroes. This was particularly pronounced in communist states that had to find a replacement for religious ceremonies in their effort to push back the social function of organized religion. In others, this appropriation often took place in a symbiotic relationship with religious communities.

Religion and nationalism are particularly combustible when national movements emerge in competition to one another along religious lines. This includes: Northern Ireland where being in favor of a united

Ireland coincides with Catholicism and most Protestants support union with Britain; Bosnia, where Bosniaks are overwhelmingly Muslims, Serbs Orthodox, and Croats Catholics; Lebanon, where confessional groups are politically organized. Usually, conflicts are not based on religion, but religion is a constitutive feature of the nation and a marker of difference. Thus, the conflicts in Northern Ireland, Bosnia, and Lebanon were not religious tensions but rather competing national or ethnic claims, justified and colored by religious difference. As we will explore in the next chapter on ethnic conflict, such overlapping cleavages are mutually reinforcing. Religion and national belonging are particularly rigid. While linguistic assimilation might be possible, and other markers of difference can be ignored or forgotten, changing religion is rare and often fraught with difficulties. When religious nationalisms are in conflict, religion often serves as a justification—religious symbolism is employed, from murals in Belfast to the destruction of mosques and churches in Bosnia and Lebanon—but the conflict is usually about nationalism, not religious difference.

Race and nation

Just as nationalism interacts with religion, gender, and socio-economic position, nationalism forms a complicated relationship with race. Race, unlike the others, constitutes a sometimes competing and at times reinforcing identity category based on ascribed markers that combine (real and imagined) physical markers and descent. Just like nations, race is not based on biological reality but on social construction that attributes certain "color" or other labels to individuals based on their physical features and descent. Race and nation intersect, but they can be mutually enforcing or can weaken each other. When race is a constitutive feature of the nation, it makes the understanding of the nation more rigid and exclusive, whereas if a nation is understood to be multiracial, it can weaken the significance of race.

Debates about nation and race have been dominated by the case of the United States, which is only partially representative for a broader range of countries. Race has been a potent category of exclusion since the rise of the idea of racism in the nineteenth century. Racial hierarchies had existed earlier, such as the notions of European colonizers in the Americas who did not consider the native populations to be human or, if they did, saw them as inferior. Similarly, the exclusion of Jews in many European societies was not just based on religion but also on racial grounds, namely the idea that descent trumps religious affiliation. In Spain and Portugal, the *limpieza de sangre*, the purity of the blood, was grounds for excluding Christians who had converted from Islam or Judaism as a result of the violent *Reconquista*, the conquest of the Iberian Peninsula by the Christian kingdoms against the Moors that also led to the forced conversion and expulsion of Jews. Only by the nineteenth century did the importance of "pure" Christians or Christians of Jewish or Muslim descent fully cease to matter. Thus, the distinction between people based on descent existed before the rise of the nation and the emergence of the biological underpinnings of racism. However, it was the combination of imperialism, which sought to justify a rule over supposedly inferior peoples, and nationalism, which categorized people into groups based on shared identity, often based on supposed descent, that gave rise to racism as a distinct category.

Nationalism and racism are, as a result, closely intertwined, and in the nineteenth century, the terms were frequently used interchangeably, while in other contexts, larger groups were widely described as races, such as the Germanic or Slavic race. Racial categories also included visible markers such as skin color, and common distinctions set out white (European), black (African), yellow and brown (Asian), and red (American) races. While these distinctions did not hold up to scientific scrutiny, they are an important backdrop to the rise of nations and nationalism. It was not only radical groups and thinkers, such as the National Socialist German Workers Party in Germany, that thought of the world as divided into nations and races. Thus, an early journal devoted to international affairs that would later merge to become *Foreign Affairs* was originally called the *Journal of Race Development* highlighting how race and nation were used interchangeably.

With the collapse of National Socialism, the pseudoscientific justification for racial discrimination and hierarchies went into decline. Yet this did not spell an end of nationalism with strong racist foundations. The most extreme case was the white settler nationalism in Africa, discussed in the previous chapter. However, the importance of race prevailed also in the Americas. In the United States, Jim Crow laws at the state and local level excluded blacks in the South and curtailed their civic and political rights. While the laws were lifted as a result of the civil rights movement, patterns of discrimination and exclusion have persisted. For the nation, this has meant that the category of race excluded certain citizens from full citizenship rights and membership in the nation.

In Latin America, there is no tradition of legislative exclusion of the black population. Nevertheless, racial hierarchies have remained potent, and being "whiter" has been closely associated with high political and social rank. As European settlers dominated over the indigenous population and African slaves, socio-economic position and skin color have been closely associated. Most Latin American countries differ from the United States, however, in terms of "racial mixing." In the United States, cross-racial relationships had long been limited, initially mostly as a result of sexual abuse by slave owners and later, in the North, where freed slaves settled. Segregation made racial mixing difficult and less common than in Latin America. Here, a larger share of indigenous populations and a smaller number of European settlers has resulted in the emergence of nations that imagined themselves as more "mixed" than in the United States.

The election of Barack Obama in the United States, who was not just the first African American president but one who is one half African American and half white, signified to some the rise of multiracial or maybe even post-racial America. Following desegregation and decades of affirmative action and other policies to remedy the entrenched discrimination, the significance of racial distinctions appeared to be in decline. While most earlier debates were about racial equality, hybridity and diversity emerged as key themes. The "one drop rule" had historically meant that a person with just limited African origin would be "black," no matter how small that share was. This understanding is still deeply entrenched, as Barack Obama was widely understood as an African American president rather than being of both European and African descent. This concept draws on notions of white racial purity and was echoed in Nazi German racial policies, where Germans had to prove their descent and having one Jewish grandparent was enough to be considered to be of mixed descent.

Maintaining a rigid distinction between blacks and whites, as well as other racial categories, has bedeviled debates in the United States, as censuses and other official documents ask citizens to identify with such racial categories. The rise of more mixed-race couples, the endorsement of hybridization and individual choice undermines the idea of homogenous racial groups and rather highlights the flexible and changing nature of identity. At the same time, it risks overemphasizing individual choice and obscures the collective nature of discrimination.[19]

The dilemma of choice and identity is encapsulated by DNA testing. These commercial tests have become popular, particularly in immigrant societies, as they claim to provide individuals with detailed and apparently scientific data on their ethnic heritage. Based on an analysis of a DNA sample, these companies offer an estimate of the different ethnic backgrounds people might have. On the one hand, these tests highlight the diverse backgrounds most people hail from, disproving the myth of ethnic "purity." On the other hand, they also suggest that ethnic belonging is a matter of biology, i.e., descent is reflected in one's DNA rather than by upbringing and cultural exposure. Thus, it reintroduces the biological assumptions of ethnic groups and nations as fixed and natural categories that can be determined by a DNA test. This became apparent in the debate around the DNA test taken by the American politician Elizabeth Warren in 2018. She published the result to disprove claims by US president Donald Trump that she had falsely claimed Native American heritage. While the test showed that her DNA appeared to suggest Native American ancestry, it also raised controversy about whether such a claim could be legitimate without being culturally identified with the community. Native American leaders have challenged Elizabeth Warren's claims for appropriating a Native American identity without being part of the community and accepting the implicit racial logic of DNA tests.[20]

Who owns identity has become a central question in recent years, as reflected by this controversy. This question has come to matter in debates about identity in the United States over the cultural appropriation ranging from the origin of foods, such as Greek Feta, to clothing, such as the Mexican sombrero. Nations define themselves through a changing and, as noted above, often recently invented set of traditions, symbols, and myths. Many of these are not unique to any one nation, like music, clothing, food, and other features that are taken as constitutive of a nation travel, move, are copied and transferred. Foods often travel and are then claimed by many nations, so that what used to be known as Turkish coffee in the Balkans has become Greek, Serbian, "domestic" or "national" coffee to lay claim to the coffee tradition, brewed from coffee beans that do not have even a remote connection to the countries in question. The traditional dress of Herero women in Namibia offers another example. These *ohorokova* dresses, colorful and lavish, with a high neck and full-length skirt, are inspired by the dresses German colonists wore during the brief and brutal German colonial rule: the same rule that saw the genocide against the Herero by the German colonial army. There is an inherent tension between the borrowing and transfer of such dresses, foods, and traditions and the claims to authenticity of nations. These claims are reinforced through the rise of the global marketplace of products and tourism, as explored earlier.

First, the concept of nation-branding and the idea of claiming foods through trademarking the protected origin, for example, the protection that Parmesan cheese can only come from the Italian region around Parma, rather than from Wisconsin, creates a commercial link between products and the nation. Beyond the marketing of the nation, certain dishes are presented as national rather than shared, from Greek or Bulgarian yogurt to the origins of pasta, with the Italian-based International Pasta Organisation claiming that pasta has its origins in Etruscan cuisine and was thus not imported to Italy from China by Marco Polo.[21]

Another level of ownership has emerged in the debates about cultural appropriation. This question is intertwined with the debate about Orientalism, namely the idea that Europe and later the United States have viewed the rest of the world through the lens of colonial powers. This perspective often exoticized other regions and considered them unequal or inferior. Orientalism and the subsequent debate about postcolonialism reflect on the Eurocentrism of power and, by extension, of science and culture. As we have discussed in the previous chapter, colonial rule and the understanding of Africa and Asia created and reinforced ethnic identities, imposed state structures, and established deeply embedded power structures that often still prevail today.[22] The display of other cultures, such as in European ethnographic museums, was often less about respect for different cultures and more about showing the exotic and primitive, justifying European superiority and control. In Belgium, for example, the Africa Muséum reopened only in 2018 after a ten-year closure and reevaluation. It still contains a statue of a European missionary and an African boy with the inscription "Belgium brings civilization to Congo."[23] This view, combined with stolen artifacts, represents the engrained European and American imbalance of power reflected in the colonial and postcolonial experience.

From this perspective, the discussion about cultural appropriation emerged, suggesting that features of identity from marginalized groups should not be copied or emulated by those coming from a position of privilege. This goes beyond stamping out everyday racism, such as blackface, but focuses on the ownership of culture. Thus, can an American of European descent wear a sombrero, or can a non-Roma make Roma music? In Poland, can non-Jews dress up as Jews for a "traditional" Jewish wedding?

On the one hand, using recognizable features of a different culture might appear disrespectful and often stereotypical, including a sense of hierarchy and implicit power-relations. On the other hand, the idea of cultural appropriation suggests a very static understanding of these markers as belonging to a particular group, even though hybridity and transfer are inherent parts of processes of national identity formation.

These dilemmas and debates highlight that we do not live in a post-national, post-ethnic, or post-racial world. These concepts remain potent and vary between exclusionary and inclusionary, latent and virulent expressions. As the nation-state is an inherently incomplete construct, states and non-state actors evoke the nation at moments of need. This idea of the nation intersects with other forms of social belonging, such as class, gender, and race. As this chapter has highlighted, there is also space for the hybridity of identity, i.e., the combination of multiple national identities or their features, in terms of language or religion. The idea of purity is a myth, even if it has been potently cultivated by radical movements over the past centuries. Hybridity does not imply that "anything goes." The identity choices of individuals are confronted by the society around them and might be accepted or rejected. Take two very different examples. In the United States, Rachel Dolezal was the president of a chapter of the National Association for the Advancement of Colored People (NAACP) in

Spokane, Washington, and positioned herself as an African American activist. In 2015 it emerged that she was not of African American descent. She had to resign her post and was criticized for being a fraud and falsely appropriating an African American identity, even though she claims to identify as black. The second example is Tomio Okamura, who was born to a Czech mother and a Japanese-Korean father and moved to Czechoslovakia in the 1980s. By 2012, he had become a successful far-right politician in the Czech Republic. His party, called "Freedom and Direct Democracy" and founded in 2015, is a right-wing anti-EU, anti-immigrant party, an unexpected career considering that far-right parties and their electorate are defined by their xenophobia and rejection of foreigners. Origin and context matter when it comes to the acceptance and the apparent paradox that a half-Japanese Czech politician can make a career in the far-right of European politics, while a Caucasian American is disgraced for identifying as an African American activist.

Thus, nationalism remains potent after the creation of nation-states. More importantly, nationalism permeates and interacts with a variety of other social identities, such as class, gender, and race. Everyday nationalism thus does not just entail the mechanisms through which nationalism remains relevant in nation-states as a top-down process, driven by states and elites, but is also a reflection of how nationalism is reproduced and shaped in everyday life, from waving the flag on social media to national stereotypes told through jokes.

6

Ethnic Conflict

Ethnic conflict is both common and exceedingly rare. Common, because most armed conflicts today are motivated at least in part by antagonisms over identity that can be subsumed under the heading of ethnic conflict. Rare, because despite great levels of ethnic diversity around the world, conflicts remain the exception. Ethnic conflict is a term to describe the violent conflict that has ethnic identity at stake. Even the concept itself is misleading. As we have discussed nations and nationalism in this book, the term "ethnic" appears to fall out of the framework. However, ethnic conflict is better understood as ethnonational conflict: that is, conflict based on national identities that are defined along ethnic lines. If the previous chapter explored everyday nationalism, some of it exclusionary, this chapter examines the causes and dynamics of virulent exclusionary nationalism, i.e., when nationalism becomes a justification for violence.

Most conflicts have multiple causes and continue for a variety of reasons, and ethnonationalism is frequently just one of them. During the Cold War, for example, many proxy wars were ostensibly about allegiance toward the Soviet Union or the United States. Both superpowers supported governments or insurgents who claimed to be communist or anti-communist respectively. In Angola, for example, the National Union for the Total Independence of Angola (UNITA) and the Popular Movement for the Liberation of Angola (MPLA) first both fought Portuguese colonial rule. After independence in 1975, MPLA took control of the country and built a communist regime with Cuban and Soviet support, whereas UNITA staged an insurrection that lasted until the early 2000s. What looked like an ideological conflict also had

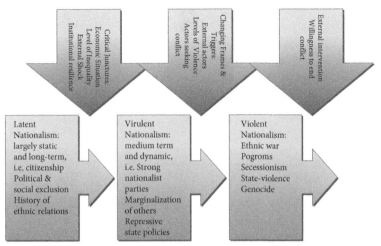

FIGURE 6.1 *Dynamics of nationalism.*

ideological proxy wars take on ethnic dimension

ethnonational undertones. The UNITA leader, Jonas Savimbi, hailed from the Ovimbundu, the largest single ethnic group in Angola. The Ovimbundu became the main basis of support for UNITA, which over time shaped the perception of both UNITA and the Ovimbundu, who also became politically and socially marginalized after UNITA lost the civil war. The ruling MPLA recruited mainly from the second-largest group, the Ambundu, who lived in the region around the capital, Luanda. Thus, the ideological proxy war had ethnic undercurrents, serving both to recruit supporters and to exclude and marginalize others. This does not mean that ideology did not matter and that the only line of confrontation was ethnicity: there were also rural versus urban divisions and other fault lines that fueled the conflict. As in many other conflicts, ethnicity was one but not the only cause of the conflict.

Thus to describe a war as an ethnic conflict does not imply that ethnic nationalism is the only or even the main causal factor, or that it is a cause by itself, i.e., without its deliberate use by particular groups. Ethnicity by itself needs to be harnessed in political discourse, in media reporting, through social movements, or in the writings of intellectuals; it does not exist in a social vacuum nor

ethnicity becomes the theme of the conflict when people deliberately make it so imposes itself as a source of violent conflict without human agency. Sometimes, conflicts reinforce and strengthen national identities and thus conflicts become more ethnic over time. As such, violence can create identity, especially if individuals are targeted for their identity. This was aptly described by Eldar Saraljić, a Professor of Philosophy with a Bosnian Muslim background:

> Being persecuted for being Muslim generated a personal and cultural resistance in me. I adopted and celebrated that scorned identity. Gradually, I *became* a Muslim. I embraced the target on my back and made it my own. But adopting an identity as a form of resistance, as I learned quickly, can take one only so far. Like an ill-fitting polyester suit, this identity itched, and I yearned to wear something more comfortable.[1]

This often-traumatic experience can shape and increase the salience of national identity, making violence into a generator of identity.[2]

Mass violence motivated by ethnicity and nationalism comes in multiple forms. Classic interstate war can be fueled and motivated by ethnonationalism. In the First World War or the Iran–Iraq war (1980–1988), governments appealed to nationalism to motivate citizens to support the war, to sign up to fight, and to otherwise endure the horrors of war. During the First World War, propaganda posters, articles, and speeches appealed to the greatness of their own nations and the threat posed by the enemy often described as a barbaric and essential threat. An example is the British propaganda poster "How *The Hun* Hates!," referring to the German enemy. Leaflets dropped by the fledgling Italian air force over Vienna in 1918, under the command of the nationalist poet and proto-fascist Gabrielle D'Annunzio, similarly explained: "we wage war against your government, the enemy of national freedom, with your blind, obstinate and cruel government, which can give you neither bread nor peace and feeds you only on a diet of hatred and elusive hopes."[3] In the era of mass wars, where the morale of the population (and that of the enemies' population) mattered, appeals to nationalism became an essential part of warfare. Interstate wars are rarely described as ethnic conflicts, but the claims made on people or territories are often ethnonationalist.

In the Second World War, Nazi Germany sought to establish a racial empire centered on Germany, and together with its ally Italy it justified the invasion of neighboring countries with ethnonational claims to territory, such as Dalmatia and Albania, or the protection of people, such as the Sudeten Germans in Czechoslovakia.

Interstate wars are also used by regimes to kindle nationalism, such as the war between Argentina and Great Britain over the Falkland Islands or Malvinas in 1982. The Argentinian military junta instigated the war as a distraction from the economic crisis and domestic unrest, striking up nationalist fervor over the islands, which were ruled by Britain but claimed by Argentina. After the ten-week war, the victory of the British armed forces, in turn, brought about a wave of nationalism in the UK, while in Argentina the military rulers soon had to relinquish power. Interstate war, as this example shows, is not just the result of nationalism but can be instrumentalized by regimes for a number of reasons, including a crisis of legitimacy, as a distraction, or to use nationalism either to mobilize citizens or to demobilize them from other forms of political engagement.

Riots and terrorism

Today, most conflicts, and with them most victims, involve not states but at least one non-state actor. These conflicts are most commonly civil wars, i.e., wars fought either by non-state actors against a government or among different non-state actors. In addition to such wars, there are also different types of violence within states, such as race riots or one-sided violence described as ethnic cleansing or genocide. Ethnic riots are described by Donald Horowitz as "an intense, sudden, though not necessarily wholly unplanned, lethal attack by civilian members of one ethnic group on civilian members of another ethnic group, the victims chosen because of their group membership."[4] Such riots have a history in Central and Eastern Europe, targeting Jews, as well as in India, often involving Muslims and Hindus. One example is the 2002 Gujarat riots. These erupted in the Western Indian state after a train with Hindu pilgrims caught fire and fifty-nine pilgrims perished. The fire broke out following a confrontation with Muslim vendors at a train station. While the fire appears to have been caused by accident, the chief minister of the state, Narendra Modi, and others called the incident a terrorist act, blaming Muslims for the deaths. In the aftermath, the radical nationalist *Hindu Vishva Hindu Parishad* (VHP) called for a strike that escalated into riots against Muslims throughout the state. After three days of rioting, including revenge attacks against Hindus, more than 1,000 people died and 2,500 were injured. The riots appear not to have been a spontaneous occurrence but preplanned by nationalist groups. Riots often involve some element of planning and are rarely entirely spontaneous. Key is the role of state authorities. Riots frequently become possible because the state or the main source of authority encourages the violence or at least turns a blind eye. Examples include the mass pogroms against Jews by Poles in Jedwabne in 1941 during the German occupation and the anti-Jewish pogroms in Russia, including in Kishinev (present-day Chişinău in Moldova) in 1903 and Odessa (present-day Ukraine) in 1905, which were made possible by a state that tolerated and even facilitated and encouraged mass violence. In other cases, riots occur in the absence of a state or where the state is weak, such as 1969 riot in Malaysia that later spilled over into Singapore, triggered by elections in which radical Malay ethnonationalists targeted ethnic Chinese in Malaysia.

Nationalist terrorism is another type of ethnic violence, defined by indiscriminate violence that aims to achieve a political goal, employed outside the context of a war. Religious terrorist groups, such as Al-Qaeda or ISIS (Islamic State of Iraq and Syria), have dominated headlines over the past few decades, while ideological groups, such as the far-left German Red Army Faction (RAF) or the Revolutionary Armed Forces of Colombia (FARC), dominated during the Cold War. Both in the past and today, many terrorist groups base their claims on nationalism. The term terrorism has to be used with great care, as governments often label insurgent groups as terrorists, whether they use violence or not.

Classic examples include groups that seek secession and resort to targeted or indiscriminate violence against a government, its representatives, or even the entire population. The Basque Euskadi Ta Askatasuna (ETA), which began its campaign in 1959 against the Franco government, or the Irish Republican Army (IRA), which fought the British government in Northern Ireland, are classic examples of ethnonationalist groups employing terrorist strategies, including the bombing of government officials and symbols of the state, assassinations, and kidnappings. The line between insurgent groups in a civil war and terrorism is fluid and often in the eye of the beholder. The groups see themselves as freedom fighters, whereas states brand them as terrorists. Such groups also shift over time and might even become legitimate political parties. Take the Kosovo Liberation Army (KLA), which fought the Serbian security forces that occupied Kosovo and harassed its Albanian population in the 1990s. The KLA initially targeted high-ranking representatives of the Serbian state through bombs and assassinations, classic features of a terrorist strategy. As the repression by the Serbian police increased, including the murder of KLA leader Adem Jashari and around fifty members of his extended family and fellow fighters in March 1998, the conflict escalated into a full-scale civil war, with the KLA resorting to conventional guerrilla warfare. In Sri Lanka, the Liberation Tigers of Tamil Eelam (LTTE), commonly known as the Tamil Tigers, similarly sought to carve out a homeland in the north of the island for the Tamil minority. The group emerged after anti-Tamil programs, state repression, and rising Sinhalese Buddhist nationalism among the majority. Besides waging a conventional guerrilla war to control the Tamil majority areas, the group also employed suicide bombers and assassination attempts against military officials.

Causes of ethnic violence

Ethnic violence does not emerge out of the blue nor can it be reduced to ethnic diversity itself. Papua New Guinea could be described as the most ethnically diverse country in the world, as there are more than 800 different languages spoken among its eight million inhabitants, mostly not mutually comprehensible and stemming from several language groups. The most significant language besides the dominant creole language based on English, Tok Pisin, is spoken by only around 200,000 citizens. Besides, citizens identify with a similarly large number of different ethnic groups belonging to the broader categories of Papuans, Melanesians, Negritos, Micronesians, and Polynesians. There was a significant ethnic conflict when the population of Bougainville, an island East of New Guinea itself, formed a movement seeking independence in ten years of strife between 1988 and 1998, and there was also a less violent insurgency in the highlands of New Guinea. Yet, overall, considering the extreme linguistic and ethnic diversity, the intensity of ethnic conflict in Papua New Guinea has been low. Thus, ethnic diversity, even at its greatest extreme, does not breed conflict. In fact, even the conflict in Bougainville brought together a linguistically and ethnically diverse population in the insurrection against the government of Papua New Guinea. Other highly diverse countries, such as Tanzania, have also experienced little ethnic conflict. On the other hand, countries with a relatively low level of fractionalization, i.e., the degree of diversity in a society based on both the number of groups, criteria such as language or religion, and their size, have experienced high levels of violence, such as Yemen, Somalia, or Libya. All of these are formally homogenous in terms of language and religion, but have fractured along the lines of tribes and other extended networks of descent that have trumped national or supranational loyalties, such as Arab nationalism or Islam.

Ethnic conflict does not occur between ethnic groups. Just as nations are not homogenous blocks that act in unison, neither are ethnic groups. While membership in an ethnic group or nation requires the idea of belonging to a shared community, distinct from others, such an identity is neither static nor fixed. The relative importance of ethnic or national identity will vary in an everyday context, where gender, friends, social status, class, or place of residence might easily matter more than ethnic identity. Thus, ethnic groups need to be "made," which involves not a one-off process of convincing individuals to join a group, or gain awareness of belonging to one, but repeated reinforcement, as discussed in the previous chapter. Creating such a "groupness," as American sociologist Rogers Brubaker has called it,[5] strongly relies on the role of elites, often also described as ethnic entrepreneurs, in strategically enhancing group identity and distinction. Ethnic entrepreneurs might be deeply convinced about the importance of ethnic and national identity, or they might be cynically manipulating identity politics for their own advantage. Ethnic conflict is often a part of (re-)creating groups rather than the outcome of a confrontation between fixed groups. Here, internal control and external conflict are important in understanding the dynamics of ethnic conflict.[6]

Ethnic entrepreneurs need to convince their constituency not only that they are best at representing them but also that they should think "ethnically" when making political choices. In the first free elections in Yugoslavia in 1990, ethnonationalist parties often competed against more civic-minded centrist parties, which contested the elections over economic reform, not ethnicity. Ethnic and nationalist parties had to convince voters that what mattered was not economic reform but a threat to the nation. This was particularly pronounced in Bosnia, where three nationalist parties appealed to their respective national groups: Muslims, Serbs, and Croats. They faced little competition between each other, as Muslims would not vote for a Serb nationalist party and vice versa. Instead, they had to convince each of their constituencies that they should not vote for either the reformed League of Communists or the Reformist Party of the popular Yugoslav prime minister Ante Marković. The voters' choice could be understood as an ethnic prisoner's dilemma, where individuals from different groups make suboptimal choices because of the lack of trust among them. In brief, the fear that others would vote for nationalist parties that would pursue exclusionary policies makes support for your "own" ethnic party more appealing, not out of support for ethnic politics but to avoid being marginalized by the success of others.[7]

Thus, ethnic polarization is also based on intragroup polarization and the ability of ethnic entrepreneurs to persist over either political parties that reject ethnic categories altogether or more moderate leaders. The polarization and radicalization can be part of electoral campaigns and outbidding among candidates, but in many cases, the radicalization occurs outside the context of elections and has other goals. Thus ethnic conflict is not a mere consequence of ethnic polarization but is part of the polarization process.

In the postcolonial context, ethnic or tribal identities, as they are often known, are easily dismissed as backward and parochial. Instead, as discussed earlier, national movements often promoted new national ideas to transcend ethnic identities. The underlying assumption, like that of John Stuart Mill and other European liberal nationalists of the nineteenth century, was that the particular ethnic identities would be overcome and absorbed into larger national identities. While this succeeded in some cases, ethnic identity and the tensions that arose were not a holdover from premodern societies. In fact, modernization itself enhanced ethnic tensions. Modernization resulted, for example, in urbanization. As new administrative and economic capitals emerged in Africa and Asia, rural populations moved to the cities. Seeking new economic opportunities, migrants did not go looking for ethnicity, but they often found it. Networks based on one place of origin and kinship provide support networks for new arrivals. In this new urban environment, competition for jobs is intense, and opportunities for social advancement are scarce, particularly for new arrivals. Thus, ethnic competition based on networks of origin and familiarity is common.[8]

Ethnic conflicts are thus not some primordial holdover but a form of violence that has increased dramatically in the decades since the Second World War, reaching its peak in the early 1990s. Before decolonization, violence was perpetrated by colonial empires against restive populations, from Ireland to Namibia, and national liberation movements emerged against these empires. Some of these movements understood themselves as civic nationalist groups, often aspiring to form part of larger anti-colonial movements, such as the Congress Party in India or Kwame Nkrumah in Ghana. Others had a distinct ethnonational coloring, from radical Zionist groups in British-controlled Palestine to Jinnah's Muslim League in India, later Pakistan. As the new countries had to decide on national languages, what history to teach, and also who was to hold power, tensions within states increased. The rise of ethnic conflict was, however, not confined to the postcolonial states of Africa and Asia. As noted earlier, Europe also experienced tensions and conflicts, some violent, such as in Northern Ireland and the Basque Country, others mostly peaceful, as in Belgium or Catalonia.

The steady increase of ethnic conflict resulted in civil wars exceeding other types of war, such as interstate or revolutionary wars. The peak of ethnic conflict, based on its intensity, combining both the number of conflicts and of victims, was reached in the early 1990s, just after the end of the Cold War. A primary cause was the decline in repressive regimes that opened the door to competing and often conflictual claims. The wars in disintegrating Yugoslavia, the genocide in Rwanda, and civil strife in Somalia were the most visible reflections of the peak of ethnic conflict. As control of the superpowers over proxies waned and demands for democracy increased, so did the risk of ethnic conflict.

It might at first appear like a paradox, but countries are particularly prone to ethnic conflict in phases of democratization and transition between different types of government. Authoritarian governments can repress ethnic insurgencies by force, as in the case of China toward Uyghur demands for greater autonomy or independence in the Xinjiang Uyghur Autonomous Region of Western China. Here, as in other authoritarian regimes, claims for greater self-rule are often met by outright repression, giving insurgent groups limited space for action.

When authoritarian or totalitarian systems collapse or are overthrown, a new system of government needs to take their place. This is a challenging process at the best of times, with strong anti-democratic actors often seeking to save their power, weak political alternatives, and institutions beholden to the old regime. When different nations or ethnic groups enter the fray, things can get more complicated. First, politicians need to organize parties and movements on a blank slate, in which case identity is a readily available criterion. While ideology or other programmatic details require explanation, evoking membership in a group, be it ethnic, national, or otherwise based on identity, is easy to communicate, especially if group differences have been or are politically salient. Furthermore, a new political system requires answers to crucial questions that might favor one or another group. The election system might prefer one group over the other, and choosing the executive or the administrative organization of the country is all-important and potentially divisive. With high stakes and ethnic identity a potent political marker, these moments of transformation are particularly susceptible to ethnic conflict.[9] This was the case in Yugoslavia in the late 1980s. As the communist system was undergoing an economic crisis and the ruling party's legitimacy was declining, the main political challengers that emerged were nationalists or hailing from the communist nomenclature, reinventing themselves as nationalists to stave off the opposition. Yugoslavia was organized as an ethnofederal state, where each of the largest nations had their own republic (except Albanians) and Bosnia was a tri-national republic. Recalibrating a democratic Yugoslavia was difficult, as the elites throughout the country had diametrically opposed views: Slovenes, as well as Croats, wanted a more decentralized country, whereas the Serb leadership sought to recentralize the country, as many Serbs lived in other republics. Thus competing views over the type of democracy and the balance of power fueled ethnic tensions and facilitated conflict. The political systems discouraged transnational parties, and competing claims on the post-authoritarian organization of the country pitted republics, and with them, nations against one another. Democratization, or rather the emergence of political pluralism, was highly combustible. In nation-states, such as neighboring Hungary, or even in states with minorities, such as Bulgaria or Romania, the key questions after the collapse of authoritarian communist regimes were how to elect the parliament and how to balance power between the legislature and the executive, but there were no questions over the degree of power devolved to mono-ethnic regions or the representation of different ethnonational groups in the central government. In brief, the transition from authoritarianism to democracy in multinational or multiethnic countries raises additional challenges that raise the stakes and make violence more likely.

Ethnic conflicts emerge out of long-standing, but not ancient, tensions. As such the conflict is preceded by tensions, political disputes, and confrontation. The mere existence of ethnic groups is not a sufficient cause for ethnic conflict. Instead, the critical question is to what degree these differences are politicized and determine the political and social choices citizens make. Here, the concept of cleavages is useful. Cleavages are lines of division that divide citizens into stable, well-defined groups. These could be based on religion or the relationship between church and state, rural versus urban, or class. Rather than political choices, which can easily shift, cleavages mark more profound divisions that individuals cannot easily cross. These often translate from politics into society: for example, each community might have their own clubs and associations, and share few points of contact in everyday life. Ethnicity and other features of identity can constitute such cleavages. If ethnicity coincides with religion, language, class, or other markers of difference, these cleavages are mutually reinforcing and create the makings of a fragmented society.

In Northern Ireland, identification with Ireland versus the UK closely correlates with citizens who are Catholic and Protestant respectively; so much so, that many describe the conflict as being between Catholics and Protestants. While there were religious wars in the seventeenth century and earlier, today there are no conflicts between Catholics and Protestants elsewhere. Germany, for example, is divided between Protestants and Catholics (today with a substantial number of agnostics, atheists, Muslims, and others), yet this division has not become a national cleavage in German society, as citizens of both religions identify as Germans. Protestantism and Catholicism matters in Northern Ireland because religious affiliation and national identity closely overlap.

These lines of divisions do not appear by themselves, they need to be politicized and reinforced. Thus, there is no automatic progression from ethnic difference to cleavage to conflict; these differences need to be promoted and strengthened, and there has to be limited or no resistance to such efforts.

While ethnic cleavages provide for a distinction between countries that are characterized by ethnic diversity without much political conflict and others where ethnic difference is socially and politically salient, they do not explain why and when conflicts break out.

There is not a single universal trigger that could explain the outbreak of conflict. Conflicts are often multicausal, and reducing them to one factor would ignore their complex genesis. The dissolution of Yugoslavia and the subsequent wars, for example, had a number of explanatory factors. The factors that contributed to the collapse of the country and the subsequent wars were: the death of the dominant leader, Tito, in 1980; the economic crisis and growing social inequality between the republics; the ethnofederal structure of the country that empowered regional or statewide elites; the rise of nationalist elites; historical grievances, in particular, those dating back to the Second World War that had never been addressed in a nuanced manner; and the collapse of the Cold War system and with it Yugoslavia's strategic position. Different scholars may give varying weight to these factors, but none of them can be ignored. In a multifaceted approach to explaining ethnic conflict, it is useful to distinguish between underlying, structural features, such as colonial legacies, socio-economic differences that overlap with ethnic identity and other types of cleavages, medium-term factors such as the political system, which might exclude or include some groups, and growing economic inequalities or the shifting social prestige of belonging to a particular group. Finally, triggers facilitate the outbreak of violence, such as the availability of guns or a sudden change of government.

Dynamics of ethnic conflict

Most explanations for conflicts can be summarized as focusing either on opportunities or on grievances.[10] The opportunities focus on the structural factors that enable a conflict. These range from the geography of a country or region, which might make an insurgency easier due to the availability of resources and weapons. In Kosovo, the Kosovo Liberation Army might have wanted to start an uprising against the Serbian authorities before 1998, but it was the collapse of the Albanian state and the ransacking of army barracks the previous year that made Kalashnikovs and other light weapons readily available and cheap. Resources matter too, as it is not cheap to fight a war or insurgency. While states have armies and the means to fund wars, insurgent groups lack such easily available sources to fund their campaign. Sometimes they might gather money from the diaspora, as the IRA had done for decades among Irish Americans. Others might tax or extort money from citizens living in their area of control. Another source of income can be valuable raw materials, such as gold and diamonds. "Blood diamonds," so called because they fund wars, have been essential motivators of civil wars in Liberia, Sierra Leone, and Côte d'Ivoire. Sometimes, these resources might be used to enrich rebel leaders, such as Charles Taylor in Liberia. Opportunities might be crucial in enabling conflict but grievances are important for motivating the participation. Grievances are complex and can draw on the real or imagined disadvantages that individuals experience and which they associate with being a member of a particular group. This does not need to be the result of specific discrimination, but socio-economic differences might disadvantage some and favor others in a manner that could be attributed to being a member of a particular group. Grievances commonly draw from three sources: political exclusion, economic disadvantage, or cultural and social position.

Grievance and competition might occur between citizens of different linguistic, religious, or ethnic backgrounds competing on the same playing field. However, individuals often perceive, rightfully or wrongly, that another group is privileged. This might be an ethnic group that has traditionally held political power, social prestige, or economic power.

Political exclusion or marginalization can stem from systematic government policies directed against specific groups. In Northern Ireland, for example, the Catholic minority has long been marginalized in institutions and decision-making positions in the province. The result is often that groups do not identify with state institutions and consider them hostile. During the conflict in Northern Ireland, for example, the police force was known as the "Royal Ulster Constabulary." It recruited members predominantly from the Unionist population, and even its name favored the Protestant and Unionist community by using their preferred name of the province—Ulster—and by emphasizing "royal," as the monarchy is seen more favorably by Unionists than by Nationalists, who seek to leave the UK and join Ireland. Institutions that are seen as closed and hostile are thus often rejected by citizens from the group that feels excluded, reinforcing the antagonistic relationship between the state and the group in question.

Political power can also be a source of conflict when the relative balance of power is shifting. In Belgium, the Francophone elite dominated after its independence in 1830, and the rapid industrialization of Wallonia reinforced the dominance of the French language. A small Flemish national movement emerged in the early twentieth century and was encouraged by the German occupation during both World Wars. However, the conflict grew, especially after the Second World War, with Flemish demands for greater language rights and representation. The economic decline of Wallonia aided this shift, as Flanders became the economic powerhouse and French lost its prestige. The social and economic shift took decades to translate into political changes that offered a greater role for Flemish speakers and the region of Flanders.

In Lebanon, demographic shifts undermined the balance of power in the institutions. When the country became independent in 1943, the elites from different religious communities agreed on an unwritten "National Pact." Christian Maronites and Orthodox, Sunni and Shia Muslims, as well as the Druze—a small heterodox offspring of Shia Islam—established a division of key positions and the political orientation of the country. The president would be Maronite, the prime minister Sunni, the speaker of the parliament Shia, and so on, whereas in parliament Christians would have a slight advantage of 6:5. In terms of political orientation, the diverse religious makeup resulted in a carefully maintained balance between East and West, i.e., close ties to France and a position in the Arab world. This agreement, based on the problematic 1932 census and the careful power-sharing system, held until 1975. A demographic shift in favor of the Sunni and Shia communities put pressure on the system, as did the increasing tensions over the substantial presence of Palestinian refugees, mostly Sunni, in the country. Once the civil war broke out, it would take fifteen years, until 1990, to recalibrate the distribution of power, and even then the shift was minor, with political power balanced between different Christian and Muslim communities based on parity.

In addition to political exclusion, as well as the shift of political power and demographic dominance, economic and social exclusion are crucial contributors to ethnic tensions. Economic exclusion can be the result of group discrimination or simply the region of a country where the group lives. It also does not mean that members of a particular group are objectively worse off. In Yugoslavia, many Slovenes and Croats felt disadvantaged because their republics were more productive and economically advanced, yet they had to contribute disproportionally to economic support for less-developed regions. In turn, poorer republics felt exploited by the richer and saw the gap between them grow. As a result, at both ends, economic arguments served to buttress demands against the other. Similar arguments can be found in nation-states, such as in Italy between the North and the South, but here, such claims are moderated by shared national identity, no matter how weak.

Beyond real and imagined economic discrimination, specific groups might be singled out for economically benefiting at the expense of others. Such market-dominant minorities, a term coined by the American lawyer Amy Chua, easily become the target of the majority.[11] In some cases, economic wealth or dominance in certain professions might coincide with group membership, but often this perception by a majority grossly overstates the influence of a group or assumes that an economically affluent minority represents the larger community. Perceptions of wealth and influence might thus diverge considerably from the reality.

These groups may include imperial merchant minorities, such as Armenians and Jews in the Ottoman Empire, Lebanese in West Africa, or Indians in Uganda, or minorities that achieved such a reputation for other reasons and are often seen as alien, such as Chinese in Southeast Asia. These Chinese minorities in the Philippines, Vietnam, and Indonesia are small in size, mostly making up just 1 percent of the population (except for Malaysia, where around a fifth of the population are of Chinese origin), yet they exercise considerable economic influence. This gap has often resulted in ethnic violence and pogroms. Indians held a similar position in Uganda, but they were expelled en masse in 1972 by Idi Amin, who came to power in a coup the previous year and used anti-Indian sentiment to force most of the country's 75,000 Asians out of the country.

In Europe, the anti-Semitism of the late nineteenth and early twentieth centuries illustrates this dynamic and highlights that economic grievances need not be based on actual ethnoeconomic stratification but merely on the perception. Even if most Jews were no better off than other citizens, common anti-Semitic tropes described Jews as economically exploiting gentiles. The *Protocols of the Elders of Zion*, a notorious forgery written at the turn of the twentieth century in Russia as an anti-Semitic text, purports to lay out a Jewish plot to take over the world and outlines in detail the supposed plans to economically enslave non-Jews. For example, the protocols claim that a Jewish global conspiracy "shall soon begin to establish huge monopolies, reservoirs of colossal riches, upon which even large fortunes of the goyim [non-Jews] will depend to such an extent that they will go to the bottom together with the credit of the States on the day after the political smash."[12] In brief, the supposed plot the forgery outlines is to economically dominate non-Jews, to establish Jewish domination, and to support the Marxist cause. The protocols were first widely disseminated in Russia by the Imperial secret police and later spread globally as one of the core anti-Semitic texts disseminated by Henry Ford in the United States and inspiring the anti-Semitism of the Nazi movement. Thus, it is less the real economic advantage of a given group but the perception thereof that is often decisive.

Other grievances may focus on social marginalization or the perceived loss of status, thus not absolute marginalization but, rather, relative decline. Thus, Serbs in Kosovo had dominated the province until the 1970s due to their stronger position in the League of Communists and a history of mistrust between the state and the Albanian population. The Communist Party in Yugoslavia sought to enhance the powers of the province, as well as those of Albanians, resulting in Serbs losing their previously privileged position. This caused widespread resentment with the now predominantly Albanian authorities in Kosovo, furthered by cases of discrimination, and triggered Kosovo Serb mobilization against the Albanian population, seeking protection from the central Serbian authorities. The resentment was fueled by a strong narrative of cultural superiority that made the shift in power more potent.

These grievances, be they political, economic, or social, draw on emotions. Roger Petersen has argued that the key emotions driving ethnic conflict are fear, anger, rage, and resentment.[13] Resentment and anger are particularly crucial in understanding the motivation for violence. Resentment and fear are both intrinsically linked with grievances. Resentment is mostly based on the perceived injustice of one's own position and the supposedly privileged or exploitative place of others. In brief, resentment expresses the notion that another group is unfairly privileged. Fear, on the other hand, can be the result of these shifts in power (or the perception thereof) and triggers concerns over suffering disadvantages, discrimination, expulsion, or even death at the hands of another group. Fear can also emerge among members of a group that has long been marginalized.

These emotions rarely emerge on their own but are often deliberately mobilized by ethnic entrepreneurs through raising tensions in the mass media, spreading rumors, and giving political speeches. Considering that most societies are characterized by the absence of conflict, war and ethnic violence do not emerge overnight.

The stories of ethnic conflict, of neighbors killing neighbors, such as in Rwanda, suggest that the normal environment first needs to be suspended to enable mass violence. Replacing a peaceful context with a violent one where conventional restraints no longer apply can be done through state policy or by insurgent groups, sometimes as a top-down process, sometimes drawing on mass mobilization, all with the goal of replacing everyday cooperation with confrontation.[14]

Violence may be part of a deliberate political strategy. This may include the goal of using mass violence to stay in power, as ethnic conflict can impose homogenization in the name of national unity, allowing for undemocratic and unaccountable mechanisms of rule and scapegoating. Ethnic cleansing, i.e., the deliberate and planned expulsion of particular ethnic groups, may also be a wartime goal by itself. In fact, ethnic cleansing is rarely a byproduct of ethnic conflict but rather a central goal of one or multiple warring factions. Ethnic cleansing facilitates the creation of homogenous national territories and has thus played an important part in the emergence of nation-states. Various forms of ethnic cleansing have been part of nation-state formation dating back to the nineteenth century. Such policies include the expulsion of minorities in newly emerging nation-states, especially if these minorities are associated with a hostile nation-state or the previous empire. The Greek-Turkish population exchange, in which Orthodox inhabitants of the newly formed Republic of Turkey were forced out in exchange for the Muslims of Greece, amounting to a total of 1.6 million people, marks an early example of the large-scale displacement of people based on their national alliances, even if in this case it was based on the more rigid and thus more easily determinable religious identity. Later, millions of Hindus and Muslims had to leave their homes when India and Pakistan were created; Muslims and Christian Palestinians were forced from their homes at the creation of Israel and after the failed Arab alliance to stop the country's independence. Ethnic cleansing was thus the dark side of both nation-state formation and democracy, as elites seeking to consolidate the rule of the dominant nation excluded others, especially those belonging to communities which were a real or perceived threat.[15]

Similarly, genocide is based on a deliberate policy by states or state-like actors to eliminate particular groups based on their group identity. Thus, genocide is a crucial aspect of modern mass violence in the name of the nation against another nation. Most genocides, not just the Holocaust, occurred within the context of larger wars that enabled the commission of large-scale murder, as they would have been challenging to execute in times of peace. Genocide, as defined in the 1948 UN Genocide Convention,

> Means any of the following acts committed with intent to destroy, in whole or in part, a national, ethnical, racial or religious group, as such, (a) Killing members of the group; (b) Causing serious bodily or mental harm to members of the group; (c) Deliberately inflicting on the group conditions of life calculated to bring about its physical destruction in whole or in part; (d) Imposing measures intended to prevent births within the group; (e) Forcibly transferring children of the group to another group.[16]

Genocide is thus first and foremost a crime defined along identity lines that focuses on nations and ethnic groups, as this book discusses. Genocide is closely linked to the notion of exclusionary violent nationalism.

Once violence occurs, it often has a self-reinforcing effect, as it strengthens group identities, polarizes and shrinks space for a pluralist debate within and between groups. Thus, ethnic conflict is often more protracted than other types of conflict. Nevertheless, ethnic conflicts do come to an end. Some conflicts can last for decades, and ethnic conflict tends to last longer than interstate wars. The Lebanese Civil War lasted fifteen years; the Second Sudanese Civil War, in which the South sought independence, lasted twenty-one years. The duration of these ethnic conflicts is by no means exceptional. Wars end either with the victory of one party, by some negotiated settlement, or by a truce. One-sided victories are the most common in civil wars. Of the 108 civil wars recorded between 1945 and 1999, around half ended with the victory of one side, whereas the other half is divided between settlements, truces, and externally imposed settlements.[17] While military victories may be slightly more common, they are also more likely to relapse into violence, as the victor could be tempted to impose their dominance or even engage in genocide or ethnic cleansing. Such policies often trigger new waves of violence. There are less drastic options for victorious parties in ethnic conflict to impose themselves. One option is called the control model, wherein one party does not ban or destroy other groups or their identities, but dominates the political system and marginalizes others. The best example is the case of Israel. After Israel gained the West Bank and Gaza in the 1967 war, it did not expel the Palestinian population but also did not make an effort to include them in the Israeli political system, which most Palestinians would have rejected and would have posed a threat to Jewish dominance in the state. What is more, it also did not offer meaningful self-rule. As a result, the Palestinian population remained under the hegemonic control of the Israeli state, resulting in the continuation of the conflict until today.

Another option is the creation of an overarching identity. In Rwanda, the Rwandan Patriotic Front (RPF) won the civil war following the 1994 genocide. The RPF had fought the Hutu-dominated government since 1990, until the Arusha Accords of 1993 provided for a temporary peace agreement under a UN mandate. However, a radical Hutu movement associated with the government planned genocide against the Tutsi minority, represented by the RPF. Following the assassination of the Hutu president and long-term dictator, Juvénal Habyarimana, in April 1994, the genocide began, claiming nearly one million victims, primarily among Tutsis, within 100 days. Despite the mass killing of Tutsis, the RPF successfully conquered the country by July of the same year, forcing the perpetrators to flee, mostly to neighboring Zaire, today's Democratic Republic of Congo. The RPF took control of Rwanda, and, under the leadership of Paul Kagame, has dominated the country since. The new government, dominated by the Tutsi minority, could not impose minority rule, as Tutsi made up only around 15 percent of the population before the war and were much diminished by the genocide. Instead, the RPF-dominated government banned any reference to Hutu or Tutsi identity and systematically promoted a transcending Rwandan identity. Considering the deadly consequences of a highly ethnified society, this was not unreasonable but also served the new ruling elite, which came from a minority.

Other conflicts end with a truce, which might lead to either a resumption of the conflict, a permanent settlement, or remain a frozen conflict. Frozen conflicts can last for decades, with large parts of a country de facto independent. At times, these de facto independent parts might receive support from external patrons, such as some of the post-Soviet territories. Transnistria, a mostly

Document: Genocide Survivor Testimony from Rwanda, 1994

A testimony of Gilbert Masengo Rutayisire, 1994.[18]

I saw a white Pajero jeep driven by presidential guards, this jeep came and found us where we were standing and ask us: "Who are you?" One boy, unfortunately he died, he said to them: "We are citizens in this Rugenge sector." They said no, we want to know you ethnics. He did not know what was going on, he said to them: "We are Tutsis." You are Tutsis and you dare stand there. There did not add any other word, they went.

... We hid; I first hid myself at a neighbor who allowed me to hide in the ceiling of his house. There was a man called Nsababera Eraste, he left these neighbor's place when he was still young and come to work at our home for a longtime. When he became old, my mother got him a small plot in which she enabled him to build a small house and later on he got married.

... [He] finally knew where I was hiding and he was dying to kill someone. He wanted to kill, but he could always remember all the good things that my mother did to him and felt discouraged.

... They continued to search for others, but in the meantime I have already sent my prayers to God because I felt it was my last moments. They cut bananas that were closer to me, God always does miraculous things, these bananas fell down and covered my legs. Finally they went away but I heard them whispering where did this cockroach pass, where is this cockroach?

...

I tried to search if there is any one of my family who is still alive unfortunately all of them died except one girl called Chantal who was out of the country. She was out of Rwanda during the war time. I knew about the death of everyone, my siblings, my mother and I accepted what happened.

Russian-speaking sliver of land east of the Dniester River in Moldova, achieved de facto independence during the dissolution of the Soviet Union and preserved it with the help of Russian military support in the early 1990s. Similarly, South Ossetia and Abkhazia have been able to attain their de facto independence from Georgia, first in the

1990s and then reinforced during the Russian-Georgian war of 2008. Lastly, the Ukrainian conflict created Russian-supported regions in eastern Ukraine that are similarly de facto states without much international recognition. While external support is often crucial, such de facto states can also emerge when the central state disintegrates or is too weak to take control, as has been the case in Somalia since 1991, when the longtime dictator Siad Barre was overthrown and the central government collapsed. Since then, Somaliland and to a lesser degree Puntland have been able to secure a fairly steady de facto independence. The most enduring frozen conflict can be found in Cyprus. The conflict between Greek and Turkish Cypriots had been ongoing since before independence from the UK in 1960, but it was the coup in 1974, the leaders of which sought unification with Greece, that triggered the Turkish invasion and subsequent occupation of the northern parts of the island. Since the island was partitioned, and despite numerous international efforts to find a negotiated settlement, the status quo prevails. This is in part due to the presence of Turkey, including the army in the north. This mirrors Russia's presence in the post-Soviet frozen conflicts, which has made a resolution more difficult, as the status quo has been working reasonably well there, reducing the pressure to find a negotiated settlement.

There are a few instances where a settlement can result in formal independence. Usually, governments are reluctant to see a part of their territory go, and most other countries are reluctant to recognize secessionist states unilaterally. Mostly, independence only succeeds if the country or region it secedes from accepts this decision: a rarity. This occurred in 1991 when Eritrea managed to become independent from Ethiopia. It was possible as two resistance movements, the Eritrean People's Liberation Front and the Ethiopian People's Revolutionary Democratic Front, jointly fought the repressive Marxist government of Ethiopia, and after its overthrow agreed on Eritrea's independence. In Sudan, the protracted civil war stretched the resources of the government and forced it to accept the 2005 Comprehensive Peace Agreement that granted South Sudan autonomy and allowed it to hold a referendum on independence, which it did in 2011.

As outright independence is rare, most ethnic conflicts end with a negotiated settlement that keeps the borders intact and seeks to satisfy the different parties. It is unsurprising that these settlements often do not last, as no party is fully satisfied. The settlement of an ethnic conflict needs to include not just a ceasefire, as this would only result in a frozen conflict, but a readjustment of the political system that gave rise to the dispute in the first place. Thus, ending ethnic conflict often involves constitutional and institutional changes that are more significant changes than in the resolution of interstate wars. The toolkit for addressing ethnic conflict involves three key features: mechanisms to include different ethnic groups in the governing of the country, varying forms of territorial autonomy, and minority or group rights. In brief, these can be understood as either offering self-rule, inclusion, or joint rule. If an ethnic conflict is focused on a territorially concentrated minority, territorial autonomy is an obvious choice. For example, South Tyrol gained the status of an autonomous province within Italy following decades of negotiations with Austria, resulting in a treaty outlining the self-rule of the region with a German-speaking majority in 1992. Regional autonomy is a common feature in agreements, from the Good Friday Agreement for Northern Ireland to to the regional autonomy granted to the island of Bougainville following the civil war between rebels and the government of Papua New Guinea in 2000.

In many cases, territorial autonomy is not enough, especially if the group is too large to be just satisfied with self-rule alone or the region is not only populated by members of the group but also others, requiring some form of minority rights.

Minority rights can be wide-ranging but commonly include language and education protection. Language rights allow a group to use their mother tongue in private as well as in its dealings with the state, for example, in administration, for street signs, or in institutions. Educational rights, which help to preserve a group's identity, include language teaching in schools, as well as other subjects taught in the mother tongue, and history lessons reflecting the minority perspective. Such a curriculum may be offered in integrated or separate schools, ranging from primary schools only to all the way up to universities. These rights are usually insufficient in the aftermath of ethnic conflict, as disputes often also include demands for political participation and trust along ethnic lines is low. Political representation ensures that different ethnic groups, particularly smaller ones, are able to shape the decision-making process. This allows participation in decisions that directly affect the community members and inclusion in other key issues impacting the community, both directly and indirectly. In some cases, this includes easier or guaranteed representation in parliament and other quotas. Such access to parliament can be found in countries such as Romania or Slovenia, but it is usually only effective as a tool to prevent conflict rather than to end it, as parliamentary representation does not prevent representatives from smaller groups from being ignored. After all, in post-conflict settings, trust is low, and the risk of political exclusion remains high.

Thus the most common response, besides territorial autonomy, in peace settlements is power-sharing. Power-sharing describes a range of agreements that provide for institutionalized tools for the inclusion of different groups in the political system. Some power-sharing deals can be temporary, resolving a political dispute that might have little to do with ethnicity per se. There is a pattern that such temporary power-sharing arrangements seek to address political stalemates following inconclusive or disputed elections in Africa. This approach has been used in Zimbabwe and Kenya over the past decade to patch up contested elections, but it often resulted in protracted political instability and no genuine sharing of power. More enduring power-sharing mechanisms require constitutional changes and institutional redesign that provide access to representatives of different ethnic groups to the government. Most prominently, this is the consociational approach, which rests on the proportional inclusion of groups in parliament, government, and public administration, coupled with veto powers and a certain degree of self-rule. Such agreements have been put into place statewide, such as in Bosnia and Herzegovina, Burundi, or North Macedonia, or at the regional level, as in Northern Ireland. Besides, power-sharing institutions have been adopted as a political settlement to prevent the escalation of conflicts, including in South Tyrol and Belgium. Consociational arrangements are often complex and include a plethora of mechanisms to safeguard group rights.

Bosnia and Herzegovina serve well to highlight the complexity of such a system. Here, power-sharing was established by the Dayton Agreement that ended the war in 1995. Following three and a half years that saw more than half of the population displaced by ethnic cleansing and over 100,000 dead, the country had been weakened

Document: Constitution of Bosnia Herzegovina[19]

The constitution is Annex 4 to the Dayton Peace Agreement negotiated between Bosnia and Herzegovina, Croatia and Yugoslavia (Serbia and Montenegro) in 1995.

... Bosniacs, Croats, and Serbs, as constituent peoples (along with Others), and citizens of Bosnia and Herzegovina hereby determine that the Constitution of Bosnia and Herzegovina is as follows:

...

Art. I.3. Composition. Bosnia and Herzegovina shall consist of the two Entities, the Federation of Bosnia and Herzegovina and the Republika Srpska (hereinafter "the Entities").

Article III: Responsibilities of and Relations Between
The Institutions of Bosnia and Herzegovina And the Entities

1 Responsibilities of the Institutions of Bosnia and Herzegovina. The following matters are the responsibility of the institutions of Bosnia and Herzegovina:
   (a) Foreign policy.
   (b) Foreign trade policy.
   (c) Customs policy.

...

2 Responsibilities of the Entities.
   (a) The Entities shall have the right to establish special parallel relationships with neighboring states consistent with the sovereignty and territorial integrity of Bosnia and Herzegovina.

   ...

   (d) Each Entity may also enter into agreements with states and international organizations with the consent of the Parliamentary Assembly. The Parliamentary Assembly may provide by law that certain types of agreements do not require such consent.

Article V: Presidency
The Presidency of Bosnia and Herzegovina shall consist of three Members: one Bosniac and one Croat, each directly elected from

the territory of the Federation, and one Serb directly elected from the territory of the Republika Srpska.

Article IV: Parliamentary Assembly

The Parliamentary Assembly shall have two chambers: the House of Peoples and the House of Representatives.

1 House of Peoples. The House of Peoples shall comprise 15 Delegates, two-thirds from the Federation (including five Croats and five Bosniacs) and one-third from the Republika Srpska (five Serbs).

   (a) The designated Croat and Bosniac Delegates from the Federation shall be selected, respectively, by the Croat and Bosniac Delegates to the House of Peoples of the Federation. Delegates from the Republika Srpska shall be selected by the National Assembly of the Republika Srpska ...

2 House of Representatives. The House of Representatives shall comprise 42 Members, two-thirds elected from the territory of the Federation, one-third from the territory of the Republika Srpska.

by mass violence, perpetrated foremost by the Bosnian Serb Army, alongside conflicting claims over whether the country should exist. The peace settlement sought to satisfy the mutually exclusive claims through power-sharing. The central institutions are weak and ensure that the three dominant groups—Bosniaks, Serbs, and Croats—are equally represented, including a three-member state presidency and quotas in the government and in one of the houses of parliament. In addition, multiple veto mechanisms ensure that no group can be overruled. In terms of self-rule, the country is divided into two entities, with the Republika Srpska overwhelmingly populated by Serbs (primarily as a result of ethnic cleansing during the war) and the other entity, the Federation, mostly inhabited by Bosniaks and Croats. In the latter, ten cantons create more units in which one of the two groups mostly dominates and enjoys considerable powers. Thus, power is highly deconcentrated along ethnic lines, and where joint decision-making is required, it allows for representatives of each group to block nearly any decision. While the power-sharing system in

Bosnia is very complex and particularly prone to blockages, it illustrates the dynamics of consociational power-sharing. While it allowed for an end to the conflict and created a minimalist consensus based on a weak state with high levels of self-rule, it also resulted in considerable difficulties. The numerous veto possibilities make it easy for a party to bring the institutions to a standstill. In a politically contested postwar environment, in which the existence of the state and its powers is far from shared among all key political actors, such blockages have been common, obstructing the functioning of the state, while the more homogenous substate units continue to operate. The system also gives considerable weight to ethnic belonging, as electoral units are largely mono-ethnic and many elected offices are assigned by ethnicity. There is thus an institutional reward and emphasis on candidates running as representatives of a particular ethnic group or nation, rather than by appealing to more than one group. Thus, power-sharing risks reinforcing ethnicity, keeping the political basis of the conflict alive, and perpetuating tensions.

Power-sharing systems are thus not just institutional responses to ethnic conflict; they institutionalize ethnic tensions and ethnify the political system. There are of course variations, and some systems are more inclusive, often called liberal consociational systems, such as those found in Iraq, Afghanistan, and Malaysia. Bosnia, together with Belgium and Northern Ireland, belongs to the group of more rigid, corporate consociations.

Beyond consociational approaches, other power-sharing mechanisms can foster inclusion and cooperation among groups in a post-conflict environment without such a strong emphasis on the elites who represent each group. These tools are often described as centripetal power-sharing, which emphasizes shared institutions and a diffusion of power rather than ethnic quotas. In practice, such approaches are more likely to succeed when there has been no violent conflict, with higher levels of trust and less polarized ethnic groups.

Beyond institutional arrangements, the ethnic conflict also requires more complex approaches for dealing with the consequence of war. These include tools of transitional justice which deal with war crimes and other abuse, including special courts, forms of truth and reconciliation commissions, and indigenous tools to close the gap between communities. Unresolved tensions are a major contributing factor to renewed conflict and political settlements often institutionalize difference rather than reduce it. Truth and reconciliation commissions and civil society organizations' process can deal with the mass violence, including gender-based violence, divergent and confronting views on the past, and other aspects of the conflict.

Since the early 1990s ethnic conflict has declined globally, but this should not lead to the conclusion that the era of ethnic conflict is over. Ethnonational diversity is not a cause of ethnic conflict but a prerequisite. Most states are not nation-states in the sense that they are populated by citizens who identify with only one nation. Instead, most states are torn between claims to represent a particular nation and a reality that is more complicated. Conflict emerges out of a complex constellation of factors that include grievances, based on real or perceived disadvantages and threats, and facilitated by opportunities for those seeking to redress their demands through violence. The risk of ethnic conflict is thus deeply embedded in the age of the nation. As long as the logic of the nation and the nation-

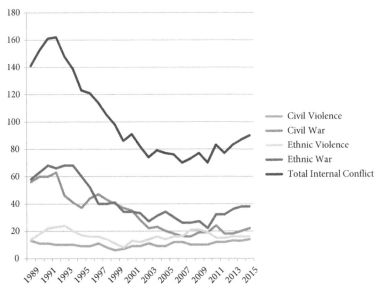

FIGURE 6.2 *Trends in armed conflict.*[20]

state is the prevailing theme of the international system, the ethnic conflict will be a feature. Diversity, be it based on different groups preceding the modern state or new groups based on migration, as we will discuss in the next chapter, is a constant irritant to nation-states, and thus tensions are an intrinsic aspect of the discrepancy between the ambition of the nation-state and the reality of far greater diversity. This tension can express itself in a variety of manners, from subtler repression to outright ethnic cleansing and genocide. The tools employed vary depending on the nature of the regime, the degree of polarization, and the particular opportunities (or lack thereof).

7

Migration and the Politics of Diversity

Migration has always been a building block of human society. Human migration throughout history means that there is no human whose ancestors were not migrants. While most people may not move far from their place of birth, living their lives in a small area, societies expand, and individuals move for work or survival over long distances. Migration is thus not a phenomenon of modernity. People have moved for work or due to persecution for centuries, and large groups often moved with conquering armies or in flight. For example, in 1492 Isabella I of Castille and Ferdinand II of Aragon forced the Jews of Spain to either convert to Catholicism or leave their realm. Many of those expelled found refuge in the Ottoman Empire and settled in its metropolises, such as Istanbul and Salonika (present-day Thessaloniki, Greece). Similarly, in Northern Europe Jews, as well as Huguenots and many others, fled their homes due to their religious identity, as rulers often did not tolerate religious diversity. While some fled from kingdoms and empires, at times others moved with expanding empires, like the Armenians, Greeks, and Jews who moved to the most remote corners of the Ottoman Empire, from today's Bosnia to the North African shore.

With the colonial expansion of European powers to the Americas and elsewhere, migration to places with no predetermined religious or other identities from the European framework became possible, allowing religious and other persecuted minorities to start new lives overseas. Once states had formed in these places of European migration, they began to discriminate in favor of some migrants over others.

Migration and citizenship

Thus, the mass migration of Europeans to the Americas in the late nineteenth century was hardly unprecedented in human history. What changed was the nature of the state. As modern countries established regimes of citizenship, it mattered who was a newcomer and who was a citizen. At the same time, borders became firmer and were no longer amorphous regions, where, as the rule of one empire declined that of another grew stronger. There are two features that matter: the time of migration and the migrant's similarity or difference to the majority. Thus, as discussed in the previous chapter, an ethnic German from Kazakhstan migrating to Germany might gain citizenship easily, whereas a Kazakh, coming from the same country as the ethnic German, would face much more significant obstacles to acquiring citizenship and acceptance, not to mention residence. Traditional minorities are also often distinguished from migrants by how long their ancestors have lived in the country. Some countries offer a specific cut-off date to distinguish between minorities with full rights of minority protection and migrants, who lack most of these legal safeguards. In Hungary, for example, a minority needs to have lived in the country for 100 years to be recognized as such. Laws often implicitly or explicitly draw a distinction based on the creation of the nation-state. A group that lived in the territory before the establishment of the state is a minority; those who come later are migrants. International human and minority rights bodies, such as the Advisory Committee overseeing the Framework Convention for the Protection of National Minorities of the Council of Europe, the most important international minority rights treaty, has challenged this approach, but it remains common in most state policies and laws. Thus, a majority of states in Europe (and beyond) consider those who lived on their territory before the country was established to be minorities, while migrants are those who have moved to the new state. Of course, this can create the paradoxical situation of minorities and migrants being of the same national background, with the country grouping them in different categories. For example, Austria recognizes the historical Croat minority in the eastern region of Burgenland, who settled there during Habsburg times, but does not recognize Croat migrants from Yugoslavia or, later, Croatia and Bosnia as a minority, even though they are more numerous.

The history of migration and nation-states is complex. In the nineteenth and most of the twentieth century, nation-states were places from which citizens emigrated. If arriving in a new place was usually not easy or open, neither was leaving. Many European states worried about their citizens leaving and imposed restrictions. Some of the states' concerns were borne out of economic considerations: emigrating farmers would not till the soil at home. But often states feared that they would suffer if their citizens left, thus diminishing the nation-state in terms of size and weakening it vis-à-vis its neighbors and competitors when it came to soldiers and the workforce. Therefore, migration was restricted not only by the destination countries but also the states from which would-be migrants sought to leave.

In terms of immigrant societies, legal recognition, social acceptance, and economic opportunity are the essential aspects of inclusion or exclusion in a new community, often framed as nations.

Immigrant states

When considering migration, we can distinguish between six types of states that have experienced large-scale immigration. Classic immigrant states are based on the immigration of the majority of their populations, and therefore immigration is a constitutive element of their national identity, making them more accepting toward migration. This does not mean that these states do not discriminate against some groups of migrants, or that they are encouraging immigration at all times. These countries include classic cases such as the United States, Canada, and Australia as well as several South American countries, such as Argentina and Brazil.

The second category includes former colonial states with policies of accepting migrants from former colonies and experience with diversity through their colonial policies. The UK, France, and the Netherlands are representative cases.

Third, nation-states that have been sources of emigration are distinct, as immigration is not part of the constitutive narrative of the nation-state and diversity is, at best, associated with historical minorities. The transition from an emigrant nation-state to an immigrant society is thus often characterized by anti-immigrant attitudes. Besides Germany and Italy, most Central European countries fall into this category.

Fourth, some countries have allowed for large-scale immigration but prevent any legal, social, or political inclusion for those migrants. This type of policy could be found in Germany during the early "Gastarbeiter" phase of labor migrants, and today it characterizes policies toward migration in rich Gulf states, such as the United Arab Emirates.

Fifth, there are many countries which have experienced immigration, often informally, including refugees, ranging from Lebanon hosting Palestinian and later Syrian refugees, to the Democratic Republic of Congo, which became the destination for millions of refugees from Rwanda. Sometimes, acceptance is possible due to ethnic and other connecting features of identity and weak state capacity. These might make it easier for migrants to move to these countries than to European or North American countries with more established systems of the border and administrative control. At the same time, integration, including citizenship, might be more difficult.

Sixth, we are seeing the emergence of "transit" countries that are seen both by themselves and by migrants as waystations toward more attractive destinations. These countries often treat migrants well, as they are seen as a transitory group without the perceived risk of remaining, but the states may also engage in repressive policies as the migrants may appear to be an economic threat, or they may execute repressive policies at the behest of the destination countries. Such regimes can be found in Libya, a stopping point for many refugees and migrants from sub-Saharan Africa, as well as countries in Southeastern Europe that are stopping points for those traveling toward Western Europe, such as North Macedonia or Serbia. Mexico is another example.

These different categories highlight that migration is a global phenomenon and states respond based on their own experiences with migration and their locations within global migration patterns. State policies and social attitudes are often shaped by earlier experiences of immigration and the degree to which migration is part of the self-identification of the nation and state. While richer countries might be more attractive destinations for immigration, much of global migration and refugee flows take place elsewhere.

Migration and the making of new states

In all societies, one can observe policies and attitudes described as nativism, which holds "that states should be inhabited exclusively by members of the native group ('the nation') and that non-native elements (persons and ideas) are fundamentally threatening to the homogenous nation-state."[1] Such nativism has also been an important feature in classic immigrant societies, such as the United States, Canada, or Australia, where the acceptance of migrants has never been without backlash or stereotyping.

For example in the United States, after the anti-Irish, anti-Italian views became widespread as immigration shifted from Northern to Southern Europe. In 1891, an editorial in *The New York Times* justified the mob that killed eleven Italians in New Orleans thus: "These sneaking and cowardly Sicilians, the descendants of bandits and assassins, who have transported to this country the lawless passions, the cut-throat practices, and the oath-bound societies of their native country, are to us a pest without mitigation."[2] Such views would also be directed against Jews and Chinese. The latter's immigration was restricted in the 1882 Chinese Exclusion Act, the first legislation in the United States to regulate immigration.

Document: The Immigrant Problem 1892

*D*iscussion on Chinese and Irish Immigration in the United States among scholars.[3]

Charles B Spahr: ... I am for the protection of American civilization against the Asiatic. We have here a certain territory, and in it we have a high state of civilization or a low one. As in former days we had a class favoring the introduction of slavery into new

States and Territories, and another opposing it, so now we have a class opposing the introduction of Chinese labor and the sweating system. ... Ten years ago Mr. Beecher disposed of this question in a single sentence. He said: "An ox eats hay; but the ox does not turn into hay; the hay turns into ox." And so it was thought we could receive, without hurt, unlimited immigration from every country on the globe. But we have found one kind of immigrant that can not be turned into ox. The Chinese ranks not as hay, but as garbage, and if the ox takes too much, the change takes place in the wrong way.

Robert G. Eccles: ... The danger to health comes not from individual bacteria, but from bacteria settling in certain localities in colonies, and there breeding and increasing. All dangerous diseases begin in such colonies and spread through the body. The analogy holds good in the nation. The danger from foreigners comes when they form a nidus, as it were—when the Chinese cluster together as they do in San Francisco and defy our Government and civilization, and send out thence a poisonous influence, just like the bacteria in our bodies. Such performances as those of the Clan-na-Gael in Chicago, and of the Irish in New York on St. Patrick's Day, are examples. We should not allow foreigners to foster foreign ideas in this country. As long as they do it we are in danger from such organizations as the Mafia in New Orleans. The concentration of foreign elements from one nation in one place and the development there of their national characteristics is dangerous. Our safety lies in letting the evil tendencies of different nations check each other. Let one evil kill another. Let the mean, selfish characteristics of the Irish clash with and kill the mean, selfish characteristics of the Germans, and so forth. Immigration free and unrestricted, save by the imposition of the tax of which I spoke, means safety and improvement of the standard of American people. "Assisted" immigrants should be sent back home.

In 1924, the Immigration Act restricted overall immigration, setting an annual limit of 165,000 and prohibiting all immigration from Asia (including Japan, China, and India as well as Southeast Asia). Only immigration from the Americas remained unrestricted. These laws were a close reflection of public opinion. A political cartoon of 1921, for example, shows Uncle Sam hammering a sign on the American continent reading "No dumping ground for refuse" with a caption on the hammer reading "U.S. public sentiment." On the other side of the Atlantic, an old lady, representing "Some European officials," is seeking to dump a barrel on the United States, labeled "Undesirables for America."[4]

The United States was the primary destination for European migrants in the late nineteenth and early twentieth centuries: around thirty-two million people arrived in the United States between 1820 and 1932. Five million more moved to Canada, and more than thirteen million moved to Latin America, particularly to Argentina, Brazil, Cuba, and Uruguay. The tolerant policy toward migration in Latin America was strongly motivated both by economic considerations and racial ideas that the European migrants would "whiten" the population, a view widely held among the elites, who were primarily drawn from Spanish and Portuguese settlers. Non-European migrants were often not welcomed, just like in the United States or Australia, and laws and social attitudes discriminated against Chinese or Black migrants, including those from some Caribbean islands such as Haiti.

Migrants faced less discrimination based on their socio-economic status than in the United States, as the average population was often no better off than the immigrants. In addition, Latin American nation-building saw European migrants positively rather than defining itself against them. This only changed in the interwar period, when, as in the United States, economic crisis and isolationism led to more restrictive policies by the 1930s.[5]

In Australia, immigration was similarly based on the distinction between Europeans and non-Europeans, known as the "White Australia Policy," which came into effect at the beginning of the twentieth century.

Document: Immigration Restriction Act 1901, Australia[6]

*P*assed by the Australian Parliament in 1901 to prevent immigration from non-European countries as part of the "White Australia" policy.

> The immigration into the Commonwealth of the persons described in any of the following paragraphs of this section (hereinafter called "prohibited immigrants") is prohibited, namely:— (a) Any person who when asked to do so by an officer fails to write out at dictation and sign in the presence of the officer a passage of fifty words in length in an European language directed by the officer.

In particular, Asian migrants were seen as a menace to Australia, a threat accentuated by the fear of Japanese invasion during the Second World War. This widely held position was reflected by Arthur Calwell, the Australian minister of immigration from the Labor Party, who argued in 1947 that "we have 25 years at most to populate this country before the yellow races are down on us."[7] During these postwar decades, more than three million migrants from Europe moved to Australia, increasing the population by nearly half by 1972. In the subsequent years, immigration based on racial preference for "whites" was eventually abandoned.

Migration in Europe

Until the mid-twentieth century most European countries, including Britain and Germany, were places from which people emigrated. Immigration before then was exceptional. There were small groups of emigres across Europe, from Russian revolutionaries and anarchists in Geneva, Munich, Paris, and London, to students from the colonies in Paris and London, East and Southeast European students in the Habsburg Monarchy and Germany. These were small in number, and neither saw themselves nor were seen by the majorities as immigrants but, rather, as citizens who were temporary residents, even if "temporary" could mean decades.

The UK together with France, as the major colonial powers, were among the first European countries to be confronted with large-scale migration from their colonial possessions, both from near domains such as Ireland to far-flung overseas possessions. The UK thus had an Islamic community in the late nineteenth century and hosted lascars (sailors) from the Indian subcontinent from the eighteenth century. Migration accelerated after Indian independence and became a source of controversy. The turning point came shortly after the Second World War, when in 1948 the HMT *Empire Windrush* brought 800 Jamaicans to the UK. These Jamaicans could settle in the country and obtain British citizenship as a result of the 1948 British Nationality Act, which offered a legal path to British citizenship for all inhabitants of the Commonwealth. These would be the first groups of around half a million Caribbean migrants to the UK that could benefit from the law until 1970. The ship's name also became the synonym for these migrants, known as the Windrush generation, and in 2018 it gave the name to a discrimination scandal involving the illegal deportation of some of those early migrants. Later migration predominantly came from other former colonies, particularly the Indian subcontinent.

In the UK, the uncertain status of some communities living in former colonies generated migration. In particular, South Asians who had migrated to East Africa during the colonial period found themselves in a precarious position after Kenya, Uganda, and other countries became independent. After independence, many did not take citizenship of the new countries and were left in legal limbo. The new nation-states sought to marginalize and exclude such communities associated with the colonial period, and as these minorities had few links with India or Pakistan, the UK became an important refuge and destination.

It is this postcolonial immigration that created the first noticeable backlash in British debates. In 1968, Enoch Powell, a Conservative MP, gave a rousing speech against immigration in Birmingham that became known as the "rivers of blood" speech. What made the speech significant was its open rejection of immigration and the idea of integration as well as some of the key themes that would turn out to be recurring in anti-immigration rhetoric. Powell cited a constituent who wanted to leave the country, worrying that whites would become powerless in the country:

The existing population were never consulted, they found themselves made strangers in their own country. ... Now, at all times, where there are marked physical differences, especially of colour, integration is difficult though, over a period, not impossible. Here is the means of showing that the immigrant communities can organise to consolidate their members, to agitate and campaign against their fellow citizens, and to overawe and dominate the rest with the legal weapons which the ignorant and the ill-informed have provided. As I look ahead, I am filled with foreboding; like the Roman, I seem to see "the River Tiber foaming with much blood."[8]

The threat of being dominated by the immigrants, the inability to integrate the new arrivals, and the danger their customs pose have remained recurring themes of nativist claims. Powell, who would not make a political career out of the topic, was more of a classic conservative politician than a populist benefiting from anti-immigrant rhetoric. However, his speech pioneered many themes that would become increasingly important in European anti-immigrant discourse in the subsequent decades.

France had experienced immigration earlier than the UK, predominantly from its Southern European neighbors Spain and Italy. In addition, Algerian Muslims had moved to France, just as French settlers had moved to Algeria. Algiers was occupied by France in an ill-fated attempt by the French king Charles X to bolster his popularity at home. The occupation of Algiers succeeded but did not prevent the king from being overthrown shortly afterward in 1830. Rather than a mere isolated French port, French rule spread to encompass a large tract of land, the start of European colonization of Africa. In 1848, Algeria had been divided into several French departments, making it an integral part of the country, a level of integration into the metropolitan state that did not occur in Britain. Nevertheless, Algeria was not just a part of France: it was also a colony, and its settlers were treated differently to its Muslim population. Before the end of the Second World War, few Algerian Muslims had permanently moved to metropolitan France, yet the country strongly relied on them—just as Britain relied on its colonies—for soldiers during the two World Wars. Besides, France also recruited colonial workers to fill labor shortages during the war. During the interwar period, up to half a million Algerians were on temporary contracts in France, concentrated in Paris and Marseille. This pattern was disrupted by the Second World War, but like in the UK, migrants from the colonies, whether they were administratively separate as in the UK or integrated like Algeria in France, constituted an obvious source of labor, even though European labor was preferred.

The tensions between migration and the anti-colonial struggle became visible in October 1961. By that point, the Algerian War of Independence had been raging for seven years, with the National Liberation Front (FLN) waging a guerrilla war against French colonial rule. Some 150,000 Algerian Muslims lived in Paris, holding French citizenship. In the context of bombings in France, including Paris, by the FLN, some 30,000–40,000 protestors, mostly Algerians, demonstrated against French policy and in favor of the FLN. In response, the Parisian police detained and killed a large number of demonstrators. The numbers are contested, ranging from 40 to more than 200 who were killed and thrown into the River Seine. Anti-immigrant policies began to emerge, like in the UK, by the late 1960s and early 1970s, but they were closely linked to opposition to decolonization, especially in the case of Algeria. A violent far-right movement, the Organization of the Secret Army (*Organisation armée secrète*, or OAS), included officers of the French Army and Algerian settlers opposed to President Charles de Gaulle's policy of granting Algeria independence. While white settler regimes in Rhodesia and South Africa had little impact on British politics, the OAS sought to assassinate De Gaulle and later provided the kernel for French far-right politics. Jean-Marie Le Pen, a former soldier of the French colonial wars in Indochina and Algeria, would become the most visible political representative of far-right anti-immigrant politics after he established the National Front (*Front National*, FN) in 1972, following his earlier engagement in less prominent far-right campaigns and groups.

Germany had virtually no colonial migration, having lost its few colonies after the First World War. Most labor migration had been internal, with Poles from the East seeking jobs in the industrial Ruhr area. An unprecedented number of migrants entered Germany during the Second World War when the Nazi government used forced and voluntary labor from occupied and allied Europe to make up for labor shortages caused by the war. Millions of forced laborers worked in inhuman conditions and were literally worked to death, while voluntary labor was treated better—this included civilians from allies in

Scandinavian and Western European countries. Forced labor included Jews, prisoners of war, and civilians from Eastern Europe, especially occupied Poland and the Soviet Union. Altogether, Germany became more diverse under the Nazis than it had ever been before. In total, around 6.5 million non-German civilians and 2 million prisoners of war were forced (or to a much smaller extent volunteered) to work in Nazi Germany in 1944.

Most of these workers, if they survived, returned home at the end of the war, as millions of Germans settled especially in West Germany, having been driven from their homes in Eastern Europe. The continuous emigration of East Germans until the building of the Berlin Wall in 1961 provided a labor force for the soaring economy. After the closing of the inner-German border, new sources of labor were needed. Early worker programs attracted Italians, with similar programs in Switzerland and the Benelux countries. West Germany concluded further agreements on recruiting workers in the 1960s with Spain, Greece, Turkey, Morocco, Tunisia, and Yugoslavia. By mid-1973, 2.6 million workers from Mediterranean countries were employed in Germany, amounting to around 4 percent of the population. During this period about half a million new workers came to Germany, as others returned home. The term "Gastarbeiter," guest worker, circumscribed the common understanding of this migration. The German authorities and society thought of these workers as temporary residents, i.e., as guests, who would eventually return home to their countries of origin. Accordingly, the residence permits were linked to specific jobs and were often temporary. This phase of large-scale immigration came to an end with the oil shock of 1973. Shortly afterward, a ban on further labor immigration from outside the European Community came into effect. The share of foreigners increased nevertheless, as "guest workers" stayed and brought their families to live in Germany, reaching 4.7 million by the early 1980s. Thus Western Germany became an immigrant country without a deliberate policy of immigration or a broad social consensus. The term "guest workers" remained in use, and only in the late 1980s did a gradual recognition emerge that these foreigners were indeed migrants and were here to stay. This dynamic was closely mirrored in other neighboring states, such as Switzerland, Austria, and the Benelux countries.

In Eastern Europe, in East Germany in particular, similar labor migration took place to countries with labor shortages, including around 60,000 Vietnamese who worked in the German Democratic Republic. In addition, students from allied socialist countries were educated in Moscow, East Berlin, or Belgrade. However, the workers and students were often segregated from the population, and the socialist governments did consider them temporary residents.

Altogether Europe had become considerably more diverse in the postwar decades as a result of migration from former colonies and Southern European countries along the Mediterranean, from Portugal to Turkey. However, this transformation was unplanned, and governments and societies implicitly or explicitly assumed that these migrants would be temporary. The European economic crisis as a result of the 1973 oil shock resulted in stricter limits on immigration in most West European countries. Britain was the first country to deal with diversity, while Germany was less willing to adopt policies toward migrants in what could be described as "willful neglect."[9] The fact that the policy toward migrants was called "Ausländerpolitik," i.e., policy toward foreigners, highlighted the long-prevailing understanding of the migrants as foreigners, not as new or future Germans.

The rise of anti-immigrant politics

The 1980s witnessed the rise of anti-immigrant parties. In France, the *Front National* achieved some electoral successes in national, local, and European elections. In Austria, Jörg Haider transformed the Freedom Party (*Freiheitliche Partei Österreichs*, FPÖ) into a far-right anti-immigrant party in 1986, resulting in rising support for the party. In Germany, the far-right Republicans (*Die Republikaner*) and other far-right parties entered the European Parliament and state parliaments but failed at elections to the federal parliament; their successes were short-lived and marked by fragmentation and a highly volatile support basis. However, it was not only parties on the far-right that adopted anti-immigrant positions. European center-right parties campaigned on limiting immigration, epitomized by Margaret Thatcher's campaign speech in 1978, in which she expressed the fear that the country "might be rather swamped by people with different cultures."[10]

Anti-immigrant violence had been rare, but it began to occur across Western Europe, including the Notting Hill riots in 1958, in which working-class whites attacked Afro-Caribbean migrants in a London neighborhood. In the early 1990s, a series of anti-immigrant attacks occurred in Germany, shortly after unification, such as the Hoyerswerda riots, in which Vietnamese and Mozambican workers were attacked and an asylum seekers' residence was burned down. Similar attacks occurred elsewhere in Eastern Germany, where far-right groups successful organized after unification, including in Rostock-Lichtenhagen in 1992. Incidents also occured in Western Germany, including the arson and murder of five members of a Turkish family in the small town of Solingen in 1993. There have been subsequent attacks against foreigners by neo-Nazi, Skinhead, and other such extreme-right groups across Europe. While immigration became a source of far-right mobilization in terms of political parties and violent groups, the country also became more accepting of being an immigrant country. The turning point toward integration occurred from 1999 to 2000, when a coalition government of Social Democrats and Greens liberalized the citizenship law allowing migrants to obtain German citizenship, while not granting dual citizenship.

By the 1990s, migration had become a critical theme not just in Europe's Northwest but also in countries such as Italy and Greece, where migrants were beginning to settle. Some arrived from Africa and the Middle East, and with the collapse of communism hundreds of thousands of Albanians moved to both countries. Again, the transformation from a country of emigration to one of immigration met with opposition. As overall numbers were relatively small and Albanians did not constitute a visible minority, migration only became a salient cause for political parties in the 2000s. In Italy, the Northern League, initially a northern secessionist party, took on an anti-immigrant line, whereas in Greece, the economic crisis catapulted the ultra-nationalist far-right party Golden Dawn (*Chrysí Avgí*) into parliament. Golden Dawn organized soup kitchens and other social services for Greeks only and campaigned against migrants. Its supporters have attacked foreigners and left-wing political opponents.

There have been two crucial turning points in North America and Europe regarding migration. The September 11, 2001, attacks on the

World Trade Center and the Pentagon were a watershed in the United States, and to some degree in Europe. Since then, immigration, especially Muslim immigration, has been repeatedly politicized and media and politicians have described Islam as a threat to the United States. The US president George W. Bush described the world in stark Manichean terms in the aftermath of the attacks, noting that "every nation, in every region, now has a decision to make. Either you are with us, or you are with the terrorists." [11]

In Europe, the so-called refugee crisis of 2014 to 2015 proved a similar turning point. The number of immigrants seeking asylum in the EU increased steadily in the previous years, reaching 626,960 in 2014 and doubling to 1.3 million in 2015. The numbers slowly declined in the following years, but the images of hundreds of thousands of migrants seeking their way to Europe—mostly Western Europe—by sea across the Mediterranean and on land along the Balkan route shaped discourses. At first, governments and citizens welcomed refugees in some key destination countries, such as Germany, Sweden, and Austria, epitomized by citizens welcoming refugees at train stations with food. However, public perception shifted toward framing migration as a constitutive threat. Triggers across Europe were the sexual assaults by presumed non-European migrants in and around the Cologne train station during the New Year's celebrations of 2015–6, and several high-profile terrorist attacks, such as the shooting at the French satirical magazine Charlie Hebdo in January 2015, linked the threat of radical Islam and migration.

With these events, migration and especially the migration of Muslims became a central focus of the debate. Far-right parties shifted from a broad anti-foreigner line in the 1980s to an anti-Muslim focus. Besides the rise of radical Islamic terrorism, a number of other issues caused this shift. In Britain, the Salman Rushdie affair in 1989, when the supreme leader of Iran, Ayatollah Ruhollah Khomeini, called for the killing of Rushdie for his book *The Satanic Verses*, raised the question of the compatibility of Islam and Western liberalism. In France, bans on headscarves in schools in the name of the principle of *Laïcité*, the strict separation of state and religion, shifted attention to the question of women's rights. The main arguments in these debates centered on the incompatibility of Islam, or particularly radical Islam, and Europe.

New political movements, such as Dutch politician Geert Wilders' Party for Freedom, focused on the supposed threat of the Islamification of the Netherlands and argued against Islam and migration from Muslim countries on the grounds that the conservatism of Islam threatened women's rights as well as other forms of liberalism, including LGBTQ (lesbian, gay, bisexual, transgender and questioning) rights. Thus instead of arguing against migration from the perspective of classic conservatism or Christianity, these new parties claimed to defend European secularism from immigration.

Migration is not automatically a central aspect in debates over national identity and the nation. The intensity of immigration-related debates in North America and Europe in the past decade would suggest otherwise, but migration is often ignored or discussed in a different conceptual framework to national identity. The significance of migration for debates about the nation and national identity is thus not just about the numbers of migrants but also about the framing of migration in the discourse. In Hungary, the issue of migration has been central to political debate since 2015, and Prime Minister Viktor Orbán has made the fight against immigration a defining feature not just of his government but also of national identity. The total number of refugees that entered the country has been insignificant, and those who arrived in large numbers in 2014 were seeking to pass through on their way to other countries such as Austria, Germany, or Sweden. Thus, what is crucial is not migrants themselves but the threat they are supposed to be.

On the other hand, Lebanon has witnessed the influx of nearly one million refugees, more than 20 percent of the population of around five million. While this has put the country in a precarious position in terms of political stability and economic resources, refugees have been depicted as less of a core threat to the nation than in Poland, which hosts a few thousand refugees. This is even more surprising as the Palestinian refugees in Lebanon were important catalysts for the civil war, and in a country with a fragile confessional division the massive influx of refugees placed a considerable strain on the political balance of power, not to mention economic resources. Only by 2019 did more pronounced demands for the return of Syrian refugees emerge, including at a rally under the slogans "Employ a Lebanese" and "Syria get out."[12] The importance of migration to narratives of national identities is thus variable and circumstantial.

State policies toward migration

Migration and the response from the state and society are constantly renegotiated, both in countries with a historical record as immigrant societies and in those with a more recent history of migration. Immigrant societies, such as the United States, Canada, Australia, and Latin American countries, defined their national identity through migration, not in opposition to it. Yet that did not mean that they endorsed universal immigration or immigration at all times. Those societies not traditionally exposed to immigration had formed an understanding of what it meant to be a member of the nation that excluded migrants. If citizenship is defined through residence, as in France or the UK, it might facilitate integration over countries such as Germany, where descent prevailed until recently as the critical criterion for citizenship and inclusion.

Based on different historical experiences with migration and divergent conceptions of the nation, and the role of the state in reaffirming the nation, state approaches toward diversity vary. We can distinguish between assimilation, integration, multiculturalism, and control.

Control is a type of state policy toward national, ethnic, or linguistic diversity that does not seek to deny diversity, while at the same time not offering equal access to state and societal inclusion. This best describes German policy until the 1980s, when the state and society did not prevent the immigration of guest workers and their families, but provided no path for them to become German citizens. Thus, it was near impossible to achieve social and political inclusion on a permanent and equal basis.

An assimilationist approach describes state policies under which migrants are required to give up public manifestations of their identity and take on the dominant language and habits. This has been the prevailing approach in France, which assumed that in order to become French, migrants had to accept the strict separation of religion and state. The assumption of assimilation, i.e., that once migrants had fully accepted the dominant identity they would be fully included in the nation, is flawed. Discrimination against French of North African origin remains pronounced, even if the individual's only visible distinctiveness is their name. Furthermore, after the end to mass immigration in the mid-1970s, policies pronouncing the distinctiveness of immigration were promoted to facilitate or encourage an eventual "return" of the migrants to their countries of origin.

In the United States, the conventional term used to describe policies toward migration is that of the "melting pot," an image in use since the early twentieth century and popularized by a play with the same name written by Israel Zangwill. The melting pot implied that the different national identities would merge into an American identity through intermarriage and a common language and customs. This concept, while seemingly inclusive, originally conceived primarily the merging of European nations at the expense of Americans of non-European origin. The mixing of Europeans with African Americans was banned either by the Jim Crow Laws or by social taboos. Besides, the culture into which migrants were supposed to melt was not just a combination of the different immigrant cultures but was instead predefined by the white Anglo-American Protestant heritage, which favored English, whiteness, and Protestantism. Consequently, until the mid-twentieth century at least, the melting pot rather meant assimilation into the prevailing cultural package. Although integration in this context allowed immigrants to preserve their heritage to a greater degree, as embodied by the emergence of hyphenated identities such as Irish-American, there were in-built biases in favor of European migrants.

The most controversial response to immigration in recent years has been multiculturalism. Multiculturalism first emerged as a down-to-earth response to the different challenges of diversity in Canada. When Prime Minister Pierre Trudeau declared in 1971 that "there is no official culture, nor does any ethnic group take precedence over any other,"[13] it was both groundbreaking and pragmatic. His policy grew out of the work of the Royal Commission on Bilingualism and Biculturalism, appointed in 1963 to address the difficult relations between French speakers, primarily in Quebec, and the Anglophone majority. In Quebec, an independence movement was growing in strength, and many Québécois felt disadvantaged in the mostly English-speaking country. The Official Languages Act gave French and English formally equal status, and while assuaging the Francophones it alienated many English speakers and other immigrant groups. At the same time, migration had become a divisive issue. Like Australia or the United States, Canada had historically allowed immigrants only from some countries, usually favoring Europeans. These restrictions on migration were gradually lifted after the Second World War, but non-European immigration remained controversial. The policy of multiculturalism provided for a broader justification for the inclusion of French speakers and color-blind migration policies. Finally, it also allowed Canada to address the inclusion of the first nations. At first, the policy of multiculturalism was mostly symbolic, with the state recognizing diversity as a positive value rather than funding multicultural policies actively.

In practice, multiculturalism does not entail the formal recognition of all the groups the term might encompass. Thus, unlike minority rights, which might include the recognition of language rights, the right to education, and similar collective rights, multiculturalism emphasizes the value of diversity, and later this would also entail funding for activities that promote difference. Beyond funding the cultural activities associated with different communities, it meant for example that the state would reflect the diversity of its society. This was embodied by the 1991 Canadian Broadcasting Act, which required the public broadcaster to reflect "the linguistic duality and multicultural and multiracial nature of Canadian society" and "the special place of Aboriginal peoples within society."[14] Multiculturalism can also mean that public administration offers materials in multiple languages used by the constituents. While falling short of formal language rights, it constitutes a pragmatic recognition of linguistic diversity.

The conceptual and practical challenges over multiculturalism focused on the balance between protecting individual rights and the collective rights of the group. For example, women wearing a veil could be viewed as reflecting the cultural identity of the group—North African Muslims in France, for example. Alternatively, they might also be seen as women oppressed by backward religious traditions. Whereas some practices might be clearly prohibited, such as female genital mutilation, with others the state response might be less clear. The issues are reflected in the debates between communitarian and liberal proponents of multiculturalism. Communitarians emphasize the importance of collective identities and the need to preserve them, even at the risk of infringing on individual rights. Liberal multiculturalism, on the other hand, emphasizes the importance of individual choice over collective restrictions. This dilemma also has repercussions for state policies regarding how to protect group traditions, from Inuit whale-hunting to slaughtering techniques for kosher and halal meat, raising complex questions about the give and take of social norms and traditions of the society in large and particular groups.[15]

By the early 2010s, multiculturalism came under criticism from the political mainstream, reflecting the broader crisis of migration. German Chancellor Angela Merkel noted in a 2006 speech that "multiculturalism [*Multikulti*] has fooled Germany, multiculturalism has failed."[16] Five years later, British Prime Minister David Cameron took a similar position, arguing that "we have encouraged different cultures to live separate lives, apart from each other and apart from the mainstream. We've failed to provide a vision of society to which they feel they want to belong. We've even tolerated these segregated communities behaving in ways that run completely counter to our values."[17]

In Europe, multiculturalism became a byword for the lack of integration of migrant communities rather than multiculturalism as it evolved as a pragmatic government practice in Canada. Ironically, the criticism has been stronger in European countries that lack strong multicultural state policies. Most European countries only recently began conceiving themselves as immigrant societies, and the criticism reflected in the speeches of Merkel and Cameron highlights the neglect toward migrant communities that shaped policies in many European countries rather than multiculturalism. The crisis of multiculturalism is thus less of a crisis of the deliberate policies of including migrants into the society by transforming nation-states into states that do not favor one nation over others, and more of a failure and willful neglect of European states to turn themselves into immigrant societies.

Crisis of integration

Controversy over immigration emerged in countries with diametrically opposed models of inclusion and exclusion. This includes France, which has not endorsed the multicultural approach but instead state policy has promoted the idea of a republican civic nation to which all immigrants are expected to assimilate. Other countries, such as Germany or Italy, maintained a close link between national identity based on descent and citizenship. In Belgium, the lack of integration of Muslim communities and the radicalization within these communities has been a particularly controversial topic. The consequence has resulted in the rise of repressive policies, including the ban on full veils, the so-called burqa ban imposed in 2011, and policing the Brussels neighborhood of Molenbeek, widely considered a "breeding ground" for radical Islam, with a proportionally high number of terrorists and volunteers for the Islamic State (ISIS) hailing from the community. However, Belgium's policies toward the mostly Turkish and Moroccan migrants in these and other neighborhoods could not be considered multiculturalism. Radicalization occurred in the context of socio-economic marginalization, with high levels of youth unemployment, low levels of education, and a strong sense of isolation from mainstream society. This problem has emerged across Europe, where the largest non-European migrant groups are usually Muslims from the Middle East. Most migrants come from less developed and more traditional regions and found manual labor that did not require higher levels of education. This precarious position gradually became consolidated over several generations, especially where immigrants lived in compact neighborhoods, such as the desolate high-rise suburbs around Paris, the *banlieue*.

The failure to integrate migrants and their children into society is thus a real challenge in some countries, especially in Western and Southern Europe, which shifted from emigrant to immigrant societies only in recent decades. The difficulties that arise derive from a complex link between exclusion and marginalization by mainstream society, based on their presumed cultural inferiority, often also compounded by the marginalized socio-economic background of many migrants and their families. Where migrants could form compact communities, these facilitated coping with social pressure but also rendered integration more difficult. Thus, practical dynamics, rather than multiculturalism as an approach, conditioned these challenges.

Diasporas and identities in-between

Migrants often find themselves in-between in terms of identity. In a world divided into nation-states, migrants do not "fit" where the state or society does not include them into the community. One option is assimilation into the new nation, i.e., giving up language and cultural markers to become American, French, British, or German. As noted earlier, this option depends on whether this is possible in practice. There is evidence that, for example, migrants are less likely to be hired for a job based on their name.[18] In such a context, assimilation is only open to some, either those who change their name or are able to assimilate because they have no visible markers that set them apart. The alternative is to remain part of a distinct community.

Another possibility is to maintain a dual or hyphenated identity, such as being Irish-American, Turkish-German, or otherwise emphasizing the duality of identity. This duality can be reduced to a mostly folkloric recollection of an ancestral home, with links that are expressed through tourism and lore. Alternatively, it can be an important feature of identity. However, the terminology matters. While there are German-Americans, there are also African Americans, with one category evoking a distinct nation, the other encompassing an entire continent. In the case of slavery, the country or nation of origin might be impossible to ascertain and usually did not exist at the time, yet this distinction in categories of hyphenated identities highlights how they might be driven by outside, state-led categorization, as discussed above in the context of censuses, and not by self-identification. Hyphenated and dual identities also can be restricted by the acceptance of this duality. Most European countries and nations offer little space for double identifications. Citizenship laws are a reflection of this, where dual citizenship is often prohibited for immigrants who also express identification with their family's country of origin. They are viewed with suspicion, particularly when relations are tense.

Migrants were and are not just the subject of state policy and social attitudes in the country they move to, they often maintain a connection to their homeland and form identity communities in their new homes. Thus, in addition to the relationship between the state and society and immigrants, we also need to consider the connections migrants might maintain with their or their family's country of origin. One dimension of this connection could take the form of long-distance nationalism. Beyond the idea of belonging to a nation back in the country of origin, this can manifest itself in political and social engagement, both in the place of origin and the new home, ranging from lobbying, voting, protesting, and supporting identity politics back in the country of origin. For example, this can entail collecting money in Irish pubs in Boston for the Irish Republican Army (IRA) during the "troubles" in Northern Ireland, to Swiss and US diaspora Albanians joining the Kosovo Liberation Army (KLA) to fight Serbian security forces between 1998 to 1999. Such engagement is by no means a recent phenomenon: the Armenian diaspora mobilized against the oppression of the Ottoman Empire more than a century ago, and some German immigrants in the United States supported Hitler and the Nazi movement during its rise to power.

It would be misleading to conceptualize migrants as a unified nationalist community engaging back home. The relationship is more complicated. Many migrants do not organize and assimilate or integrate into the new country, keeping family ties, maybe for one or two generations, yet do not become politically engaged. Nationalist activists from the homeland have often been disappointed that many emigrants care so little. The Croatian politician and writer Ante Tresić-Pavičić visited the United States in 1905 to establish contacts with migrants and reports with disappointment that some told him "What have you come to tell us about the homeland? The old homeland that bore us was a stepmother to us .... to us the homeland is where life is good to us, and that is here ... Tell your fairy tales in the old homeland but leave us here in peace for this is now our home."[19] Many thus had little interest—not just in the Croat case—in keeping in touch with the state or nation that they had left. Diasporas, migrants who are organized to keep social, cultural, and political contacts with the country of origin, are self-selecting groups.

Besides, migrants often "discover" or form their national identity once they live in their new home. For example, the millions of Europeans who left for the Americas in the late nineteenth century frequently had no strong sense of national identity when they left, just like their kin who stayed behind. Once in the diaspora, networks based on shared language, background, and cultural familiarity were often crucial for "making it," and thus national identity often only evolved in the new home. In Australia, for example, migrants from the region of Macedonia in Southeastern Europe often only "discovered," or instead decided, that they were Greeks, Bulgarians, or Macedonians, depending on which community they encountered. The Yugoslav guest workers in Germany similarly arrived as Yugoslavs, organized into clubs by Socialist Yugoslavia and opening "Yugoslav" restaurants. However, once the country dissolved in the early 1990s, the Yugoslavs of Germany and elsewhere followed suit to become Croats, Serbs, Macedonians, etc.

The discovery of the original identity can also be reactive. If the majority excluded and discriminates against migrant communities, they might adopt their family's national identity as a form of protest and reaction.[20] This rediscovery of national belonging should not be understood, as many other forms of national identification, as discovering the "real" nation but as a hybrid that incorporates family traditions and knowledge as well as newly acquired and sometimes reactive elements of identity.

Diasporas are not just members of the nation geographically removed to a different country or continent: they raise questions about citizenship and how to imagine the nation. Countries of origin also view their current and former citizens and co-nationals abroad from a variety of angles. Some states actively court their diaspora. Classic European emigrant countries, such as Ireland and Italy, have made it easy for former emigrants to obtain citizenship and voting rights. Others see or saw migrants as betraying the nation for leaving the nation-state. In the nineteenth and early twentieth centuries, some European countries made it difficult for their citizens to leave their country, including Hungary and Bulgaria. During the Cold War, all socialist countries (except Yugoslavia from the early 1960s) restricted the movement of their citizens and viewed the anti-communist diaspora as a threat. Similarly, other political emigrants are often seen not as a resource but a threat by hostile states.

Distance also gives nationalism a different significance. If nationalism is about the self-rule of the nation, long-distance nationalism focuses on self-rule elsewhere, and not where immigrants live. Distance often creates an idealized vision of home, and nationalism can compensate for distance. Thus, there are examples of diasporas supporting radical nationalist causes at home, from Tamils in the UK, and Kurds across Western Europe, to Indians in the United States, who fund nationalism from the relative safety of their homes.

Migration is often not permanent, as many of those who left later returned their home country. This goes not just for guest workers in Germany but even for migrants in the Americas. Thus, the connection is an important reference not just for long-distance nationalism but as part of the idea of return. This return might take place through regular visits, more easily possible today than a century ago or by permanently returning back to ones' country of origin. The myth of return informed the connection to home and the nation.

For states, especially nation-states, long-distance nationalism—real or imagined—raises questions about loyalty. Migrants have thus often been excluded for fear that they might support their country of origin in times of conflict. The best example is the mass internment of Japanese Americans during the Second World War. Around 110,000 to 120,000 Japanese Americans were interned by the American authorities, although the majority were second or third-generation immigrants with American citizenship based on the ill-founded suspicion of collective disloyalty. Similarly, Muslim Americans and Europeans have come under suspicion of states and societies in the aftermath of 9/11 and terrorist attacks in Europe.

Migration in modern nation-states raises the question of membership in the nation and, with it, citizenship. Migration has been rejected in states that were founded on the premise of immigration, such as the United States during the 1920s and more recently, as well as in nation-states that have defined themselves through a community of common descent. The latter might offer citizenship to and even encourage the immigration of ethnic kin, including countries such as Israel, Hungary, and Germany, as explored in Chapter 5. On the other hand, hostility toward immigration of people from different backgrounds is often caused by a self-understanding as a homogenous nation-state and the perceived threat of immigration to the dominance of the nation.

Conclusion

Migration has become a defining topic in policy debates across Europe and North America, especially since 2014, when over a million refugees came to Europe from Africa and the Middle East, in particular from Syria. The images of large numbers of refugees crossing the borders triggered fear of uncontrolled mass migration, reflected in terms associated with migrants such as "invasion" and "flood." This anxiety over refugees is often most pronounced where refugees are few in number, including countries such as Hungary and Poland, suggesting that the fear of migrants has reasons other than migration itself. The underlying argument of anti-migrant rhetoric, as will be explored in more detail in the next chapter, is the fear of being overwhelmed by foreigners in what far-right writers, groups, and parties have called the "replacement" of indigenous populations by foreigners. Hungarian prime minister Orbán defined this threat as part of a wider challenge to the nation in a July 2018 speech: "In today's open-society Europe there are no borders; European people can be readily replaced with immigrants; the family has been transformed into an optional, fluid form of cohabitation; the nation, national identity and national pride are seen as negative and obsolete notions; and the state no longer guarantees security in Europe."[21] The presumed threat of migration merges with a great menace to the nation posed by liberalism and global elites, with a strong conspiratorial undertone that blames particular groups and individuals, such as the Hungarian-born philanthropist George Soros, for promoting the supposed replacement of Europeans with immigrants. This claim was first articulated by the French writer Renaud Camus[22] and has been adopted by a wide spectrum of far-right groups and activists from the French *Front National* to the Australian terrorist Brenton Tarrant, who killed fifty people at a mosque in Christchurch, New Zealand, in March 2019, and who referred to the "great replacement" in a manifesto he wrote to justify the shooting.

Thus, migration has become a defining feature of nationalism in Europe and North America over the current decade. In particular, the attention of nativist movements has focused on migrants with a Muslim background. This is grounded in the perceived antagonism between the "West" and "Islam," a view that draws on long-established historical motifs from the crusades to the Ottoman Empire. The contemporary antagonistic view emerged through the rise of anti-Western radical Islamic movements since the late 1970s and a long legacy of Western colonialism. Nationalist opposition to migration is thus framed in larger categories based on religion, such as the notion of Judeo-Christian culture, or normative and geographic categories such as "the West." As a result, nationalist anti-immigrant movements portray themselves as defending "civilizations" or larger "cultures" rather than just particular nations. For example, *Pegida*, the German far-right protest movement that emerged in Dresden in 2015, stands for "Patriotic Europeans Against the Islamization of the Occident," explicitly considering themselves not just Germans but Europeans. This framing of anti-immigrant groups as being European and protecting Europe distinguishes not only between nations but also larger groups based on religion or origin. This approach enables far-right groups to seek cooperation along the lines of anti-immigrant positions and reflect the transnational nature of nationalist movements and the exchange of ideas that occur among them. In the next chapter, we will explore in more detail what explains the significance of nationalism today, with anti-immigrant and anti-Muslim groups and ideas playing a central role.

8

New Nationalism and Populism

As Nazi Germany began its war of conquest in Europe, the well-known Austro-Hungarian economist Karl Polanyi found refuge in the United States, having fled Austria in 1933. At a lecture given at Bennington College, Vermont he noted that "the more intense international cooperation was and the more close the interdependence of the various parts of the world grew, the more essential became the only effective organizational unit of an industrial society on the present level of technique: the nation. Modern nationalism is a protective reaction against the dangers inherent in an interdependent world."[1] Polanyi's emphasis on the links between global connection and nationalism resonate to this day. While nationalism might appear to be the anthesis to globalization, it is also closely intertwined with it. This chapter will explore how nationalism remains a relevant idea in today's world and how it interrelates with the recent increase in populism and authoritarian trends around the world. Subsequently, it will explore different explanations for the apparent rise of nationalist politics, followed by a discussion of the global networks and nationalism.

This chapter draws on Florian Bieber, "Is Nationalism on the Rise? Assessing Global Trends," *Ethnopolitics* 17, no. 5 (2018): 519–540; and Florian Bieber, "Ethnopopulism and the Global Dynamics of Nationalist Mobilization," *Ethnopolitics* 17, no. 5 (2018): 558–562. Both are published under Creative Commons Attribution License.

During the nineteenth century, nationalism correlated closely with the emergence of modern states that were a response to the demands of modernity, including unified economic units with an educated and mobile workforce. Earlier, trading cities, such as Venice or the Hanseatic League, could outperform large territorial states. Now, nation-states could unify economic spaces and bind citizens to them through bonds of loyalty that empires could not offer. Arguably, nation-states, with the partial exception of the largest of them, such as China or the United States, have outlived the usefulness as viable economic units. Nation-states cannot be autonomous economic actors, even the largest of them is too much embedded in global economic trade networks.

Thus, it is easy and tempting to describe nationalism as backward and anachronistic, as indeed it often is. In the enthusiasm of the end of the Cold War, some considered nationalism to be a dying breed and the violent conflagrations of the period to be the last spasms of an idea that would not survive the rise of a globalized postmodern and post-national world. In this regard, the liberal logic resembled the Marxist understanding of nationalism as a phase of social development that would be overcome either through liberal globalization or socialism. Neither was right, as nationalism has remained relevant and has not shown any sign of withering away. Of course, this does not mean that nationalism is going to remain a permanent fixture of human society. After all, nations and nationalism are relatively recent phenomena and thus might be replaced as they displaced earlier types of collective identity. Yet, it is a deeply ingrained feature of societies and the international system and offers a strong category responding to the human need to belong to an identifiable group.

Nationalism and globalization are thus intertwined. The current wave of globalization, which could be understood as "the widening, deepening and speeding up of global interconnectedness,"[2] is not the beginning of this process. Arguably, globalization emerged in the early modern era as a world economy surfaced that linked the continents in an ever-increasing network of trade and cooperation. This system was long dominated by Europe, in particular through the colonial possessions and trade posts of Europe's great powers, and saw its first peak in the decades before the First World War. Both World Wars were a product of globalization—the globalization of war—and highly disruptive to global trade. However, globalization as it is understood today, is just part of this long-term process, in which the rise of the nation is deeply embedded. The political theorist Benjamin Barber argued already in 1996 that the conflict between McWorld, representing global consumerist and capitalist domination and identity politics, represent the essential global conflict.[3] Of course, nations and other aspects of identity politics can themselves become consumer products and rely on global media, but in a nutshell, globalization and identity politics are two often conflicting sides of the same coin. Nationalism is not the only form of identity politics, and since 9/11 and the rise (and fall) of the Islamic State (ISIS) more attention has been focused on religious extremism. However, it is useful to consider both as closely interrelated phenomena as identity politics. Religious extremism is often a more visible and transnational threat than nationalism. Since nationalism is directed toward the nation and thus inherently fragmented, whereas religious radicalism can be universal in scope and its followers, individual nationalisms are more restricted.

Religious extremism often comes to the foreground when nationalism is not a strong source of identity or has become discredited. In particular, in many Arab countries of the Middle East, nation-building has had only limited success. States are often closely identified with conservative and repressive regimes that have dominated the states since their establishment. The consolidation of these states as nation-states has been disrupted by ideas of pan-Arab cooperation, as discussed in Chapter 3, to which many leaders paid lip service. The rise of political Islam as the dominant force of identity politics in the Middle East in the late 1970s has been closely linked to the failure of the states and their leaders to create a plausible nationalism.

Whether religious radicalism or nationalism, both are a response to globalization. Globalization, combined with its power structures, often favoring Western capitalist countries due to the long history of global economic dominance has triggered a reaction through nationalism and other particularisms. These, in turn, rely on the techniques of global exchange and copy modes of communication themselves. Today's nationalism is as a result also globalized. Globalization also challenges established orders and promotes hybridity and cultural mixing. Frequently, the main line of confrontation is not between competing nationalisms, as it was a century ago, but the competition with cosmopolitan and hybrid identities that reject the singular importance of the nation.[4] The potency of virulent nationalism was visible during the 1990s, when there was a sharp rise in ethnic conflict during the first years of the decade, as discussed in Chapter 6. What appeared as the victory of liberal internationalism in Western Europe and North America was entirely different in many other regions of the world where the collapse of the Cold War was both caused by nationalism and enabled the emergence of new and violent nationalism. The decline of ethnic violence in the late 1990s might have appeared to be the peak of global cooperation based on liberal values. Yet already September 11, 2001, cut this trend short politically with the subsequent wars waged by the United States and economically with the crisis of 2008. If there was a liberal, post-national moment, it was brief and fleeting.

In turn, in recent years, rising nationalism is seen everywhere and in everything. From the election of Donald Trump to Brexit in 2016, the nationalist policies of the Japanese Prime Minister Shinzō Abe, his Indian counterpart Narendra Modi, and the Turkish president Recep Tayyip Erdoğan, the success of far-right parties in Italian, German, and Austrian elections in 2017 and 2018, nationalism appears to be on the rise globally.[5] When accused of being nationalists, some world leaders have openly accepted this label, as US president Trump did in late 2018 when he stated: "You know what I am? I'm a nationalist. OK? I'm a nationalist."[6] Just a few years earlier, such an admission would have been unimaginable. While nationalism might not have been dead, it was indeed not an acceptable label to describe oneself, in particular among leading global politicians.

Document: Remarks by President Trump to the 73rd Session of the United Nations General Assembly

Speech given at the UN General Assembly, New York on 25.9.2018.[7]

... The United States is stronger, safer, and a richer country than it was when I assumed office less than two years ago.

We are standing up for America and for the American people. And we are also standing up for the world.

... That is why America will always choose independence and cooperation over global governance, control, and domination.

... As my administration has demonstrated, America will always act in our national interest.

... We will never surrender America's sovereignty to an unelected, unaccountable, global bureaucracy.

America is governed by Americans. We reject the ideology of globalism, and we embrace the doctrine of patriotism.

Around the world, responsible nations must defend against threats to sovereignty not just from global governance, but also from other, new forms of coercion and domination.

... We recognize the right of every nation in this room to set its own immigration policy in accordance with its national interests, just as we ask other countries to respect our own right to do the same—which we are doing. That is one reason the United States will not participate in the new Global Compact on Migration. Migration should not be governed by an international body unaccountable to our own citizens.

Ultimately, the only long-term solution to the migration crisis is to help people build more hopeful futures in their home countries. Make their countries great again.

...

The whole world is richer, humanity is better, because of this beautiful constellation of nations, each very special, each very unique, and each shining brightly in its part of the world.

In each one, we see awesome promise of a people bound together by a shared past and working toward a common future.

...

Inside everyone in this great chamber today, and everyone listening all around the globe, there is the heart of a patriot that feels the same powerful love for your nation, the same intense loyalty to your homeland.

The passion that burns in the hearts of patriots and the souls of nations has inspired reform and revolution, sacrifice and selflessness, scientific breakthroughs, and magnificent works of art.

Our task is not to erase it, but to embrace it. To build with it. To draw on its ancient wisdom. And to find within it the will to make our nations greater, our regions safer, and the world better.

To unleash this incredible potential in our people, we must defend the foundations that make it all possible. Sovereign and independent nations are the only vehicle where freedom has ever survived, democracy has ever endured, or peace has ever prospered. And so we must protect our sovereignty and our cherished independence above all.

...

So together, let us choose a future of patriotism, prosperity, and pride. Let us choose peace and freedom over domination and defeat. And let us come here to this place to stand for our people and their nations, forever strong, forever sovereign, forever just, and forever thankful for the grace and the goodness and the glory of God.

Thank you. God bless you. And God bless the nations of the world.

Thank you very much. Thank you. (Applause.)

As outlined in this book, nationalist leaders often target those co-nationals who are "unreliable" members of the nation, scapegoat other nations or minorities or they direct their grievances against some global elite. These are structural features of nationalist movements going back to their origins in the late eighteenth century and are by no means novel. The specific targets might shift. Thus, nationalism in North America and Europe has been directed against migrants from the global South, in particular from Muslim countries. The neighboring nations are less a target than they would have been a century ago. It was thus rather surprising when the leader of the French far-right Marine Le Pen described the new Franco-German friendship treaty, signed in Aachen in January 2019, as selling out the French region of Alsace to Germany (without any evidence, of course). Such anti-German rhetoric pales in comparison to the anti-Muslim line.

Nationalism, authoritarianism, and populism

The rise of nationalism, so it would seem, is closely tied to the rise of populism and authoritarianism as the three defining and global political trends of recent years. However, what is the relationship between the three and what role does nationalism play in bolstering the other two?

Authoritarianism has been making a gradual comeback following the end of what has been called the "third wave of democracy"—the most rapid and universal spread of democracy that began in Southern Europe and Latin America in the 1970s and spread to Eastern Europe and later to Asia and sub-Saharan Africa in the late 1980s and early 1990s. Since it became clear that democracy would not take hold in many countries as easily as optimists had hoped in the early 1990s, embodied by Francis Fukuyama's argument that the end of history meant an end to ideological competition to liberal democracy. First, there has been the spread of hybrid regimes that combine formal democracy with varying types of authoritarian restrictions, these could be called most aptly competitive authoritarianism.[8] Many regimes only formally became democratic, adopting democratic institutions, while retaining autocratic control, such as Russia, there has also been a decline of democracy since the mid-2000s. This decline affected liberal democracies, such as Poland and Hungary, as well as many more restricted democracies, such as Turkey. Finally, competitive authoritarian regimes, such as Russia, have become more entrenched. More recent waves of democratization, such as in Arab countries in 2011, largely failed and led to war and the retrenchment of authoritarianism with the sole exception of Tunisia.

There is no direct or inherent link between authoritarianism and nationalism. Authoritarian regimes can draw on different types of legitimacy, including output legitimacy, such as economic growth, as has been the case of China, or input legitimacy, such as theocracy and communism. Nationalism can provide, however, an important source of legitimacy, either as building legitimacy against external actors or against domestic others (minorities and opposition). It is often unconsolidated democracies and hybrid regimes that are the most susceptible to virulent nationalism. This is for two distinct reasons:

1. During periods of democratization, new institutions and rules have to be set that define the political community, the constitution needs to be revised or rewritten, citizenship or electoral laws need to be determined: is the state a nation-state, does a core nation have privileged access to citizenship, are ethnic kin allowed to vote or some groups excluded? With crucial questions related to the political community being under discussion, membership in the nation is renegotiated and nationalism can frequently gather in salience.

2. During the period of political opening, competition is imperfect, and nationalism provides for an easy and ready-made ideology that can compete on the "marketplace of ideas."[9] Furthermore, authoritarian attitudes among citizens often correlate closely with nationalist worldview.[10] As regimes move toward greater authoritarianism, they often resort to nationalism to justify this shift. For example, Turkey under President Recep Tayyip Erdoğan initially engaged in many liberalizing reforms in the 2000s, including greater rights for minorities, such as Kurds. As the government became increasingly authoritarian following the challenge in the 2013 Gezi protests in Istanbul and the failed 2016 coup, it adopted a more nationalist tone and resorted to repression against Kurds and other minorities. Similarly, Russia under Vladimir Putin has been emphasizing its distinctiveness from the West and played up national interest in a revisionist military policy toward its neighbors, including the invasion of Georgia in 2008 and Ukraine in 2014. In particular, as the post-Cold War hegemony of the West linked Western dominance and liberal democracy, nationalism has facilitated the ability to justify authoritarianism as a counterweight to Western influence.

It is populism, however, that can provide for the most plausible link between nationalism and authoritarianism. Similar to nationalism, populism is a versatile ideology. It seeks to represent "the people" against an elite that might be understood as a political or economic elite, or potentially a foreign elite that dominates. It thus promotes majoritarianism and rejects institutions that restrain the supposed will of the majority.[11] Populism per se is able to embrace all political ideologies. On the Left, grassroots movements such as *Podemos* in Spain and the radical leftist coalition and later party *Syriza* in Greece adopted populist policies and rhetoric. In Latin America, there is similarly a long tradition of populist movements and the Left from Peronism in Argentina to Hugo Chávez in Venezuela that draw on the large social inequalities. Similarly, writers such as Chantal Mouffe have argued that the political Left should adopt populist strategies.[12]

If populists define the people in national terms, populism and nationalism create a symbiosis, in what could be described as ethnopopulism.[13] Here, the "corrupt elite" can be either a minority, which is accused of holding political or economic power (as is often the case in anti-Semitic or anti-Chinese strategies) or the elite is accused of being beholden to foreign interests. The anti-elite discourse might also be directed against a foreign elite. This has been a feature of National Socialism and its nationalist and anti-Semitic precursors, reflected in the claim of a global Jewish conspiracy, such as the Protocols of the Elders of Zion, as discussed earlier. Similar motives have emerged in the discourse of European populists who target a "globalist" elite. Targets include representatives of a global economic elite, such as Brussels as a representative of the EU as a distant, undemocratic elite, or individuals, such as George Soros. The anti-Soros campaign has become a central feature of populist groups in Europe and the United States, as the Hungarian-born American billionaire combines features that make him the ideal mark: rich and liberal, a banker and Jewish, with strong global philanthropic engagement, he can be a target for all these aspects. In 2017, the Hungarian government, for example, launched a campaign against Soros with billboards under the slogan "Don't let Soros have the last laugh," accusing him of plotting to organize massive immigration to Hungary, a spurious claim. Numerous other nationalist and populist parties, politicians, and groups have targeted Soros, ranging from the Macedonian government to president Trump.[14]

Beyond Soros, populism has targeted the supposed global elite, suspect for their lack of national identity. The global elite conflates left-wing criticism of global capitalism with nationalist critiques of disloyal and disconnected global citizens. British Prime Minister Theresa May took such a view in an attack on the global elite at a Conservative Party conference in October 2016, noting that "if you believe you're a citizen of the world, you're a citizen of nowhere. You don't understand what the very word 'citizenship' means."[15] The dichotomy between a global elite, who do not appreciate the citizenship of the nation-state and the authentic population, evokes anti-elite and anti-globalist themes and pits the people against a remote and disconnected elite.

Whereas populists need not be autocrats, the implicit erosion of checks and balances and the Manichean worldview of populism does lend itself as a legitimizing strategy for autocrats. In addition, and more importantly, populists commonly drift toward authoritarianism in power and are at best restrained by strong, resilient democratic institutions. Moreover, populism rejected the political legitimacy of other parties as not speaking in the name of the people, a monopolistic claim made by populists to speak for the often "silent" majority. It is important to take such claims critically. As a leading scholar of populism has argued "the leaders described as 'nationalists' are better understood as populist poseurs who have won support by drawing on the rhetoric and imagery of nationalism."[16] This characterization applies more widely than just in the case of recent nationalists. As we saw in earlier chapters, nationalist leaders often claim to speak in the name of the nation, but this does not mean that they enjoy the support of a majority of their supposed constituency. While ethnonationalist populists, as they might be termed, claim legitimacy in the name of an exclusionary nation, including Narendra Modi in India, Jair Bolsonaro in Brasil, and Donald Trump in the United States, their support base is considerably narrower and often motivated by other consideration than what their claims would suggest. The electoral success of politicians who also have a nationalist background is thus not automatically a measure of nationalist sentiment. Instead, it is often a legitimizing strategy. The electoral victory has not been based on the popularity of their claims but often on the weakness of political opponents, including in Hungary in 2010, in Japan in 2012, the United States in 2016, and Brasil in 2018. Corruption and an economic downturn as in Hungary 2010 or India in 2014 were the crucial issues that handed Orbán and Modi the electoral victory.

For example, Narendra Modi was elected in a landslide on the nationalist Bharatiya Janata Party (BJP) ticket in 2014 in the Indian general elections and has remained popular. However, the basis for his support has been less the Hindu nationalism of his party but more his economic and social platform. The election campaign was marked by a deliberate discursive shift of the BJP away from its earlier Hindu nationalism.[17] Furthermore, the electoral victory came after an extended decline in riots in India.[18] Thus, citizens have viewed his policies on communal relations or his handling of relations with Pakistan less positively than other policies, yet these would have been the policy areas in which nationalist policies would be expected to resonate well.[19] This suggests that the popularity is grounded in economic policy rather than support for nationalism. When seeking reelection in 2019, Modi more explicitly evoked narrow Hindi nationalism.[20] Of course, nationalist parties often moderate their rhetoric, knowing that the more nationalist electorate would vote for them anyhow and might be reached through so-called "dog whistles," symbols and slogans that have little meaning for the majority but appeal to a nationalist core. Politicians of the far-right Austrian Freedom Party, for example, regularly wear blue cornflowers on their revers. Most voters pay little attention to this symbol of nineteenth-century German nationalists and of the underground National Socialists during the 1930s, but the far-right core of party loyalists take note.

Furthermore, support from established mainstream conservative political parties is often essential for the success of far-right parties and candidates. They either serve as coalition partners or became vehicles of ethnopopulist candidates themselves, such as the Republican party in the United States. Finally, if reelected in fragile democratic systems, where institutional checks and balances are less strongly developed, electoral manipulation contributes to retaining power, as has been the case through gerrymandering and changing the electoral system in Hungary and Turkey.

While there has been an apparent wave of successes of ethnopopulist parties and candidates in recent years, there is no universal or straightforward explanation. As noted throughout this book, nationalism is neither new nor has it been absent over the past decades. In some countries, nationalism might have been less exclusionary and instead a latent political force, but in crucial elections candidates who ran on populist tickets that were based on exclusionary and virulent nationalism succeeded or made strong gains. Thus, rather than seeking to explain some "new nationalism," it is more productive to understand the shift in nationalism to become more pronounced in public life and displaying more exclusionary features.

Identifying nationalist trends

Capturing nationalist attitudes is difficult, especially on a global scale. Nationalism has very different normative connotations around the world. While in Europe, few would self-identify as nationalists, nationalism is often viewed more positively in regions where the construction of an overarching national identity is taken as a desirable alternative to narrower ethnic or religious identities or not so distant memories of imperial rule. Proxies for nationalism are also not equally translatable to different contexts. Whereas in North America and Europe, anti-immigrant sentiment and nationalism closely interlink, in many Latin American countries, Africa, and Asia, migration is not a core theme of nationalism. Pride in the nationality, i.e., citizenship, low levels of trust of people of another nationality, not seeing oneself as a citizen of the world, and support for countries dealing with their problems can all be seen as questions, asked in global surveys that provide some insight into global nationalist attitudes. While there is wide variation across the globe, no single pattern emerges, neither is there a clear north-south divide nor are citizens in smaller countries displaying different attitudes than those in larger states. Importantly, when examining the trend in surveys over the past fifteen to twenty years, there is no discernible global increase of nationalist, isolationist tendencies.[21] This trend suggests that the rise of nationalist politics in many countries either has other causes than a shift in attitudes or rather the political and social expression of nationalism is not the consequence of changing attitudes but the more visible and effective mobilization of the existing nationalist sentiments.

In Europe, there has been a long-term trend in rising nationalist parties, in Western Europe discernable since the 1980s.[22] Elections and referenda in 2016 to 2017 suggest the strength of nationalist parties, candidates, and propositions but also show that there is not a universal and progressive increase in support for nationalist parties.[23]

Overall, far-right parties have made significant gains in Europe in recent years. In 2016, the far-right Freedom Party candidate Norbert Hofer gained 46.2 percent of the vote in the Austrian presidential elections, and Marine Le Pen of the National Front (*Front National*, FN)—since renamed the National Rally (*Rassemblement National*, RN)—gained 33.9 percent in the second round of the French presidential elections in May 2017. Similarly, the far-right Alternative for Germany (*Alternative für Deutschland*, AfD) entered the German Bundestag with 12.6 percent of the vote in September 2017, a first for postwar Germany. The Northern League (*Lega Nord,* LN), a party with a far-right platform, running as part of a right of center coalition in Italian election under the leadership of Matteo Salvini emerged as the third-largest single party in parliament with 17.37 percent of the popular vote. This trend was, however, not the same all across the board. In the UK, the nationalist UKIP party lost most support, gaining only 1.8 percent of votes and not a single MP, while in the Netherlands in 2017, the Party for Freedom (*Partij voor de Vrijheid*, PVV) of Geert Wilders became the second-largest party, yet his gains were smaller than widely expected. Similar trends were mirrored in the European Parliament elections in May 2019. While far-right and ethnopopulist parties did well in some countries, such as France, Italy, and Hungary, there is no clear European wave of ethnopopulist parties. Instead, there has been a normalization of such parties, with the parties or their programs becoming coopted by main-stream parties.

The increased support for nationalist parties or candidates and the absence of a large-scale attitudinal shift appears at first contradictory. However, there are two aspects to consider. First, nationalist attitudes did not rise globally—the rise of nationalist parties and candidates has been regional, focused primarily on Europe and the United States. Second, even when just considering those countries, one cannot observe a long-term shift toward more nationalist attitudes. In countries with rising nationalist politics, it is polarization and prioritization that resulted in support for nationalist candidates.

Both structural and attitudinal factors contribute to the electoral basis of nationalist parties. The voters of nationalist parties in developed postindustrial societies—often from working and lower-middle classes—are often less well educated and belong to the majority community. They experience economic and social uncertainty, frequently combined with a real or perceived status reversal and marginalization. This might be coupled with latent racism, authoritarianism, and longing for a past that is long gone (or rather that never existed).[24] The support for nationalist parties can be explained either through a cultural backlash, i.e., anxiety over social status and cultural change, be it through migration, enhancing the status of minorities—be they sexual or ethnic—or through economic causes, such as the economic precariousness of those voters that are particularly susceptible to supporting ethnopopulist candidates and parties.[25] While there is merit in understanding the relevance of one factor over the other, they are closely intertwined and point to uncertainty and loss of influence, both real and perceived, that facilitate the rise of ethnonationalist populists.

In the United States, the white working class, which disproportionally supported Trump in the 2016 elections, is more authoritarian (64 percent have an authoritarian orientation) than the average population, including support for a leader who breaks the rules. There is a strong belief that the American way of life has deteriorated since the 1950s (65 percent) and fear that the country is losing its identity and cultures (68 percent). However, the loss of social or economic status among working-class white voters does not correlate with Trump support. Support was stronger due to particular attitudes, such as perceived discrimination against white Americans, anti-immigrant attitudes, and a threat from foreign cultures.[26] The voters for Marine Le Pen display comparable features, hailing mostly from a blue-collar background, with limited education, and a high level of dissatisfaction with democracy.[27]

Support for radical right parties is not only based on nationalist positions of voters, such as anti-EU and anti-immigrant positions, but also on economic grounds, such as negative perceived economic position, and economic adversity at the country level and preference for redistributive policies.[28] Research shows that groups that experience real or perceived decline and vulnerability, as well as social marginalization, are more likely to support nationalist policies.[29] Members of groups that experience a status reversal are particularly vulnerable. This can be particularly well-identified in Eastern Germany, as it allows for comparison with the Western German population with which it shares many features, including language and the current political system. The former Socialist Eastern Germany demonstrates that voting for nationalist parties and nationalist violence, such as anti-immigrant attacks, are not necessarily a predictor of broader social attitudes. Thus, while anti-immigrant violence is higher in Eastern Germany than in the West, the variation of anti-immigrant attitudes is not significant.

A longitudinal study in Germany of attitudes toward authoritarianism, anti-Semitism, anti-immigrant sentiments, and the Nazi period shows that the overall anti-Semitic, anti-immigrant, and authoritarian attitudes did not rise over the past decade, in fact, they mostly declined. At the same time social polarization and radicalization, i.e., the willingness to use force has increased.[30] Thus, other factors have to explain the variation in voting and violence, such as weaker civil society (societal life) and the sense of greater "fraternal relative deprivation." This concept describes the discontent of members of a group arising from the perceived disadvantage an individual is suffering for being a member of this group, in comparison to others, be they migrants, West Germans, or elites. A key structural cause of nationalism is a multidimensional sense of marginalization. A study of Eastern Germany found that the local dynamics that facilitated far-right support and violence included rural (or semi-rural) versus more privileged urban centers, the sense of marginalization as East versus West Germans and finally the sense of being disadvantaged as Germans over foreigners, in particular refugees. Furthermore, the study finds great importance in authoritarian and ethnocentric worldviews stemming from the socialist period as well as a depoliticized environment.[31]

Besides, long-term structural features matter. In Germany, the far-right populist AfD has performed better in municipalities where the National Socialists did well in elections in 1933. This appears to be a better predictor than exposure to migration, the central theme of the party. As many of the supporters for the AfD were previous nonvoters, the party appears to have activated support among citizens who were not politically engaged but live in structurally conservative and nationalist environments. Considering the time of eighty years between support for the NSDAP and the AfD, the pattern is not based on the same voters but rather the transmission of patterns through families and the local environment.[32]

Altogether, ethnopopulists parties do not succeed for a single reason. First, weakness of political alternatives, other issues might matter for explaining success. Second, the electoral support includes economic, cultural, and structural factors that interlock.

Still, radical nationalist parties rarely secure elected office by themselves. At best, they become part of ruling coalitions. However, the rise of nationalist parties and candidates can shift policies of mainstream parties and larger social debates and attitudes. Ethnonationalist populists can shift the debate, even if they are not based on broad support. There are discursive practices, i.e., ways in which particular topics, such as the own nation, migrants, minorities, or neighboring nations, are discussed in public. These changes occur when topics are discussed differently in media or public debate. Such a shift might be the result of a direct policy of a ruling party—as might be the case in more authoritarian countries—or be the consequence of a more gradual change. For example, the debate in Europe about refugees underwent a shift (to varying degrees) from discussing refugees in terms of the humanitarian needs to refugees as a security threat, associated with terrorism, sexual and criminal violence.[33] This shift can be understood through the notion of a *spiral of silence* that suggests that individuals remain silent about their opinions if they perceive them not to be in line with the broader dominant social ideas.[34] This dynamic can silence nationalist or xenophobic views in a social environment that discourages it. However, if there is a discursive shift in the opinions published or publicly expressed, those who hold virulent and exclusionary nationalist views might be encouraged to voice these, while critiques might feel an increased need to remain silent.[35] Such a shift has occurred in the United States and large parts of Europe as a result of critical votes (Trump and Brexit) or moments of (perceived) crises, such as the influx of a large number of refugees in Europe in 2015 and 2016.

Nationalism in foreign policy and global links

Beyond the nationalist shift in domestic politics in some countries, nationalism is also an important force of foreign policy. Foreign policy is of course closely linked to domestic policy, as foreign policy decisions can be brought about by nationalist parties in government or other types of domestic nationalist turns. On the other hand, foreign policy can be used to rouse nationalist support. Wars and international confrontations can be instrumental in nationalist mobilization, from the effect of the Falkland War on the British public to the initial American response to the terrorist attacks on 9/11. As noted earlier, the preferred targets of many nationalist groups around the world are global elites and internal minorities and to a lesser extent other nation-states. In Europe, far-right parties were able to form a significant faction in the European Parliament for the first time in 2015. The "Europe of Nations and Freedom" faction included the French National Rally, the Italian Lega, the Dutch Party for Freedom, and the Austrian Freedom Party, among others.

Document: Speech by French Presidential Candidate Marine Le Pen, 2017

Speech held in Lyon 5 February 2017.[36]
    I am the candidate of France of the people ... From its outcome, will depend the continuity of France as a free nation and for those who like us feel above all French, our existence as a people ... I say it with gravity: the choice we will have to make in this election is a choice of civilization. Our leaders chose deregulated globalization, they wanted it to be a happy thing, it turned out to be awful. Proceeding only by the research of some of the hyper profit, it develops at a double level, globalization from below with massive immigration, global social dumping, and globalization from above with the "financialization" of the economy. The globalization that was a fact with the multiplication of exchanges, they made it an ideology: the economic globalism which refuses any limitation, any regulation of the globalization and which, for that, weakened the immune defenses of the Nation, the dispossessed of its constitutive elements: frontier, national currency, authority of its laws, conduct of the economy, thus allowing another form of globalism to be born and grow: Islamist fundamentalism ... These two globalism, today, are the short scale: The financial and business-oriented globalism of which the European Union, finance and the essence of a domesticated political class are the zealous servants;
    Jihadist globalism that undermines our vital interests abroad, but also that is implanted on our national territory, in certain neighborhoods, in certain places, in some weak minds. And both

of them work for the disappearance of our nation, that is, of France in which we live, which we love, which is why the French have a feeling of dispossession. These two ideologies want to subject our countries. One in the name of globalized finance, that is to say the ideology of all trade, the other in the name of a radicalized Islam, that is to say, the ideology of all religious ... Faced with these two totalitarianisms that threaten our freedoms and our country, we no longer have the time, nor the means of angelism, false pretenses, small arrangements, great cowardice ...

To progress, the supporters of these two globalist ideologies give the illusion of relying on our principles; in reality, they falsely invoke liberty to install their totalitarianism: it is the freedom of the fox in the henhouse ... Since we are at war against Islamist fundamentalism, we will apply to the enemies of France the legal devices of the state of war. ... Without sovereignty, no protection possible, no action possible. Without sovereignty, a project becomes a false promise. My opponents claim to control the borders, return to the right of the soil, prevent immigration, fight against unfair competition. They lie to you. ...

Everyone agrees, the European Union is a failure. That is why, once elected I will announce the organization of a referendum within the first six months of my mandate on whether to stay or leave the EU. I will then engage in talks with our partners, and trust me, they have similar aspirations to sovereignty – to renegotiate the terms of our contract with this tyrannical Europeanist system which is not a project anymore but a historical parenthesis and, hopefully one day, just a bad memory.

We open our arms to all those who share with us the love of France and who wish to engage our country on the path of national recovery ... This cleavage no longer opposes the right and the left, but the patriots to the globalists. In this presidential election, we represent the camp of the patriots ... We urge all patriots from right or left to join us. Elected or ordinary citizens, wherever you come from, whatever your commitments may have been, you have your place at our side. Patriots, you are welcome! As it is possible that presidents like Donald Trump, not only are elected against a coalition system, but above all respect their promises and act quickly and strongly in the interests and wishes of their people ...

This awakening of peoples is historic. It marks the end of a cycle.

The wind of history has turned. It will take us to the top and, with us, our country: France. Long live the people! Long live the Republic! Long live France!

European far-right leaders have met repeatedly to coordinate policy, including in Germany and Austria in 2016 and 2017 called the "Patriotic Spring." In 2016 Le Pen argued that "We are experiencing the return of nation-states."[37] Evoking the protection of European heritage and history are recurring themes in the discourse of nationalist groups that redirect historical mutual grievances toward Muslim migrants, the EU, and the dominant elites. Of course, there are key points of contention, as some nationalists lay claim on ethnic kin or territories (or both) in neighboring states. For example, Hungary under the government of Viktor Orbán has been granting citizenship to Hungarians living in neighboring countries, including Slovakia, Romania, Ukraine, and Serbia, increasing tension between Hungary and its neighbors.

Another example not based on minorities but the combination of unresolved territorial disputes and historical grievances is the tense Chinese–Japanese relationship. Disputes are based on competing historical narratives of the Second World War, two competing powers, in particular with a rising assertiveness of China and open territorial questions. These tensions in the countries' foreign policy are also reflected in popular sentiment. Thus, in 2016, 91.6 percent of Japanese and 76.7 percent of Chinese had an unfavorable or relatively unfavorable impression of the other nation. These negative views of the other are visible in a variety of fields, from stereotypes about the supposed national character to the past and the current political system.[38]

However, they are highly volatile and depend mainly on trigger events. A peak of mutually negative views was reached in 2013 during the conflict over the Senkaku/Diaoyu Islands between the two countries. Once such an escalation occurs, governments, including in more autocratic regimes, can become subject to nationalist pressure groups.[39] Thus, foreign policies are both a result of nationalist sentiment, often willfully incensed by governments and media, and shape public perception.

Even when populists come to power without much reference to nationalism, it can provide for a useful and easily invoked resource. The electoral upset and rule of Rodrigo Duterte in the Philippines since 2016 has been marked by populism rather than nationalism. Duterte used his tough-talking style against crime and political opponents, less for a nationalist agenda.[40] However, populism is easily redirected toward a nationalist foe, be it over competing claims with China or ties with the United States.

Nationalist policies pursued by governments may not just create conflict and instability in the vicinity but also can serve as a larger model and clearinghouse of nationalist movements, as the case of Russia highlights. Since taking office, Vladimir Putin has been building his domestic legitimacy on nationalism, combined with autocratic control and reestablishing state power after a decade of weakness following the collapse of the Soviet Union. This nationalist agenda took shape in the second Chechen war and was, at first, mostly directed toward the domestic arena. However, the war with Georgia in 2008 as well as rising opposition following elections in 2011 led to a more nationalist policy and a confrontation with the West, culminating in the Russian annexation of Crimea in 2014 and the Russian instigated war in Eastern Ukraine.

Like the United States and the EU, which have been supporting democracy and the rule of law over the past two decades, Russia appears to have emerged as a champion of global nationalism. Russia under Putin became an important actor in promoting global far-right nationalist groups and actors, in particular in Europe and the United States. First, Russia serves as a model for far-right groups. As Marine Le Pen stated, "the model that is defended by Vladimir Putin, which is one of reasoned protectionism, looking after the interests of his own country, defending his identity, is one that I like, as long as I can defend this model in my own country."[41] Putin's Russia embodies the combination of nationalism, authoritarianism, and populism that many far-right nationalist groups aspire to emulate. In recent years, Russia has also clearly rejected multicultural policies, protection of sexual minorities, and otherwise aligned itself policy-wise with the Far Right. Second, many ethnopopulist parties have sought to establish formal ties with Russia, Putin, and the ruling United Russia (*Yedinaya Rossiya*) Party, including the French National Rally and the Austrian Freedom Party. Third, Russia has provided assistance to these movements, both in terms of financial support, such as the well-documented credit to Front National through a Russian backed Czech bank, and through media backing in the Russian government outlets such as RT and *Sputnik*.[42] Besides, Russia might be providing illicit support to such groups and candidates, as has been alleged in terms of interference in elections in the United States, France, and elsewhere.

However, Russia as a political actor promoting nationalist parties cannot explain the rise of these parties. While Russian media might have served as echo chambers for the ideas the parties promote and ethnopopulist messages, and the country might have provided significant backing, it has not caused substantial support for such parties.

Rejection of free trade and the nationalization of industries or resources are often associated with nationalism and has been a hallmark of anti-colonial movements. In Latin America this movement has been strong in the 2000s with left-wing populist governments that built their power base on their opposition to external intervention and anti-imperialism, such as in Venezuela, Bolivia, and Argentina. Either authoritarian drift, as in Venezuela, or economic and other legitimacy crises have weakened these regimes, even if some have become more virulent in their rhetoric. However, while these movements and governments have combined nationalism with left-wing populism, the nationalism was based on genuine grievances with foreign—in particular, United States—intervention and economic dominance. Economic nationalism highlights that nationalism, as a versatile ideology, can be associated with the political Left and Right. Left-wing nationalism, widespread in Latin America, is often directed against an external other, be it the United States or a particular multinational company. This movement had its key wave well before the global economic crisis and was largely fueled by the failure of neoliberal economic policies of previous governments.[43]

Conclusions

While there is a good reason to be cautious in accepting the narrative that there is a new global wave of nationalism, the significance of nationalism remains strong, and there is no evidence to suggest its imminent decline nor is there even a clear alternative idea to structure social relations and the global political system. In the past, empires, city-states, and theocracies have been other forms of organizing a system of rule. Today, nation-states, or at least those that claim to be, are ubiquitous. States that rule not in the name of citizens bound by the idea of self-rule and common citizenship are rare and include only such outliers as the Vatican or the short-lived and unrecognized Islamic State. This does not mean that the nation-state is unchallenged or that states could not exist without a nation. Some scholars of international relations have termed the current international order "Neo-medievalism," namely the emergence of multiple overlapping layers of political and economic authority. Considering international organizations, the treaties that bind many countries and the power of non-state actors do highlight that the nation-state is far from the only building block of the global system. In fact, it has been the rise of these challenges to the nation-state contributed to anti-globalist nationalist movements and parties. Some of those were driven by the rise of the global neoliberal economic system, others by attempts to regulate them, such as in recent years the Transatlantic Trade and Investment Partnership (TIIP) between the United States and Europe or the North American Free Trade Agreement (NAFTA) (replaced by United States–Mexico–Canada Agreement [USMCA] in 2018).

The most sophisticated and advanced attempt to restrain the nation-state has been the project of European integration since its establishment as the European Coal and Steel Community in 1952. While nation-states were the initiators, they have deliberately restricted their ability to decide on important issues autonomously and granted powers to the organizations established in the framework of European integration including the European Court of Justice. The Brexit referendum in 2016, wherein 52 percent of participating British voters supported leaving the EU, highlighted the crisis of the project as well as the high level of integration and supranational entanglement the state achieved. The outcome of the referendum triggered a radical policy shift, based on strong nationalist claims such as "taking back control" with strong anti-immigrant overtones. Despite the narrow outcome of the referendum, Brexit supporters have branded opponents as traitors and given more weight to leaving the EU than other policy issues, including preserving the Union, as in Northern Ireland the Good Friday Peace Accord came under threat and as in Scotland and to a lesser degree, Wales parties favoring independence grew. Ironically, Brexit as a vote that had strong nationalist undertones risked destroying the common British state. The difficulty of the UK to untangle itself from the dense web of ties with the European Union demonstrated the extent to which the sovereignty of the states has become integrated and intertwined.

The EU does not seek to replace nationalism, as European citizenship and identity evolved to supplement national identity and citizenship. However, in doing so, it has restricted nationalism, which is why far-right and ethnopopulist parties place such emphasis on restricting the powers of "Brussels." This restriction of the nation is based on the voluntary commitment of its members and can be undone or transformed at the will of the state and its citizens. Such self-imposed restrictions have come under duress in the light of the multiple crises the EU has faced, including the economic and currency crisis, Brexit and migration as well as the decline of liberal democracy. At the same time, the EU is enjoying continuous and increasing support, in no small degree to the disastrous handling of Brexit in the UK. Furthermore a record number of EU citizens identify as Europeans. While it might only be a small minority of Europeans who identify solely as European (2 percent according to the 2018 Eurobarometer), still, there are about the same number of Europeans as Greeks or Czechs in the EU and a greater number than citizens of sixteen EU member states. As multiple identities are possible, most Europeans see themselves as both citizens of their country and the European Union, all of which are trends that have increased during a period primarily ascribed to be one of rising nationalism.[44] This is not to argue that Europeanness is not replacing nationalism, but it is a significant countervailing trend to nationalism. Despite the existence of international organizations that emulate the EU, such as the African Union, no other supranational project of political integration has borne fruit to date. This does not mean that there are no alternatives to nations and nationalism outside the EU. According to the World Value Survey (2010–2014) a majority in the countries surveyed saw themselves also as citizens of the world with particularly high rates in countries as different as Ecuador, Ghana, Nigeria, and Qatar.[45] These numbers do not suggest that the respondents are not attached to their national or subnational identities but point to the multiplicity of belonging people can choose. The significance of national belonging is circumstantial, not absolute. Insecurity, cultural or economic fear, reinforced by a favorable political and social environment give national belonging greater importance than being a citizen of a particular town or the world, a woman or a worker, gay or old, and the many other attributes individuals choose from. Nationalism assumes the subordination of these other markers of identity. As a result, virulent nationalism is both cyclical and circumstantial and requires a subtle presence of a latent nation to draw on.

Thinking about nations

Thinking about nations and nationalism cannot be seen as a historical endeavor and virulent nationalism remains a challenge for researchers to study. Recently, the leading American historian Jill Lepore argued that national history and thus the writing about the nation should be reclaimed by historians: "When historians abandon the study of the nation, when scholars stop trying to write a common history for a people, nationalism doesn't die. Instead, it eats liberalism."[46] Her argument suggests that scholars should not abandon the task of outlining the history of nations and thus shape the narratives that national history entails. In essence, it means accepting the nation (and nation-state) framework for scholarship, while influencing it. However, this risks becoming methodological nationalism, namely accepting, and reproducing nations as the main framework for analysis and thus reinforcing the nation as the main constituent unit of social organization. National histories or other scholarship that discusses nations often assume that these are the only or at least the most important units of analysis. While this, as this book has shown, might be the case in the contemporary world, national histories often project this framework into the distant (or recent) past, when the nation was inexistent or at least less prevalent. They thus suggest that premodern states and societies are direct precursors or even early exponents of the contemporary nation.

Taking the nation and nationalism seriously and not dismissing it as a passing or backward concept is imperative for scholarship. At the same time, it has to avoid the assumption that nations are fixed units in time and place to which a predetermined group of people belong.

From a normative perspective, nationalism could be seen as inherently exclusionary and hierarchical and thus in conflict with a cosmopolitan understanding that underlines shared universal values and the multiplicity of identities.[47] On the other hand, nationalism can also be seen as integrative and inclusionary, as it provides identification for its members irrespective of gender or class, at least in its more liberal variant.[48] Both normative approaches have their merits but underline the same premise that nationalism is about creating groups that foster inclusion among their members and exclusions of others. Modern states rest on the premise of a community of citizens. They need not belong to the same nation, and in many countries, they do not. Yet, for the rule to be legitimate and accepted in the eyes of citizens, the rule—including ruler and rules—has to be self-determined. That "self" is often a nation, ranging from the notion of "constitutional patriotism"[49] where the quality of the rule generates loyalty with and of the community it rules to virulent and exclusionary nationalism that rules in the name of some against others.

As the British cultural theorist Stuart Hall (1932–2014) noted, "identity becomes a 'moveable feast': formed and transformed continuously in relation to the ways we are represented or addressed in the cultural systems which surround us. Within us are contradictory identities pulling in different directions, so that our identifications are continuously being shifted about."[50] As a result, nationalism is competing and interlocking with other forms of identity.

Whereas nationalism might be ubiquitous, it is also versatile. As this book has shown, nationalism cannot be relegated to radical far-right movements. Latent nationalism is an important force in most societies across a wide political and social spectrum. Rather than conceptualizing nationalism as single and homogenous force, it takes on a multitude of variations that are often competing within a nation. From exclusionary understanding that seeks to expel minorities to inclusionary conceptions of the nation, most societies experience conflicting nationalisms. Which form of nationalism prevails is neither predetermined nor is it fixed permanently. Certainly, the historical evolution of national movements, as discussed throughout this book, matters whether the nation were based the inclusion of immigrants or whether it established itself on the basis of descent. Numerous examples also highlight that the original self-understanding where the boundaries of nations lie changes and are renegotiated. The "other" from which nations distinguish themselves is never one and the same, they can range from minorities to neighbors, imperial and colonial powers to some global elite. The nature of the other contributes to the exclusionary and virulent nature of the nation. Nations aren't simply, but they became, are transformed, and are changed by those who claim to speak for them, by the choice of its members and others who shift boundaries.

Thus, nations are often defined and redefined by competing nationalism that all offer different interpretations as to how to define the share political community. For all its internal diversity, nationalism has also been an important mechanism of homogenization. Nationalism imagines the nation in a particular way and forces or encourages members of the community to adhere to this vision. This can often overshadow and dismiss much more complex individual dynamics of identity that involve multiple language, family histories, and traditions. Nationalism is thus rarely respectful of the complexity of tradition and the past, but often imposes a corset that has to fit all its members. The rigidity of this structure and the forceness of its imposition will vary depending on the type of nationalism. In the end, nationalism has become and remains a potent simplifier and structure for human relations that denies much of human complexity and organizes it along on single line of difference: the nation.

9

Further Reading and a Guide to Key Debates

This book has outlined the emergence and rise of nations and nationalism around the world, including multiple forms this phenomenon can take, from banal and everyday nationalism to violent ethnic conflict, from policies and attitudes toward migration to the recent rise of nationalism. While key authors are noted throughout the book, the chapters do not aim to provide a systematic discussion of important debates or theories of nationalism. This concluding section will serve as a guide for further reading and critical debates, identified in the previous chapters, point to the most important texts in the field for further reading as well as internet resources for primary sources and repositories of secondary literature. These texts are just the tip of the iceberg as there is a rich and extensive body of literature on nationalism in multiple disciplines and in interdisciplinary research, both from a theoretical and comparative perspective as well as numerous case studies.

Scholars have been dealing with the question of nations and nationalism since its origins in the late eighteenth and early nineteenth century. In the early 1800s, many of those who wrote about nations were "inventors" or as they perceived themselves discoverers of nations. Early scholarship focused on describing the characteristics of their own nations, codifying languages and histories.

These contributions count rather as primary sources than as advancing an academic understanding of nationalism. One of the first scholars to discuss nationalism with a greater critical detachment was Ernest Renan who in a lecture at the Sorbonne in 1882 on "What is a Nation?" offered important insight on the centrality of individuals and their identification with a nation.[1]

Key scholars from the fields of sociology and history that contributed to the early development of research on nationalism include Max Weber,[2] Karl Deutsch,[3] and Hans Kohn,[4] reflecting a central European perspective, shaped to an important degree by German and Jewish heritage. Later, Elie Kedourie, himself a British historian hailing from an Iraqi Jewish background, developed a more global perspective on nationalism and criticized nationalism from a conservative perspective.[5] In addition, historians wrote national histories, but these are mostly narrative and few studies offered a systematic, theoretical, and comparative perspective.[6]

A breakthrough in scholarship on nationalism occurred in the early 1980s, when three scholars, the British Historian Eric Hobsbawm, the British Sociologist Ernest Gellner, and the American political scientist Benedict Anderson, published three crucial texts on the origins and development of nationalism. All three argue that the rise of nationalism is closely linked to modernization and the consolidation of the modern state. Anderson placed greater emphasis on the tools that made a nation possible, such as the vernacular, secular language.[7] Hobsbawm, coming from a Marxist perspective initially focused on the class aspects of nationalism but made his most significant contribution by defining nationalism as an ideology and outlining the mechanisms through which nationalism is understood as inventing nations.[8] Gellner places greater weight on industrialization and the emergence of a modern state, placing him firmly in a European understanding of the nation.[9] Anderson, on the other hand, offered a more global perspective and reflected on how nationalism spread through colonial empires. All three were modernists who rejected the notion of premodern nations. Less prominent, yet still an important author of this wave of nationalism literature is the British scholar John Breuilly, who also contributed to the modernist approach and focused on the role of the state.[10] Besides developing a wide range of explanations of the rise of nationalism in the modern period, this scholarship also conceptually distinguished between nations and nationalism and explored their causal relationship.

Other scholars, including Anthony Smith, a British historian, and Walker Connor, an American political scientist, have focused on the premodern ethnic origins of nations and the importance of symbols and myths in their evolution. While they do not argue that nations existed before the modern era, they point to historical continuities and the ethnic identity that had preceded the rise of the modern nation.[11]

A key contribution was made by Michael Billig in his book *Banal Nationalism* in which he shifts the focus from the revolution and conflict-centered perspectives on nationalism to its banal and everyday manifestation.[12] With it, he opened a large field of research into everyday nationalism that highlights the practices that nation-states and societies promote to install a sense of national belonging. This is also the focus on Siniša Malešević's work, who argues that nationalism is not a phenomenon on the fringes or subject to sudden rises, but rather it is entrenched and embedded in the structure of modern states and societies.[13] This view is supplemented by a constructivist perspective, such as by American sociologist Rogers Brubaker, who draws attention to not just how nations and nationalism are the product of earlier processes and actors, but require reaffirmation and thus are continuously constructed and reconstructed.[14] Consequently, this approach has been less concerned with the emergence of nationalism and its historical evolution and more concerned with the mechanisms of how it remains salient once the nation-state comes into existence.

Another strand of nationalism literature argues that nationalism is closely interlinked with democracy and modern community and thus could be interpreted as a positive force that creates bonds of solidarity in modern society. This approach is represented by Liah Greenfield, an American historian,[15] and Yael Tamir, an Israeli scholar and former politician.[16] Greenfield emphasizes the logical link between nation and democracy, as nationalism creates a community of equals. Similarly, Swiss sociologist Andreas Wimmer has argued that nation-building, understood as the process of the creation of a political community around a nation, is a crucial feature of successful states.[17]

Other researchers have explored the interlinkages between mass violence and nationalism. The role of ethnic cleansing and violence has been a growing field, with key contributions by sociologist

Michael Mann on the links between democracy and ethnic violence.[18] Ethnic cleansing has been explored as a state policy by American historian Norman Naimark[19] and German historian Philip Ther.[20] Both demonstrate that mass expulsions, be they called ethnic cleansing or population exchanges, have been an integral part of democratization and nationalism, in particular when nations and states are incongruent and dominant nations seek to assert the dominance or see it threatened.

With the rise of a postcolonial perspective and a critique of Orientalism, scholars have also tackled the Eurocentric view of nationalism and the degree to which nationalism outside Europe is merely an imitation of European trends.[21] Edward Said himself critiqued the European understanding of the Orient and underlined the links to colonialism. At the same time, he both highlighted the positive function nationalism could have in the national liberation movements, including the Palestinian one, but also worried about how it could descend into chauvinism.[22]

Others, such as Homi K. Bhabha, an Indian English scholar, emphasize the uneven and unequal global power distribution and the role the nation plays in it, exploring mimicry and liminality.[23]

Besides a critical postcolonial perspective, feminist scholarship and gender studies have provided important input into the study of nationalism. Scholarship on nationalism has long ignored its gender dimension. This has changed in recent decades as gender studies have focused on nationalism and gender roles as well as sexuality increasingly becoming a subject of research. Nira Yuval-Davis, a British sociologist, has been pioneering this field in arguing that nationalism often presupposes and reinforces particular gender roles.[24] Other scholars have noted that feminist movements and nationalism are not inherently contradictory and often overlap, and there is feminist nationalism.[25] Recent scholarship on the interrelationship of sexuality, gender, and nation emphasize that the relationship is complicated as nationalist movements might appropriate feminism or rights of sexual minorities and incorporate divergent understandings of masculinity.[26] This research also incorporates sexual orientation and other sexual violence as themes where gender and nationalism studies intersect.

Ethnic conflict has spawned its own extensive body of literature, seeking to explain the causes and dynamics of violence over identity.

A comprehensive and classic study of ethnic conflict, as well as its causes, focusing on the development of ethnic conflict in Africa and Asia has been *Ethnic Groups in Conflict* by American political scientist and lawyer Donald Horowitz. In it, Horowitz seeks to explain why some groups rebel against the state and how polarization occurs in ethnically divided societies.[27] Subsequent literature on ethnic conflict has focused on different themes and explanations of ethnic violence.[28] Some have emphasized grievances, such as deprivation and relative deprivation,[29] others the use of emotions.[30] Rational choice approaches, on the other hand, have placed more emphasis on opportunities and structures that enable conflict,[31] such as economic factors and resources, the demographic makeup of a society, and the geography as contributing factors, advanced by authors such as the economists Paul Collier and Anke Hoeffler[32] and American political scientist David D. Laitin.[33]

In recent years there has seen a large number of books published on populism and the Far-right as well as on what has been called "new" nationalism.[34] Much of this literature focuses less on nationalism and more on nationalism or nativism as one of the contributing factors to populism or authoritarianism.[35] Others have sought to explore the politics of far-right parties in Europe and North America, such as Dutch political scientist Cas Mudde.[36]

A multitude of disciplines, historians, political scientists, sociologists, economist, anthropologists, and cultural studies have, among others, made significant contributions to the field of nationalism studies. Today, libraries can be filled with the subject, including case studies focusing on small communities, towns, and regions, states and nations, and continents. Often the dialogues are so diverse and narrow that there is hardly a single debate on nationalism but a multitude. This is both beneficial as it recognizes the complexity of the phenomena but also risks fragmenting the debate into ever specialized subsections that have little communication with each other.

In this book, I have often noted the "nationality" of the key scholars I refer to. This is both a signpost to the reader to highlight the context in which they are active but also as a little reminder, how the nation can become an important marker that probably most readers barely notice.

Further resources

There are several texts that effectively outline the key theoretical debates[37] and recent development in the field of nationalism studies.[38] In terms of overviews and essay collections, the *Oxford Handbook of the History of Nationalism*[39] stands out. There are no recent readers of nationalism, but a number of collections of both primary and secondary texts on nationalism, mostly published in the 1990s continue to remain relevant.[40]

Key online resources include "The State of Nationalism: An International Review," which offers state of the art articles written by key scholars in the field and bibliographical source.[41] The "Nationalism Project" has not been updated since 2010, but contains some useful resources, including key definitions and texts.[42] H-Nationalism[43] and Ethnopolitics[44] are important mailing lists, offering listings, book reviews, debates, and conference announcements.

The most important journals in the field include *Nations and Nationalism, Ethnopolitics, Nationalism and Ethnic Politics, Ethnic and Racial Studies, Nationalism and Ethnic Politics,* and *Nationalities Papers and Studies in Ethnicity & Nationalism.*

Notes

Chapter 1

1 Eric J. Hobsbawm, *Nations and Nationalism since 1780: Programme, Myth, Reality* (Cambridge: Cambridge University Press, 1990), 192.

2 Anthony D. Smith, *The Nation in History: Historiographical Debates about Ethnicity and Nationalism* (Hanover, NH: University Press of New England), 76.

3 Peter Alter, *Nationalism* (London: Hodder Education, 1994), 2.

4 Emmanuel Macron, "Discours du Président de la République, Emmanuel Macron à la cérémonie internationale du Centenaire de l'Armistice du 11 Novembre 1918 à l'Arc de Triomphe," *Élysée*, November 12, 2018, available online: https://www.elysee.fr/emmanuel-macron/2018/11/12/discours-du-president-de-la-republique-emmanuel-macron-a-la-ceremonie-internationale-du-centenaire-de-larmistice-du-11-novembre-1918-a-larc-de-triomphe (accessed August 16, 2019).

5 Andreas Wimmer, "Why Nationalism Works," *Foreign Affairs*, March/April 2019, 27.

6 James Boswell, *Life of Johnson*, abridged and edited, with an Introduction by Charles Grosvenor Osgood (Project Gutenberg EBook, 2006).

7 Yael Tamir, "In Defense of Nationalism," *Project Syndicate*, December 19, 2018, available online: https://www.project-syndicate.org/commentary/nationalism-often-beneficial-by-yael-yuli-tamir-2018-12?barrier=accesspaylog (accessed August 16, 2019).

8 See Umut Özkırımlı, *Theories of Nationalism: A Critical Introduction* (New York: St. Martin's Press, 2000).

9 Mark Mazower, *No Enchanted Palace: The End of Empire and the Ideological Origins of the United Nations* (Princeton, NJ: Princeton University Press, 2009).

10 J. V. Stalin, *Marxism and the National Question* (1913), available online: https://www.marxists.org/reference/archive/stalin/works/1913/03a.htm (accessed August 16, 2019).

11 Max Weber, *From Max Weber: Essays in Sociology* (Abingdon: Routledge, 2009), 172.

12 Karl Deutsch, *Nationalism and Social Communication* (Cambridge, MA: MIT Press, 1953), 101.

13 Ernest Gellner, *Nations and Nationalism* (Ithaca, NY: Cornell University Press, 1983), 6–7.

14 Andreas Wimmer, *Nation Building. Why Some Countries Come Together While Others Fall Apart* (Princeton, NJ: Princeton University Press, 2018).

15 Rogers Brubaker, *Nationalism Reframed: Nationhood and the National Question in the New Europe* (Cambridge: Cambridge University Press, 1996), 6–7.

16 Michael Billig, *Banal Nationalism* (London: Sage, 1994).

17 Rogers Brubaker, *Ethnicity without Groups* (Cambridge, MA: Harvard University Press, 2004).

18 Kohn's distinction has been criticized from a number of perspectives, see, for example, Stephen Shulman, "Challenging the Civic/Ethnic and West/East Dichotomies in the Study of Nationalism," *Comparative Political Studies* 35, no. 5 (2002): 554–585; Rogers Brubaker, "The Manichean Myth: Rethinking the Distinction between 'Civic' and 'Ethnic' Nationalism," in *Nation and National Identity*, ed. Hanspeter Kriesi, Klaus Armington, Hannes Siegrist, and Andreas Wimmer (Chur: Verlag Rüegger, 1999), 55–71.

19 Rogers Brubaker, *Citizenship and Nationhood in France and Germany* (Cambridge, MA: Harvard University Press, 1992).

20 Cas Mudde, "Introduction to the Populist Radical Right," in *The Populist Radical Right. A Reader*, ed. Cas Mudde (London: Routledge, 2017), 4.

21 Fredrik Barth, "Introduction," in *Ethnic Groups and Boundaries. The Social Organization of Cultural Difference*, ed. Fredrik Barth (Oslo: Universitetsforlaget, 1968), 15.

22 Andreas Wimmer and Nina Glick Schiller, "Methodological Nationalism and Beyond: Nation–State Building, Migration and the Social Sciences," *Global Networks* 2, no. 4 (2002): 301–334.

Chapter 2

1 Ernest Renan, "Qu'est-ce qu'une nation?" (Paris: Presses-Pocket, 1992). Ernest Renan, "What is a Nation?," trans. Ethan Rundell, available online: http://ucparis.fr/files/9313/6549/9943/What_is_a_Nation.pdf (accessed August 16, 2019).

2 Hellenic Republic Ministry of Foreign Affairs, https://www.mfa.gr/en/fyrom-name-issue/ (accessed January 1, 2019), removed following the ratification of the name agreement between Greece and North Macedonia.

3 Ministry of Foreign Affairs of the Republic of Armenia, "Nagorno-Karabakh Issue," available online: https://www.mfa.am/en/nagorno-karabakh-issue (accessed January 1, 2019).

4 Republic of Azerbaijan Ministry of Foreign Affairs, "Ancient History: Etymology, Territory and Borders," available online: http://www.mfa.gov.az/en/content/801 (accessed January 1, 2019).

5 Eric Hobsbawm and Terence Ranger, "Introduction," in *The Invention of Tradition*, ed. Eric Hobsbawm and Terence Ranger (Cambridge: Cambridge University Press, 1983).

6 Derek Hastings, *Nationalism in Modern Europe* (London: Bloomsbury, 2018), 59.

7 Renan, "What is a Nation?."

8 Anthony D. Smith, *Ethno-symbolism and Nationalism: A Cultural Approach* (London: Routledge, 2009).

9 Adrian Hastings, *The Construction of Nationhood: Ethnicity, Religion and Nationalism* (Cambridge: Cambridge University Press, 1997), 5.

10 Charles Tilly, *The Formation of Nation States in Western Europe* (Princeton, NJ: Princeton University Press, 1975), 42.

11 Andreas Wimmer, *Nation Building. Why Some Countries Come Together While Others Fall Apart* (Princeton, NJ: Princeton University Press, 2018).

12 *Source:* "Emmanuel-Joseph Sieyès, *What is the Third Estate?* (1789)," available online: https://pages.uoregon.edu/dluebke/301ModernEurope/Sieyes3dEstate.pdf (accessed June 24, 2019).

13 Benedict Anderson, *Imagined Communities, Reflections on the Origin and Spread of Nationalism*, Rev. and Ext. edn. (London: Verso, 1991).

14 Nicholas Tackett, *The Origins of the Chinese Nation: Song China and the Forging of an East Asian World Order* (Cambridge: Cambridge University Press, 2017).

Chapter 3

1 *Source:* Johann Gottlieb Fichte, "Addresses to the German Nation/Thirteenth Address," trans. Reginald Foy Jones, available online: https://en.wikisource.org/wiki/Addresses_to_the_German_Nation/Thirteenth_Address (accessed June 24, 2019).

2 Derek Hastings, *Nationalism in Modern Europe* (London: Bloomsbury, 2018), 28–49.

3 Ernest Gellner, *Nations and Nationalism* (Ithaca, NY: Cornell University Press, 1983), 55.

4 Jürgen Osterhammel, *The Transformation of the World: A Global History of the Nineteenth Century* (Princeton, NJ: Princeton University Press, 2015).

5 John Stuart Mill, *Considerations on Representative Government*, available online: https://www.gutenberg.org/files/5669/5669-h/5669-h.htm (accessed August 17, 2019).

6 Charles L. Killinger, *The History of Italy* (Westport, CT: Greenwood Press, 2002), 1.

7 Graham Robb, *The Discovery of France: A Historical Geography from the Revolution to the First World War* (New York: Norton, 2007), 10–15.

8 David A. Bell, *The Cult of the Nation in France: inventing nationalism, 1680–1800* (Cambridge, MA: Harvard University Press, 2001), 208.

9 Eugene Weber, *Peasants into Frenchmen. The Modernization of Rural France* (Stanford, CA: Stanford University Press, 1976), 485.

10 Andreas Wimmer, *Nation Building: Why Some Countries Come Together While Others Fall Apart* (Princeton, NJ: Princeton University Press, 2018), 45–68.

11 Tara Zahra, "Imagined Noncommunities: National Indifference as a Category of Analysis," *Slavic Review* 69, no. 1 (2010): 98.

12 Ernest Renan, *Qu'est-ce qu'une nation?* (Paris, Presses-Pocket, 1992). Ernest Renan, "What is a Nation?," trans. Ethan Rundell, available online: http://ucparis.fr/files/9313/6549/9943/What_is_a_Nation.pdf (accessed August 16, 2019).

13 Miroslav Hroch, *Social Preconditions of National Revival in Europe* (Cambridge: Cambridge University Press, 1985).

14 Voltaire, "Essai sur les mœurs et l'esprit des nations," in *Oeuvres completes de Voltaire*, edited by Louis Moland, vol. 11 (Paris: Garnier, 1877–1885), 542, available online: https://fr.wikisource.org/wiki/Essai_sur_les_m%C5%93urs (accessed August 17, 2019).

15 Luciano Monzali, *The Italians of Dalmatia: From Italian Unification to World War* (Toronto: University of Toronto Press, 2009).

16 Otto Bauer, *The Question of Nationalities and Social Democracy* (Minneapolis: University of Minnesota Press, 2000).

17 Andreas Kappeler, *The Russian Empire: A Multi-ethnic History* (Abingdon: Routledge, 2001).

18 Nicholas Mansergh, *The Irish Question, 1840–1921* (London: Allen & Unwin, 1965).

19 Robert Lansing, *The Peace Negotiations. A Personal Narrative* (Boston, MA: Houghton Mifflin Company, 1921), 97.

20 Robert O. Paxton, *The Anatomy of Fascism* (New York: Vintage, 2004).

21 Ion S. Munro, *Through Fascism to World Power. A History of the Revolution in Italy* (London: Alexander Maclehose, 1933), 303–304, 307–308.

22 Joseph Goebbels, "Nun, Volk steh auf, und Sturm brich los! Rede im Berliner Sportpalast," in *Der steile Aufstieg* (Munich: Zentralverlag der NSDAP, 1944), 167–204, English translation available online: https://research.calvin.edu/german-propaganda-archive/goeb36.htm (accessed August 17, 2019).

23 Paul Hanebrink, *A Specter Haunting Europe: The Myth of Judeo-Bolshevism* (Cambridge, MA: Belknap Press, 2018).

24 Vladimir Ilyich Lenin, "The Right of Nations to Self-Determination," in Vladimir Ilyich Lenin, *Collected Works*, vol. 20 (Moscow: Progress Publishers, 1972), 393–454, available online: https://www.marxists.org/archive/lenin/works/1914/self-det/ch05.htm (accessed August 17, 2019).

25 In 2010 less than 1 percent of the 176,558 inhabitants were Jewish.

Chapter 4

1 Partha Chatterjee, *The Nation and its Fragments. Colonial and Postcolonial Histories* (Princeton, NJ: Princeton University Press, 1993), 5.

2 Ibid., 6.

3 Anne McClintock, *Imperial Leather. Race, Gender and Sexuality in the Colonial Contest* (London: Routledge, 1995), 5.

4 Benedict Anderson, *Imagined Communities Reflections on the Origin and Spread of Nationalism*, 2nd edn. (London: Verso, 1991), 4.

5 Michael Hechter, *Internal Colonialism: Celtic Fringe in British National Development, 1536–1966* (Berkeley: University of California Press, 1975). In France, Corsica had a similar role as a Celtic fringe, but it was also a prime source of colonial settlers and administrators, making it a colonized and colonizing region. Robert Aldrich, "Colonialism and Nation-Building in Modern France," in *Nationalizing Empires*, eds. Stefan Berger and Alexei Miller (Budapest: CEU Press, 2015), 135–194.

6 *All African People's Conference*, Accra, 1958, available online: http://credo.library.umass.edu/view/pageturn/mums312-b148-i017/#page/1/mode/1up (accessed August 17, 2019).

7 *Source:* United Nations, "The United Nations and Decolonization," available online: https://www.un.org/en/decolonization/declaration.shtml (accessed June 24, 2019).

8 Immanuel Wallerstein, *Africa: The Politics of Independence and Unity* (Lincoln: University of Nebraska Press, 2005), 88.

9 M.S. Golwalkar, *We or Our Nationhood Defined* (Nagpur: Bharat Publications, 1939), 94.

10 Mohammad Ali Jinnah, *Address by Quaid-i-Azam Mohammad Ali Jinnah at Lahore Session of Muslim League, March, 1940* (Islamabad: Directorate of Films and Publishing, Ministry of Information and Broadcasting, Government of Pakistan, 1983), 5–23, available online: http://www.columbia.edu/itc/mealac/pritchett/00islamlinks/txt_jinnah_lahore_1940.html (accessed August 17, 2019).

11 *Source:* Jawaharlal Nehru, "A Tryst with Destiny," *The Guardian*, May 1, 2007, available online: https://www.theguardian.com/theguardian/2007/may/01/greatspeeches (accessed June 24, 2019).

12 Zhaoguang Ge, *What is China? Territory, Ethnicity, Culture, and History* (Cambridge, MA: The Belknap Press of Harvard University Press, 2018).

13 Chalmers A. Johnson, *Peasant Nationalism and Communist Power: The Emergence of Revolutionary China 1937–1945* (Stanford, CA: Stanford University Press, 1962), 5.

14 *Source:* World Intellectual Property Agency, "The Constitution Law of People's Republic of China," available online: https://www.wipo.int/edocs/lexdocs/laws/en/cn/cn147en.pdf (accessed June 24, 2019).

15 Kevin M. Doak, *A History of Nationalism in Modern Japan* (Leiden: Brill, 2007), 83.

16 Ibid., 11–15.

17 Nigel Eltringham, "'Invaders who have stolen the country': The Hamitic Hypothesis, Race and the Rwandan Genocide," *Social Identities* 12, no. 4 (2006): 425–446.

18 Peter Uvin, "Ethnicity and Power in Burundi and Rwanda: Different Paths to Mass Violence," *Comparative Politics* 31, no. 3 (1999): 253–271.

19 William D. Davies and Stanley Dubinsky, *Language Conflict and Language Rights. Ethnolinguistic Perspectives on Human Conflict* (Cambridge: Cambridge University Press, 2018), 105–116.

20 Eduard Miguel, "Tribe or Nation? Nation Building and Public Goods in Kenya versus Tanzania," *World Politics* 56, no. 3 (2004): 327–362.

21 Matthijs Bogaards, Matthias Basedau, and Christof Hartmann, "Ethnic Party Bans in Africa: An Introduction," *Democratization* 17, no. 4 (2010): 599–617.

22 Jan Smuts, "The White Man's Task," *South African History Online*, May 22, 1917, available online: https://www.sahistory.org.za/archive/white-man's-task-jan-smuts-22-may-1917 (accessed August 17, 2019).

23 Eugene Rogan, *The Arabs. A History* (New York: Basic Books, 2009), 326–331, 393–395.

24 Michel Aflaq, "Our Task Is to Struggle to Safeguard the Aims of the Arabs," *Al-Baath*, December 29, 1949, available online: http://albaath.online.fr/English/Aflaq-01-arab_unity.htm (accessed August 17, 2019).

25 Fouad Ajami, "The End of Pan-Arabism," *Foreign Affairs* 57, no. 18 (1978/9).

26 Neil MacFarquhar, "Tahseen Bashir, Urbane Egyptian Diplomat, Dies at 77," *The New York Times*, June 14, 2002.

27 See Andreas Wimmer, *Nation Building: Why Some Countries Come Together While Others Fall Apart* (Princeton, NJ: Princeton University Press, 2018).

Chapter 5

1 Michael Billig, *Banal Nationalism* (London: Sage, 1995).

2 Sammy Smooha, "Types of Democracy and Modes of Conflict Management in Ethnically Divided Societies," *Nations and Nationalism* 8, no. 4 (2002): 423–431.

3 Mitchell Bard, "Understanding Israel's Nation State Law," in *Israel's Basic Laws: Israel - The Nation State of the Jewish People* (Chevy Chase, MD: Jewish Virtual Library, 2018), available online: https://www.jewishvirtuallibrary.org/understanding-israel-s-nation-state-law (accessed August 17, 2019).

4 United Nations, *Principles and Recommendations for Population and Housing Censuses*, Statistical Papers Series M, no. 67/Rev. 2 (New

York: Department of Economic and Social Affairs, Statistics Division, 2008), 23.

5 Benedict Anderson, *Imagined Communities: Reflections on the Origin and Spread of Nationalism*, 2nd edn. (London: Verso, 1991), 164–166.

6 See David I. Kertzer and Dominique Arel (eds.), *Census and Identity. The Politics of Race, Ethnicity, and Language in National Censuses* (Cambridge: Cambridge University Press, 2002).

7 *Source:* French Ministry for Europe and Foreign Affairs, "The Marseillaise," available online: https://www.diplomatie.gouv.fr/en/coming-to-france/france-facts/symbols-of-the-republic/article/the-marseillaise (accessed June 24, 2019).

8 *Source:* nationalanthems.info, "Italy," available online: http://www.nationalanthems.info/it.htm (accessed June 24, 2019).

9 Timothy Aeppel, "Americans want U.S. Goods, But Not Willing to Pay More: Reuters/Ipsos Poll," *Reuters*, July 18, 2017, available online: https://www.reuters.com/article/us-usa-buyamerican-poll-idUSKBN1A3210 (accessed August 17, 2019).

10 See Zala Volcic and Mark Andrejevic (eds.), *Commercial Nationalism: Selling the Nation and Nationalizing the Sell* (New York: Palgrave Macmillan, 2016).

11 Benedict Anderson, *Imagined Communities: Reflections on the Origin and Spread of Nationalism*, 2nd edn. (London: Verso, 1991).

12 Graham Robb, *The Discovery of France: A Historical Geography from the Revolution to the First World War* (New York: Norton, 2007).

13 Stefan Detchev, "Българска, но не точно шопска. За един от кулинарните символи" [Bulgarian, But Not Exactly Shopska: About One of the Culinary Symbols], Български фолклор 36, no. 1 (2010): 125–140.

14 Jean Comaroff and John L. Comaroff, *Ethnicity, Inc.* (Chicago: University of Chicago Press, 2009); Ulrich Ermann and Klaus-Jürgen Hermaniek (eds.), *Branding the Nation, the Place, the Product* (Abingdon: Routledge, 2018).

15 Sara R. Farris, *In the Name of Women's Rights. The Rise of Femonationalism* (Durham, NC: Duke University Press, 2017).

16 Koen Slootmaeckers, "Nationalism as Competing Masculinities: Homophobia as a Technology of Othering for Hetero- and Homonationalism," *Theory and Society* 48, no. 2 (2019): 239–265, https://doi.org/10.1007/s11186-019-09346-4.

17 George L. Mosse, *Nationalism and Sexuality. Middle-Class Morality and Sexual Norms in Modern Europe* (Madison: University of Wisconsin Press, 1985).

18 J. Christopher Soper and Joel S. Fetzer, *Religion and Nationalism in a Global Perspective* (Cambridge: Cambridge University Press, 2018), 50.

19 David Goldberg, *Are We all Post-racial Yet?* (London: Polity, 2015); David Hollinger, *Postethnic America* (New York: Basic Books, 1995).

20 Astead W. Herndon, "Elizabeth Warren Stands by DNA Test. But Around Her, Worries Abound," *The New York Times*, December 6, 2018, available online: https://www.nytimes.com/192018/12/06/us/politics/elizabeth-warren-dna-test-2020.html (accessed August 17, 2019).

21 International Pasta Organisation, "History of Pasta," available online: http://www.internationalpasta.org/index.aspx?id=6 (accessed August 17, 2019).

22 Edward Said, *Orientalism* (New York: Pantheon, 1978).

23 Daphne Psaledakis and Isabel Lohman, "Belgium's Africa Museum Reopens to Confront its Colonial Demons," *Reuters*, December 8, 2018, available online: https://www.reuters.com/article/us-belgium-museum-africa-idUSKBN1O7003 (accessed August 17, 2019).

Chapter 6

1 Eldar Saraljić, "Becoming Parents to Ourselves," *The New York Times*, June 6, 2019, available online: https://www.nytimes.com/2019/06/06/opinion/fathers-philosophy.html (accessed August 17, 2019).

2 Max Bergholz, *Violence as a Generative Force Identity, Nationalism, and Memory in a Balkan Community* (Ithaca, NY: Cornell University Press, 2016).

3 Gabriele D'Annuzio, "Viennese! Get to Know the Italians! – Leaflet Dropped by an Aeroplane," [leaflet] 1918, available online: https://www.bl.uk/collection-items/viennese-get–to-know-italians-leaflet (accessed August 17, 2019).

4 Donald Horowitz, *The Deadly Ethnic Riot* (Berkeley: University of California Press, 2001).

5 Rogers Brubaker, *Ethnicity Without Groups* (Cambridge, MA: Harvard University Press, 2006).

6 Stuart J. Kaufman. *Modern Hatreds. The Symbolic Politics of Ethnic War* (Ithaca, NY: Cornell University Press, 2001).

7 Nenad Stojanović, "When Non-Nationalist Voters Support Ethno-Nationalist Parties: The 1990 Elections in Bosnia and Herzegovina as a Prisoner's Dilemma Game," *Southeast European and Black Sea Studies* 14, no. 4 (2014): 607–606.

8 Saul Newmann, "Does Modernization Breed Ethnic Political Conflict?," *World Politics* 43, no. 3 (1991): 451–478.

9 Jack Snyder, *From Voting to Violence: Democratization and Nationalist Conflict* (New York: W. W. Norton, 2000).

10 See James D. Fearon and David Laitin, "Ethnicity, Insurgency, and Civil War," *American Political Science Review* 97, no. 1 (February 2003): 75–90; Zeynep Taydas, Jason Enia, and Patrick James, "Why Do Civil Wars Occur? Another Look at the Theoretical Dichotomy of Opportunity Versus Grievance," *Review of International Studies* 37, no. 5 (2011): 2627–2650.

11 Amy Chua, *World on Fire* (New York: Doubleday, 2002).

12 Protocol of the Learned Elders of Zion (Reedy, WV: Liberty Bell Publications, n.d.), 24.

13 Roger Petersen, *Understanding Ethnic Violence: Fear, Hatred, and Resentment in Twentieth-Century Eastern Europe* (Cambridge: Cambridge University Press, 2002).

14 Anthony Oberschall, *Conflict and Peace Building in Divided Societies Responses to Ethnic Violence* (London: Routledge, 2007).

15 Philip Ther, *The Dark Side of Nation States: Ethnic Cleansing in Modern Europe* (New York: Berghahn Press, 2014); Michael Mann, *The Dark Side of Democracy. Explaining Ethnic Cleansing* (Cambridge: Cambridge University Press, 2005).

16 Art. II, Convention on the Prevention and Punishment of the Crime of Genocide (1948).

17 Caroline A. Hartzell and Matthew Hoddie, *Crafting Peace: Power-Sharing Institutions and the Negotiated Settlement of Civil Wars* (University Park: Pennsylvania State University Press, 2007).

18 *Source*: Genocide Archive of Rwanda, "A Testimony of Gilbert Masengo Rutayisire," available online: http://genocidearchiverwanda.org.rw/index.php?title=Kmc00006-sub1-engglifos&gsearch= (accessed June 26, 2019).

19 *Source:* Office of the High Representative, "Constitutions," available online: http://www.ohr.int/?page_id=68220 (accessed June 26, 2019).

20 Monty G. Marshall, *Major Episodes of Political Violence and Conflict Regions, 1946–2015* (Vienna, VA: Centre for Systemic Peace, 2017), available online: http://www.systemicpeace.org/inscr/MEPVcodebook2016.pdf (accessed August 17, 2019).

Chapter 7

1 Cas Mudde, *Populist Radical Right Parties in Europe* (Cambridge: Cambridge University Press, 2007), 19.

2 "The New Orleans Affair," *The New York Times*, March 16, 1891, 4, available online: https://timesmachine.nytimes.com/timesmachine/1891/03/16/103299119.pdf (accessed August 17, 2019).

3 *Source:* Zabdiel Sidney Sampson, *The Immigration Problem* (New York: Appleton, 1892), available online: https://catalog.hathitrust.org/Record/012510639 (accessed June 26, 2019).

4 Lute Pease cartoon, *Newark News* (Newark, NJ), 1921, cited in Wayne Moquin (ed.), *Makers of America*, vol. 8 (Encyclopedia Britannica, 1971), 18, available online: http://digitalexhibits.libraries.wsu.edu/items/show/7984 (accessed August 20, 2019).

5 Michael Goebel, "Immigration and National Identity in Latin America, 1870–1930," *Oxford Research Encyclopedia of Latin American History* (May 2016), doi: 10.1093/acrefore/9780199366439.013.288.

6 *Source:* Australian Government, Federal Register of Legislation, "Immigration Restriction Act," 1901, available online: https://www.legislation.gov.au/Details/C1901A00017 (accessed June 26, 2019).

7 Arthur Calwell, *Commonwealth Parliamentary Debates, House of Representatives*, August 2, 1945, cited in Ingeborg van Teeseling, "Post-War Migration," Australia Explained, September 10, 2016, available online: https://australia-explained.com.au/history/post-war-migration (accessed August 17, 2019).

8 "Enoch Powell's 'Rivers of Blood' speech," *Daily Telegraph*, November 6, 2007, available online: https://www.telegraph.co.uk/comment/3643823/Enoch-Powells-Rivers-of-Blood-speech.html (accessed August 17, 2019).

9 Rita Chin, *The Crisis of Multiculturalism in Europe. A History* (Princeton, NJ: Princeton University Press, 2017), 124–125.

10 Ibid., 141.

11 "Bush: 'You Are Either With Us, Or With the Terrorists'," *Voice of America*, September 21, 2001, available online: https://www.voanews.com/a/a-13-a-2001-09-21-14-bush-66411197/549664.html (accessed August 17, 2019).

12 Sarah El Deeb, "In Lebanon, Syrian Refugees Face New Pressure to Go Home," *Associated Press*, June 20, 2019.

13 Pierre Elliott Trudeau, "Multiculturalism," House of Commons, October 8, 1971, available online: http://www.canadahistory. com/sections/documents/Primeministers/trudeau/docs-onmulticulturalism.htm (accessed August 17, 2019).

14 Canadian Radio-television and Telecommunications Commission, "Offering Cultural Diversity on TV and Radio," Government of Canada, 2017, available online: https://crtc.gc.ca/eng/info_sht/b308. htm (accessed August 17, 2019).

15 Will Kymlicka, *Multicultural Citizenship: A Liberal Theory of Minority Rights* (Oxford: Oxford University Press, 1995).

16 Angela Merkel, "Speech at CDU Party Congress," Dresden, November 27, 2016, available online: https://www.kas.de/c/ document_library/get_file?uuid=cf70cbbd-5ff1-63c9-1f80-737ac533963e&groupId=252038 (accessed August 17, 2019).

17 David Cameron, "PM's speech at Munich Security Conference," November 5, 2011, available online: https://www.gov.uk/ government/speeches/pms-speech-at-munich-security-conference (accessed August 17, 2019).

18 AFP, "North African Name 'still hurts job chances' in France," *The Local*, December 13, 2016, available online: https://www.thelocal. fr/20161213/north-african-name-still-hurts-job-chances-in-france (accessed August 17, 2019); Vikram Dodd, "Ethnic Minority Women Face Jobs Crisis," *The Guardian*, December 7, 2012, available online: https://www.theguardian.com/world/2012/dec/07/ethnic-minority-women-jobs-crisis?INTCMP= (accessed August 17, 2019).

19 Michael Palairet, "The 'New' Immigration and the Newest: Slavic Migrations from the Balkans to America and Industrial Europe since the Late Nineteenth Century," in T.C. Smout (ed.), *The Search for Wealth and Stability. Essays in Economic and Social History Presented to M.W. Flinn* (London: Macmillan Press, 1979), 49.

20 Çelik Çetin, "'Having a German Passport Will Not Make Me German': Reactive Ethnicity and Oppositional Identity Among Disadvantaged Male Turkish Second-Generation Youth in Germany," *Ethnic and Racial Studies* 38, no. 9 (2015): 1646–1662.

21 Viktor Orbán, "Prime Minister Viktor Orbán's Speech at the 29th Bálványos Summer Open University and Student Camp," July 29, 2018, available online: http://www.kormany.hu/en/the-prime-minister/the-prime-minister-s-speeches/prime-minister-viktor-orban-s-speech-at-the-29th-balvanyos-summer-open-university-and-student-camp (accessed August 17, 2019).

22 Renaud Camus, *Le Grand Remplacement* (Paris: David Reinharc, 2011).

Chapter 8

1 Karl Polanyi, *The Present Age of Transformation: Five Lectures by Karl Polanyi Bennington College, 1940*, March 1, 2017, available online: http://www.primeeconomics.org/publications/the-present-age-of-transformation.

2 David Held, Anthony McGrew, David Goldblatt, and Jonathan Perraton, *Global Transformations: Politics, Economics and Culture* (Cambridge: Polity Press 1999), 14.

3 Benjamin Barber, *Jihad vs. McWorld* (New York: Ballentine Books, 2001).

4 Arjun Appadurai, *Modernity at Large. Cultural Dimensions of Globalization* (Minneapolis: University of Minneapolis Press, 1996).

5 "Whither Nationalism?," *The Economist*, December 19, 2017, available online: https://www.economist.com/christmas-specials/2017/12/19/whither-nationalism (accessed August 18, 2019); "League of Nationalists," *The Economist*, November 19, 2016, available online: https://www.economist.com/international/2016/11/19/league-of-nationalists (accessed August 18, 2019); Ian Bremmer, "The Wave to Come," *Time*, May 11, 2017, available online: http://time.com/4775441/the-wave-to-come/ (accessed August 17, 2019).

6 Quint Forgey, "Trump: 'I'm a Nationalist'," *Politico*, October 20, 2018, available online: https://www.politico.com/story/2018/10/22/trump-nationalist-926745 (accessed August 17, 2019).

7 *Source*: White House, "Remarks by President Trump to the 73rd Session of the United Nations General Assembly | New York, NY," September 25, 2018, available online: https://www.whitehouse.gov/briefingsstatements/remarks-president-trump-73rd-session-united-nations-general-assembly-new-york-ny/(accessed June 24, 2019).

8 Steven Levitsky and Lucan A. Way, *Competitive Authoritarianism. Hybrid Regimes after the Cold War* (Cambridge: Cambridge University Press, 2010).

9 Jack Snyder and Karen Ballentine, "Nationalism and the Marketplace of Ideas," *International Security* 21, no. 2 (1996): 5–40; Marc Helbing, "Nationalism and Democracy: Competing or Complementary Logics?," *Living Reviews in Democracy* (2009), available online: https://ethz.ch/content/dam/ethz/special-interest/gess/cis/cis-dam/CIS_DAM_2015/WorkingPapers/Living_Reviews_Democracy/Helbling_updated.pdf (accessed August 18, 2019).

10 W. Eckhardt, "Authoritarianism, " *Political Psychology* 12, no. 1 (1991): 97–124; Bojan Todosijević, "Relationships between Authoritarianism and Nationalist Attitudes," in *Authoritarianism and Prejudice. Central European Perspectives*, ed. Zsolt Enyedi and F. Erös (Budapest: Osiris, 1998), 54–88.

11 Cas Mudde, and Cristóbal Rovira Kaltwasser, *Populism. A Very Short Introduction* (Oxford: Oxford University Press, 2017), 6.

12 Chantal Mouffe, *For a Left Populism* (London: Verso, 2018).

13 Erin K. Jenne, "Is Nationalism or Ethnopopulism on the Rise Today?," *Ethnopolitics* 17, no. 5 (2018): 546–552.

14 In fact, Soros has been a common target by nationalist parties in Central and Southeastern Europe since the 1990s. Kenneth P. Vogel, Scott Shane, and Patrick Kingsley, "How Vilification of George Soros Moved From the Fringes to the Mainstream," *The New York Times*, October 31, 2018, available online: https://www.nytimes.com/2018/10/31/us/politics/george-soros-bombs-trump.html (accessed August 17, 2019).

15 "Theresa May's keynote speech at Tory conference in full," *The Independent*, October 5, 2016, available online: https://www.independent.co.uk/news/uk/politics/theresa-may-speech-tory-conference-2016-in-full-transcript-a7346171.html (accessed August 17, 2019).

16 Jan-Werner Müller, "False Flags," *Foreign Affairs*, March/April 2019, 35.

17 Paula Chakravartty and Srirupa Roy, "Mr. Modi Goes to Delhi: Mediated Populism and the 2014 Indian Elections," *Television & New Media* 16, no. 4 (2015): 311–322.

18 Ashutosh Varshney. "India's Watershed Vote: Hindu Nationalism in Power?," *Journal of Democracy* 25, no. 4 (2014): 34–45.

19 Bruce Stokes, "The Modi Bounce," *Pew Research Centre*, September 17, 2015, available online: http://www.pewglobal.org/2015/09/17/the-modi-bounce/ (accessed August 17, 2019).

20 Chandrima Chakraborty, "Narendra Modi's Victory Speech Delivers Visions of a Hindu Nationalist Ascetic," *The Conversation*, May 26,2019, available online: https://theconversation.com/narendra-modis-victory-speech-delivers-visions-of-a-hindu-nationalist-ascetic-117802 (accessed August 17, 2019).

21 For a more detailed discussion of data, see Florian Bieber, "Is Nationalism on the Rise? Assessing Global Trends," *Ethnopolitics* 17, no. 5 (2018): 519–540.

22 Filip Milačić and Ivan Vuković, "The Rise of the Politics of National Identity: New Evidence from Western Europe," *Ethnopolitics* 17, no. 5 (2018): 443–460.

23 Gregor Aisch, Adam Pearce, and Bryant Rousseau, "How Far Is Europe Swinging to the Right?" *The New York Times*, March 20, 2017, available online: https://www.nytimes.com/interactive/2016/05/22/world/europe/europe-right-wing-austria-hungary.html?_r=0 (accessed August 17, 2019).

24 Daniel Cox, Rachel Lienesch, and Robert P. Jones, "Beyond Economics: Fears of Cultural Displacement Pushed the White Working Class to Trump," *PRRI/The Atlantic Report*, May 9, 2017, available online: https://www.prri.org/research/white-working-class-attitudes-economy-trade-immigration-election-donald-trump/ (accessed August 17, 2019). Studies of the US election results suggest that racist attitudes have a greater explanatory value than authoritarianism, see Thomas Wood, "Racism Motivated Trump Voters More Than Authoritarianism," *Monkey Cage, Washington Post Online*, Apeil 17, 2017, available online: https://www.washingtonpost.com/news/monkey-cage/wp/2017/04/17/racism-motivated-trump-voters-more-than-authoritarianism-or-income-inequality/?utm_term=.59c256b5cd (accessed August 17, 2019).

25 Pippa Norris and Ronald Inglehart, *Cultural Backlash. Trump, Brexit, and Authoritarian Populism* (Cambridge: Cambridge University Press, 2019).

26 Cox, Lienesch, and Jones, "Beyond Economics."

27 Daniel Stockemer and Abdelkarim Amengay, "The Voters of the FN under Jean-Marie Le Pen and Marine Le Pen: Continuity or Change?," *French Politics* 13 (2015): 370–390.

28 Jungmin Song, "Who Supports Radical Right Parties and Where Do Radical Right Parties Succeed: Multi-level Analysis of Radical Right Parties' Success," *2016 WPSA Annual Meeting*, available online: https://wpsa.research.pdx.edu/papers/docs/Jungmin%20Song%20-%20Who%20Supports%20Radical%20Right%20Parties%20 2016%20WPSA.pdf (accessed August 17, 2019).

29 Johannes Hilije, "Die Rückkehr zu den politisch Verlassenen. Studie in rechtspopulistischen Hochburgen in Deutschland und Frankreich," *Das Progressive Zentrum*, Working Paper, 2018, available online: https://www.progressives-zentrum.org/wp-content/uploads/2018/03/Ru%CC%88ckkehr-zu-den-politisch-Verlassenen_500-Gespra%CC%88che-in-rechtspopulistischen-Hochburgen-in-Deutschland-und-Frankreich_Studie-von-Johannes-Hillje_Das-Progressive-Zentrum.pdf (accessed August 20, 2019).

30 Oliver Decker, Johannes Kiess, and Elmar Brähler, "Die enthemmte Mitte Autoritäre und rechtsextreme Einstellung in Deutschland," *Die Leipziger „Mitte"-Studien*, 2016, available online: https://www.boell.de/de/2016/06/15/die-enthemmte-mitte-studie-leipzigthislinkworks (accessed August 20, 2019).

31 Danny Michelsen, Marika Przybilla-Voß, Michael Lühmann, Martin Grund, Hannes Keune, and Florian Finkbeiner, "Rechtsextremismus und Fremdenfeindlichkeit in Ostdeutschland Ursachen – Hintergründe – regionale Kontextfaktoren," *Göttinger Institut für Demokratieforschung*, 2017.

32 Davide Cantoni, Felix Hagemeister and Mark Westcott, "Persistence and Activation of Right-Wing Political Ideology," *Rationality and Competition*, Discussion Paper No. 143, February 27, 2019, available online: https://epub.ub.uni-muenchen.de/60795/1/Cantoni_ Hagemeister_Persistence_and_Activation_of_Right-Wing_Political_ Ideology.pdf (accessed August 17, 2019).

33 Bastian Vollmer and Serhat Karakayali, "The Volatility of the Discourse on Refugees in Germany," *Journal of Immigrant & Refugee Studies* 16, no. 1–2 (2017): 118–139.

34 Elisabeth Noelle-Neumann and Thomas Petersen, "The Spiral of Silence and the Social Nature of Man," in Lynda Lee Kaid (ed.), *Handbook of Political Communication* (Mahwah, NJ: Erlbaum, 2004), 339–356.

35 Leonardo Bursztyn, Georgy Egorov, and Stefano Fiorin, "From Extreme to Mainstream: How Social Norms Unravel," *NBER Working Paper* No. 23415, May 2017, available online: http://www. nber.org/papers/w23415 (accessed August 17, 2019).

36 *Source*: Marine Le Pen, "Assises présidentielles de Lyon: Discours de Marine Le Pen," February 5, 2017, available online: https:// rassemblementnational.fr/videos/assises-presidentielles-de-lyon-discours-demarine-le-pen/ (accessed June 26, 2019); and translation from Nkenganyi N'Mandela Atabong, "Immigration and the Revival of Nationalist Sentiments in France: A Nationalistic Rhetoric of Marine Le Pen," MA thesis, University of Jyväskylä, 2018, available online: https://jyx.jyu.fi/bitstream/handle/123456789/58696/URN% 3ANBN%3Afi%3Ajyu-201806213316.pdf?sequence=1 (accessed June 26, 2019).

37 "Marine Le Pen Hails Patriotism as the Policy of the Future," *BBC News*, January 21, 2017, available online: https://www.bbc.com/ news/world-europe-38705176 (accessed August 17, 2019).

38 "The 12th Japan-China Joint Opinion Poll Analysis Report on the Comparative Data," Genron NPO, September 2016, available online: http://www.genron-npo.net/pdf/2016forum_en.pdf (accessed August 17, 2019).

39 Lotus Ruan, "The New Face of Chinese Nationalism," *Foreign Policy*, August 25, 2016, available online: http://foreignpolicy. com/2016/08/25/the-new-face-of-chinese-nationalism/ (accessed August 17, 2019).

40　Nicole Curato, "Flirting with Authoritarian Fantasies? Rodrigo Duterte and the New Terms of Philippine Populism," *Journal of Contemporary Asia* 47, no. 1 (2017): 142–153.

41　Ronald Brownstein, "Putin and the Populists. The Roots of Russia's Political Appeal in Europe and the United States," *The Atlantic*, January 6, 2017, available online: https://www.theatlantic.com/international/archive/2017/01/putin-trump-le-pen-hungary-france-populist-bannon/512303/ (accessed August 17, 2019).

42　Fredrik Wesslau, "Putins Friends in Europe," *ECFR*, October 19, 2016, available online: http://www.ecfr.eu/article/commentary_putins_friends_in_europe7153 (accessed August 17, 2019).

43　Jean Grugel and Pía Riggirozzi, "Post-neoliberalism in Latin America: Rebuilding and Reclaiming the State after Crisis," *Development and Change* 43 (2012): 1–21.

44　European Commission, *Standard Eurobarometer 89: Spring 2018, Report, European Citizenship*, Feildwork, March 2018, 35–37, available online: http://ec.europa.eu/commfrontoffice/publicopinion/index.cfm/Survey/getSurveyDetail/instruments/STANDARD/surveyKy/218 (accessed August 17, 2019).

45　Ronald Inglehart et al. (eds.), *World Values Survey: Round Six - Country-Pooled Datafile* (Madrid: JD Systems Institute, 2014), available online: www.worldvaluessurvey.org/WVSDocumentationWV6.jsp (accessed August 17, 2019).

46　Jill Lepore, "A New Americanism," *Foreign Affairs*, March/April 2019, 11.

47　Kwame Anthony Appiah, *Cosmopolitanism: Ethics in a World of Strangers* (New York: W. W. Norton, 2010).

48　Yael Tamir, *Liberal Nationalism* (Princeton, NJ: Princeton University Press, 1995).

49　Jan-Werner Müller, *Constitutional Patriotism* (Princeton, NJ: Princeton University Press, 2007).

50　Stuart Hall, "The Question of Cultural Identity," in *Modernity. An Introduction to Modern Societies*, ed. Stuart Hall, David Held, Don Hubert, and Kenneth Thompson (London: Blackwell, 1996), 598.

Chapter 9

1　Ernest Renan, "Qu'est-ce qu'une nation?" (Paris, Presses-Pocket, 1992). Ernest Renan, "What Is a Nation?," trans. Ethan Rundell, available online: http://ucparis.fr/files/9313/6549/9943/What_is_a_Nation.pdf (accessed August 16, 2019).

2 Robert Bellamy, "Liberalism and Nationalism in the Thought of Max Weber," *History of European Ideas* 14, no. 4 (1992): 499–507.

3 Karl Deutsch, *Nationalism and Social Communication* (Cambridge, MA: MIT Press, 1952).

4 Hans Kohn, *The Idea of Nationalism* (New York: Macmillan, 1944).

5 Elie Kedourie, *Nationalism* (London: Hutchinson, 1960).

6 One influential work from this period was Eugene Weber, *Peasants into Frenchmen* (Stanford, CA: Stanford University Press, 1976).

7 Benedict Anderson, *Imagined Communities Reflections on the Origin and Spread of Nationalism*, 2nd edn. (London: Verso, 1991).

8 Eric Hobsbawm and Terence Ranger (eds.) *The Invention of Tradition* (Cambridge: Cambridge University Press, 1983); Eric Hobsbawm, *Nations and Nationalism Since 1780: Programme, Myth, Reality*, 2nd edn. (Cambridge: Cambridge University Press, 1992).

9 Ernest Gellner, *Nations and Nationalism* (Ithaca, NY: Cornell University Press, 1983).

10 John Breuilly, *Nationalism and the State* (Chicago: University of Chicago Press, 1985).

11 Anthony D. Smith, *National Identity* (London: Penguin, 1991); Walker Connor, *Ethnonationalism: The Quest for Understanding* (Princeton, NJ: Princeton University Press, 1994).

12 Michael Billig, *Banal Nationalism* (Los Angeles: Sage, 1994); Michael Skey and Marco Antonsich (eds.), *Everyday Nationhood. Theorising Culture, Identity and Belonging after Banal Nationalism* (Basingstoke: Palgrave, 2017).

13 Siniša Malešević, *Grounded Nationalism. A Sociological Analysis* (Cambridge: Cambridge University Press, 2019).

14 Rogers Brubaker, *Ethnicity without Groups* (Cambridge, MA: Harvard University Press, 2004).

15 Liah Greenfield, *Nationalism: Five Roads to Modernity* (Cambridge, MA: Harvard University Press, 1992).

16 Yael Tamir, *Liberal Nationalism* (Princeton, NJ: Princeton University Press, 1995).

17 Andreas Wimmer, *Nation Building: Why Some Countries Come Together While Others Fall Apart* (Princeton, NJ: Princeton University Press, 2018).

18 Michael Mann, *The Dark Side of Democracy* (Cambridge: Cambridge University Press, 2004).

19 Norman Naimark, *Fires of Hatred* (Cambridge, MA: Harvard University Press, 2002).

20 Philip Ther, *The Dark Side of Nation-States: Ethnic Cleansing in Modern Europe* (Oxford: Berghahn Books, 2016).

21 Partha Chatterjee, *The Nation and its Fragments. Colonial and Postcolonial Histories* (Princeton, NJ: Princeton University Press, 1993).

22 Edward Said, *Orientalism* (New York: Pantheon Books, 1978); see Yi LI, "Edward Said's Thoughts and Palestinian Nationalism," *Journal of Middle Eastern and Islamic Studies (in Asia)* 5, no. 3 (2011): 105–120.

23 Homi K. Bhabha, *The Location of Culture* (London: Routledge, 1994).

24 Nira Yuval-Davis, *Gender & Nation* (Los Angeles: Sage, 1997). See also Joane Nagel, "Masculinity and Nationalism: Gender and Sexuality in the Making of Nations," *Ethnic and Racial Studies* 21, no. 2 (1998): 242–269.

25 Lois A. West (ed.), *Feminist Nationalism* (New York: Routledge, 1997).

26 Jon Mulholland, Nicola Montagna, and Erin Sanders-McDonagh (eds.), *Gendering Nationalism. Intersections of Nation, Gender and Sexuality* (Basingstoke: Palgrave, 2018).

27 Donald Horowitz, *Ethnic Groups in Conflict* (Berkeley: University of California, 1985).

28 An overview over ethnic conflict, its causes, resolution, and international intervention can be found in Stefan Wolff, *Ethnic Conflict. A Global Perspective* (Oxford: Oxford University Press, 2008); and Karl Cordell and Stefan Wolff, *Ethnic Conflict. Causes-Consequences-Responses* (Cambridge: Polity, 2010).

29 Ted Robert Gurr, *Peoples versus States* (Washington, DC: United States Institute of Peace, 2000).

30 Vamik Volkan, *Bloodlines: From Ethnic Pride to Ethnic Terrorism* (New York: Farrar Straus & Giroux, 1997); Roger Petersen, *Understanding Ethnic Violence: Fear, Hatred, and Resentment in Twentieth Century Eastern Europe* (Cambridge: Cambridge University Press, 2002).

31 Russell Hardin, *One for All: The Logic of Group Conflict* (Princeton NJ: Princeton University Press, 1995).

32 Paul Collier, Anke Hoeffler, "Greed and Grievance in Civil War," *Oxford Economic Papers* 56, no. 4 (2004): 563–595.

33 David D. Laitin, *Nations, States, and Violence* (Oxford: Oxford University Press, 2007).

34 See the special section on "New Nationalism" in *Foreign Affairs* 98, no. 2 (2019); Yael Tamir, *Why Nationalism* (Princeton, NJ: Princeton University Press, 2019).

35 Pippa Norris and Ronald Inglehart, *Cultural Backlash Trump, Brexit, and Authoritarian Populism* (Oxford: Oxford University Press, 2019).

36 Case Mudde, *Populist Radical Right Parties in Europe* (Cambridge: Cambridge University Press, 2007).

37 Umut Özkirimli, *Theories of Nationalism. A Critical Introduction*, 2nd edn. (Basingstoke: Palgrave, 2010); Anthony D. Smith, *Nationalism. Theory, Ideology, History*, 2nd edn. (Cambridge: Polity Press, 2010).

38 Siniša Malešević and Tamara Pavasović-Trošt, "Nation-State and Nationalism," in *The Blackwell Encyclopedia of Sociology*, ed. George Ritzer and Chris Rojek (London: Wiley Blackwell, 2018). Eric Storm, "A New Dawn in Nationalism Studies? Some Fresh Incentives to Overcome Historiographical Nationalism," *European History Quarterly* 48, no. 1 (2018): 113–129.

39 John Breuilly (ed.), *Oxford Handbook of the History of Nationalism* (Oxford: Oxford University Press 2013).

40 Omar Dahbour and Micheline R. Ishay (eds.), *The Nationalism Reader* (Amherst, NY: Humanity Books, 1995); and John Hutchinson and Anthony Smith (eds.), *Nationalism* (Oxford: Oxford University Press, 1995) brings together primary sources and key readings. Philip Spencer and Howard Wollman (eds.), *Nations and Nationalism: A Reader* (New Brunswick, NJ: Rutgers University Press, 2005) brings together excerpts from key texts in nationalism studies. Gopal Balakrishnan (ed.), *Mapping the Nation* (London: Verso, 2012) provides for an important overview on nationalism by key authors, mostly from a leftist perspective.

41 The State of Nationalism, "Home," 2019, available online: https:// stateofnationalism.eu/ (accessed August 18, 2019).

42 The Nationalism Project, "The Nationalism Project: Nationalism Studies Information Clearinghouse," last updated December 2, 2009, available online: http://www.nationalismproject.org/ (accessed August 18, 2019).

43 Humanitites and Social Sciences Online, "H-Nationalism," Michigan State University Department of History, 1993–2019, available online, https://networks.h-net.org/h-nationalism (accessed August 18, 2019).

44 JISCM@il, "mail discussion lists for the UK Education and Research communities," JISC, n.d., available online: https://www.jiscmail. ac.uk/cgi-bin/webadmin?A0=ETHNOPOLITICS (accessed August 18, 2019).

Index

Made in United States
North Haven, CT
25 July 2023